FINAL
APPROACH

Northwest Airlines Flight 650
Tragedy and Triumph

LYLE PROUSE

Introduction by Ted Koppel

ISBN: 1460951999
ISBN-13: 9781460951996

DEDICATION

This book is dedicated to my wife Barbara. Her support and encouragement have been inspirational. She never once flinched in the face of our darkest moments.

As I sat in a courtroom and listened to myself portrayed to the world as a worthless human being, devoid of any semblance of decent character, I would sometimes glance her way. She would look at me across the large courtroom area and lovingly mouth the words, "I love you..." and I would be okay.

She is, and has always been, "The Wind Beneath My Wings..."

Retired United States District Chief Judge James M. Rosenbaum

Even though nobody died, it remains one of the most remembered crimes in history. A jetliner full of passengers flying cross-country under the "control" of a drunken cockpit crew. Late night TV's comics made the flight immortal. Who can forget Johnny Carson's, asking: "What'll you have?" Answer: "I'll take whatever the crew is having."

The flight is now history. But there remains the real and untold story. How did it happen? How did a pilot and crew, after running up a bar tab showing dozens of drinks, get behind the controls of a jet plane in the first place? And how could a person, after such a self-imposed and catastrophic fall, regain his life and his career?

Captain Lyle Prouse, for the first time tells his story. It is the ultimate story of a man coming to grips with the implacable "enemy" we all face . . . ourselves. It's the battle that never ends. Prouse fearlessly presents a life, a cataclysm, and an ultimate redemption that must be read to be believed. And it's true. After all, I was the judge.

- James M. Rosenbaum, United States District Judge (Retired)

Laura Palmer - *New York Times* bestselling author of *Escape* with Carolyn Jessop and former independent producer for ABC News "Nightline."

"There's courage...and then there's Lyle Prouse. There are heroes...and then there's Lyle Prouse. There are stories of loss and redemption...and then there's the saga of Lyle Prouse. This book will take your breath away then leave you in awe of the triumph of the human spirit...and Lyle Prouse."

- Laura Palmer

Former five term U.S. Congressman Rod Chandler (R-WA)

Lyle Prouse is a man with a remarkable story. Alcoholism took him to the depths of humiliation and rejection. He lost his job as an airline captain, he lost his licenses and he lost his freedom. Blaming no one but himself, Lyle endured the loneliness of prison and the drudgery of regaining those FAA certificates. From the depths of despair and financial ruin, Lyle emerged a sober man and returned to the vocation he loved. He reached out for help and prayed for strength. His is the story of faith, promise and hope, a story to inspire anyone.

   - Rod Chandler, Member of Congress 1983-1993

Former nine term U.S. Congressman Jim Ramstad (R-MN)

Lyle Prouse's gripping book tells all about his harrowing journey as the first pilot for a major airline to go to prison for flying drunk. Broke, humiliated and stripped of his pilot's license, Lyle sought treatment for his alcoholism and has become a powerful inspiration for countless others. From prison to a Presidential pardon, Lyle Prouse has carried the message and given hope to those still suffering.

   - Jim Ramstad, Member of Congress (1991-2009)

Captain Terry Marsh, Fleet Captain, 747 Program at Northwest Airlines

When the Flight 650 incident occurred, I'd known Lyle for more than twenty years and I was the Fleet Training Captain in charge of the Boeing 747 program at Northwest Airlines. I was shocked and embarrassed when the news broke – and even more shocked to learn that it was Lyle. We'd flown together and I considered him one of the most competent and conscientious pilots that I had ever known. Flight 650 became the 911 of commercial aviation, creating a tsunami within the industry.

Federal prosecution was also a first and when Lyle was found guilty and sent to prison there was little hope he would ever return to the profession that he loved. Most of us were sure we'd never see him in an airline uniform again but we all underestimated the incredible strength of this man. Upon his release from prison he began recertifying himself as a commercial pilot. Lyle had never flown civilian training airplanes before so the transition required even more effort. He accomplished that and with the help of the pilot community and Northwest management he returned again to his airline.

His high profile created extra attention as he made his way back. An FAA inspector watched as I gave him the final check ride of his career and he moved once again to the left seat as captain. It was one of the very best simulator check rides I'd ever seen.

Lyle continued to serve his airline and fellow pilots with distinction until his retirement.

His story is the greatest positive series of events that I have experienced in my lifetime. It would not have been possible without the help of many friends, a fiercely loyal and understanding wife, along with an incredible amount of drive and perseverance he possesses.

John Dasburg, Former President and Chief Executive Officer at Northwest Airlines

"The Playwright Aeschylus wrote two thousand five hundred years ago, 'God, whose law it is that he who learns must suffer. And even in our sleep pain that cannot forget, falls drop by drop upon the heart, and in our own despite, against our will, comes wisdom to us by the awful grace of God.' So it is that Lyle Prouse through his suffering has received wisdom and we are all the better off because of it. What he endured very few of us are even capable of imagining let alone enduring. In this book we read about how we all benefit from his good works and personal victory over one of mankind's pernicious afflictions."

- John Dasburg

"For once you have tasted flight you will
walk the earth with your eyes turned skyward.
For there you have been and there you long to return."

Leonardo da Vinci

ACKNOWLEDGEMENTS

Without the help of many people this book would never have been written. The words are mine but the effort belongs to others. Laura Palmer produced the ABC Night Line Special program about us in 1998 and pushed me for years to write the story. A published author in her own right, she spent much of her own time helping me. I loved her critique style as she crossed out paragraphs saying, "who cares?" while pointing to something else and writing "you need much more about this!"

Mickey Mills, a published author and good friend, stepped up to the editing chores. I was amazed at the differences changing a word here or there could make, or the elimination of same. He was determined to suggest only minor and subtle changes, wanting the voice to remain mine, and he spent _many_ hours helping me put this together. I am deeply indebted to him.

Peter Wold, my attorney who became my friend. He was unlike any attorney I'd ever met or heard of. In the years following the trial he remained at my side. I was broke, struggling, and trying to rise from the rubble. He continued working on my behalf and he never accepted a dime. He simply believed in me.

My deepest thanks to John Dasburg, former President and CEO of Northwest Airlines. He risked _everything_ by putting me back in the cockpit. I will always be indebted for the confidence and trust he placed in me at the risk of his own career. His decision allowed this story to end in the most wondrous way possible.

My sister, Connie Selenke, reviewed the family portion, something I hesitated to ask her to do because of the memories I knew it would dredge up. She courageously worked through it and gave me her blessing.

My trial judge was James M. Rosenbaum. I committed a grievous act, a horrendous betrayal of the public trust and I was aware that Judge Rosenbaum had strong feelings about this case. But he also maintained an open mind and he refused to permanently brand me as some had. I doubt that I could have drawn a tougher judge, but he brought an equal amount of fairness to the courtroom. Unexpectedly, he became a major part of my story many years later. I know of no other convicted felon who enjoys the same relationship I have with the judge who tried, sentenced, and sent him away to prison.

Former Marine Corps Major Don "Digger" Rowe, a Vietnam squadron mate, fact checked the story, corrected punctuation, and was of immense help. Retired Marine Lt. Col. Cary Watkins, my first flight instructor at Pensacola and Vietnam squadron mate, did likewise.

My former high school English teacher, Mrs. Corlie Mason, retrieved her red pen and corrected my punctuation as she pored through my writing – *twice*! She and her husband, Dean, were the first to urge publication and I am grateful for their support.

Captain O.C. Miller spent several years risking his reputation as he sought to bring me back to Northwest Airlines. No single pilot at Northwest Airlines enjoyed the reputation he had for integrity, wisdom, and insight. He was the lynchpin for my return to flying at Northwest. He approved the manuscript as a fact-checker and was as supportive as ever.

Dr. Audie Davis, head of the FAA's Medical Certification Branch for 34 years, personally signed my FAA Medical Certificate reinstating me as a recovering pilot. He did so without regard to political or public pressure to refuse my application, which would have prevented me from ever flying again. He became a close friend and remains so today.

State Judge Juanita Marsh founded Anchor Hospital, where I got sober. Throughout my time there, both as a patient and a staff member, she provided her kindness and support. She did many things for our entire family.

Captain Terry Marsh. Ah, my friend, what can I say except that I love you. He took me into his home, put me through his flight school free, and opened the final door towards regaining all my licenses. His wife, Susan, was equally supportive and his son, Matt, was one of my best instructors in light planes.

In memoriam to Charlie Shipp, retired Delta Airlines captain, my first mentor, who lent his guiding hand to my early efforts in recovery. And to Paul Eddy, my native brother, second mentor, and Yankton Sioux, who led by example and showed me the way. I glimpse them in the shadows and I hear their voices whispering to me in the breeze. And thank you, Ed, who has now inherited the job and does his best to keep me level and centered.

The best friend in my entire life, John Dodson, did not live to see this story written. We were closer than brothers for over 42 years until cancer took his life. We began our Marine Cadet days in the same class in 1961, were Marine officers and pilots together, survived Vietnam together, and were in the same class at Northwest Airlines. Our families grew up together. He was the funniest man I ever knew and I was the best audience he ever had. I will always miss him.

To my nine Northwest counterparts who made our house payments for four years – thank you from the bottom of our hearts. It was a gesture so far above and beyond that words fail. My thanks to all the other pilots and flight attendants who showered us with their support – cards, letters, phone calls, and often times money. Each and every person has touched our hearts.

To Ted Koppel for writing the introduction to this book. He did so in the aftermath of a deeply searing family tragedy, when most would have been too busy with their grief and their own personal problems. His reputation for integrity was one of two key factors in my decision to allow this story to be told on Nightline in 1998. I trusted Ted Koppel and I trusted Laura Palmer, the producer. I chose well.

My thanks to the thousands of fellow alcoholics I've met along the way. Thank you for sharing your experience, strength, and hope. Thank you for lighting the way so that I might follow, and thank you for my sobriety – one day at a time.

I thank my Creator for keeping me alive long enough to get sober and experience His miracles. I thank Him for the strength to persevere, the dignity to endure bad times and ignoble moments, and the unmerited gift of grace He has showered me with.

If space permitted, I would individually list the hundreds of other friends and supporters who came from everywhere at our darkest moment in time. Many provided financial support; others sent messages of encouragement and cards that lifted our spirits. One card I received in prison showed a baby bird that had fallen from the nest, hit the ground, and was flying away into the sky. It said, "Just remember...the harder the fall, the higher the bounce." I hoped so. We will never forget their love, their compassion, and their refusal to write us off as friends.

THE HISTORY OF THIS BOOK

Writing a book was never really high on my list. Barbara pushed me for years to write the story as a legacy to grandchildren and generations beyond. We'd been approached twice about a TV movie of this story. But a standard movie contract grants freedom for the producers to take as much creative license as they wish, thus making it one of those loosely "based on a true story" presentations. It was important to me that the integrity of the story not be compromised.

I drew from my personal military records, the originals sent to me years ago by the Military Records Center in Kansas City. They included every write up for every single flight during flight training, along with all my other military data. I have my military logbooks, the trial transcript, and a prison diary that had to be surreptitiously written and hidden, and personal letters. So I am able to use direct quotations, times, dates, places, and completely accurate information, and I've striven to be meticulously detailed and honest.

I have omitted the names of my two fellow crew members or changed them when necessary. I have reluctantly changed the names of prison staff and some of the reporters as well. Most of the other names are intact.

Laura Palmer told me, "If you want a true account presented then you'll have to write it yourself." I was surprised when a large publishing firm indicated interest in publishing the story. Indeed, they fast tracked it and moved another book out of the way, telling me "this will be our flagship book of the year." I worked with Becky Post, a wonderful lady who was their editorial director and we were in the very final stages by January 2007 with the book slated to hit the book shelves in September. It was a done deal and we were all set.

Suddenly, she notified me that someone above her in the chain of command wanted me to omit two very important parts of the story. They wanted no mention of my youngest son and they wanted me to "*soften*" the chapter about prison, telling me they had a "*relationship*" with the prison system they needed to retain.

I'd *already* softened the prison chapter and by omitting part of my family dynamics they were asking that the story be altered, thus presenting a picture that was incomplete and deceptive. Deception can occur through deliberate misstatement of fact, embellishment, and exaggeration – or through omission of information. I responded that the story had been fact checked several times by people who were involved, was true and accurate, and that I could not go along with what they were asking. But they insisted.

I received an advance of $8,750, half of the total, and spent it because I thought we were finished with this project. So I borrowed $8,750 from Northwest Airlines Credit Union, returned their advance, and voided the contract. I told them I could not sell my integrity for money, a book with my name on it, and royalties in the coming years. I worked too hard to keep the story truthful and accurate.

I was surprised by this turn of events but I sent the editorial director some flowers and a note that I felt worse for her than for myself. I decided to drop this project because, after all, I'd set out to leave my grandchildren the story and I'd accomplished that.

I've recently been convinced to self-publish this, something I said I'd never do. The folks at CreateSpace have been outstanding and I'm glad I've done it.

INTRODUCTION BY
TED KOPPEL

Some of the greatest figures from the Old Testament had, to put it charitably, feet of clay. King David gave orders that his loyal officer, Uriah, be abandoned to a sure death on the battlefield, because David had impregnated Uriah's wife, Bathsheba.

Jacob deceived his blind father into granting him the birthright that should have gone to his older twin, Esau.

Lot's daughters, facing a severe man shortage, got the old man drunk (as he later claimed) and used him as a stud.

Abraham, traveling with his wife, Sarah, was fearful that a powerful and hospitable Egyptian leader (it may have been a pharaoh) was so smitten by Sarah's beauty that Abraham feared for his life. He dealt with the dilemma by passing Sarah off as his sister. (Not to worry, an angel intervened in the pharaoh's dreams that night, before any damage could be done).

And need we give more than passing mention to the New Testament story of Peter, thrice denying Jesus in the Garden at Gethsemane, before beginning his more admirable career as the rock upon which Christ founded his church.

I have often marveled at the genius of those early story tellers who understood how desperately we need our heroes and spiritual leaders to have known and surrendered to moments of weakness. We are able to relate to the greatest among them because, at key intersections in their lives, they were just like us.

What people sometimes overlook in a story of redemption is that the central character needed redeeming. He may not, in other words, have always been a particularly nice person. Flawed, yes. We get that part. Everyone is flawed. Everyone needs a little redemption. But to merit an entire book, the central character needs to have made an epic journey, the course of which was predictable only in retrospect. A story of great redemption requires great failure. The emergence of incredible strength and tenacity are most impressive when they grow out of weakness and collapse. That's what makes this book worth your time.

At a certain point in his life, when his seventeen year old adopted daughter ran away from home, Lyle Prouse appears to have lost control of his life and of himself. He became totally obsessed with his sense of loss and betrayal, heedless of the pain he was inflicting on his wife, irresponsible to the point of criminality with respect to those whose lives were in his professional care. Lyle was a commercial airline pilot who flew drunk. How often is not altogether clear. Had his drinking led to an air disaster, some other book might have been written, but Lyle would have been its villain, not its hero.

Understand: Lyle Prouse appears to have a keener understanding than anyone how close he came to the abyss. His story is never less than interesting, and frequently inspirational, precisely because he makes no excuses. We know what Lyle was, because he tells us.

I should acknowledge at this point that Lyle Prouse and I have never met. I became aware of him, as most Americans did in March of 1990, when he was subjected to that uniquely American brand of scourging known as humiliation by late night comedy monologue. Lyle was a Northwest Airlines captain, who had piloted an early morning flight only a few hours after consuming fourteen or more drinks. It wasn't funny if you gave it even slightly more than a moment's thought. But most of us didn't.

Laura Palmer, however, did. Laura is an old friend who worked as a free-lance producer for Nightline. She is a woman of great empathy and patience, and she befriended Lyle; earned his trust. By the time she came to Nightline's executive producer, Tom Bettag, and me with the proposal that we devote a program to the story of Lyle Prouse, it was 1998. We had all but forgotten him. The news cycle that had produced all those "Flying High" headlines was long past. But as Laura knew, and as we learned, the real story of Lyle Prouse only moved into high gear when he was indicted and convicted. That's the story at the core of this book. This was a man who had landed his plane, but crashed his life. And then….

I mentioned that Lyle and I never met. We don't know each other well enough to be friends. We have spoken by phone a few times. We've exchanged a few letters and emails. He always signs them off with the same phrase: "Blue Skies." It's very positive, and unremittingly upbeat. He seems genuinely bewildered, or at least bemused, by the fact that this drives me nuts. Roy Rogers used to sign off in similar fashion, holding his Stetson over his head, rearing old Trigger up on his hind legs, and sending out a cheery "Happy Trails!" Even at the age of ten I was cynical about congenital optimism. But that's my problem, not Lyle's; and Roy is long past caring.

Lyle Prouse set out to write a compelling, honest book, and he's done a terrific job. Believe me. I don't owe him anything. He doesn't owe me anything. And if his worst fault is a little too much high octane optimism, he's entitled to it.

Ted Koppel

PREFACE

Life can change so suddenly – an auto accident, a random shooting, a tornado or hurricane, or some other completely unanticipated happening. Each time I watch the six o'clock news I see the faces of people whose lives have suddenly been unalterably changed in the blink of an eye.

For me, it was none of those events, but mine was just as surreal and shocking. One moment I was an airline captain, a husband and father, and thought I was doing well. The next moment I felt as though I'd stepped on a land mine. The explosion confused and bewildered me; I was bleeding from a hundred wounds, dazed, alone, and dying from the inside out. But it was my alcoholism that triggered the blast. I *never* thought I'd ever be an alcoholic…

This story began on the morning of March 7, 1990, with no hint that this would be the last day of one life and the beginning of another. It would mark a before and after that would find me drowning in the depths of a personal hell before slowly and painfully emerging into a new life in a new world.

I landed in Fargo, North Dakota, that day as the captain of a Northwest Airlines Boeing 727. A former Marine Corps pilot and Vietnam veteran, I was living out my dream of reaching the highest pinnacle in commercial aviation. The previous two years had been difficult for our family, but my wife Barbara and I had survived it together and we were two days away from our 27th wedding anniversary.

I had no reason to think it would be anything but a typical layover; I'd have some drinks, get a meal somewhere, and get back to my hotel room in time to rest up for the early morning flight the next day. But I stayed at The Speak Easy and I drank way too much.

When the alarm sounded at 4:15 the next morning, I was hung over. I shaved, showered, put my uniform on, and headed downstairs for crew pickup at 5:15 AM. As the door swung closed behind me there was no way to know nothing in my world would be routine again. A mere two hours later my nightmare would begin.

As we turned for the final approach I had no idea what lay waiting for me upon landing. When Northwest Airlines Flight 650 touched down in Minneapolis I was arrested. Mere months later I was the first airline pilot ever convicted of flying while impaired—in other words, drunk.

The last segment of any flight is the final approach phase; it didn't take long for me to realize I had just flown *my very last* final approach. My story exploded onto the national and international news scene with an unbelievable fury, and it remained a front-page item for weeks. I became a national pariah, the object of scorn, contempt, and anger. Shame, disgrace, humiliation, pain, horror, and hopelessness became my daily companions in the days and years that followed. And the worst part–I knew I deserved all of it.

I had worked hard to achieve a good life for my wife Barbara and our three children. But now I was a national disgrace and a joke. I came to redefine my personal margins for human suffering and endurance in a manner and degree never before imagined. Feelings inside me were intensified by my own inability to forgive myself. The self-torture I grimly inflicted came in unceasing and relentless ways that was impossible for me to handle.

I came from an alcoholic home but I'd vowed I would never become one of *them*. But suddenly I was faced with the question of being an alcoholic, something I found repugnant and nearly impossible to accept or digest. One of the greatest battles of my life would not take place in a cockpit or in Vietnam.

The only time I ever pondered suicide was in Vietnam as I considered what course of action I'd take if shot down and faced with capture. Captured pilots in my sector never survived long enough to make it to North Vietnam. The Viet Cong had neither the logistics nor the motivation to transport pilots several hundred miles north. So captured pilots were usually paraded from village to village as propaganda pieces until they were finally tortured and killed as an example to the local populace. I wrestled with the option of suicide or capture and could never reach a permanent decision.

But within days of the arrest in Minnesota, I found myself planning my own demise as the only available way to stop the pain that quickly reached an intolerable level. There can be no greater sense of hopelessness than when suicide becomes seductively attractive.

I never thought I would ever be jailed or go to prison. Clearly, the only possibility of that had been as a POW in Vietnam if we were to take on targets north of the DMZ. As my nightmare unfolded, I was forced to accept the probability of becoming a federal convict in an American penitentiary.

I was a proud man, proud of my Native American heritage, proud of my Marine Corps service, and proud of my personal reputation. Humility had never been a character attribute I had sought but it came to me through another form of the word – humiliation. It came from the media, the nighttime monologue of comics like Jay Leno and others, and from anyone looking for a topic to provoke laughter.

I watched nearly everything I'd worked a lifetime to achieve evaporate within a thirty day period after the arrest. Having come from a hardscrabble life, it had been a long climb to the top. Nothing was easy, but Barbara and I had finally achieved success and a level of comfort that allowed us to relax just a bit. My descent to the bottom was almost instantaneous - everything was destroyed and lost overnight.

In the process, I became acquainted with an attorney unlike any I'd ever heard about. Our relationship, forged in the midst of intense adversity, changed each of us in ways neither of us anticipated.

I walked into the depressing gray cloud of federal prison on December 5, 1990, became inmate 04478-041, a convicted felon wearing the drab khaki uniform of a federal convict. I was broke, publicly stripped of my airline career, my FAA flying certificates, and my FAA medical certificate. I had nothing left. The judge put sanctions on me that guaranteed I would never fly again. It was an extra layer of concrete over the top of my coffin and sealed my fate.

Surrounded by drug dealers and petty criminals, I took on life in a prison work camp. Living in the 24-hour insanity of the prison system severely challenged me. Nothing could have prepared me for the sickness and obscenity of our penal system.

I looked about me and there was nothing to hope for. I'd destroyed nearly everything. I knew Barbara was still with me, yet I felt so alone. My children hugged me and I drew strength from knowing they were there, but I *still* felt so alone.

I was hearing from many friends and knew it took courage for them to even admit they knew me, much less acknowledge our friendship. And while my heart was touched by their letters and cards, I could not shake the feeling of cold isolation.

As the years passed, I experienced the absolute worst of humanity and the absolute best of it. As I endured one horror after the other, I slowly made my way from the darkness into the shadows. All suffering eventually ends but I never expected to see the sunlight again.

In the months and years ahead I experienced miracles that left me awestruck. Impossible events occurred that defied all manner of odds and took my breath away. None came quickly or easily as I slowly turned my eyes skyward once more. In the aftermath there would be no way I could deny the existence of a God who provided such grace to someone who never expected or deserved it.

I never fought my termination. A grievance had been automatically filed but never activated. My termination was justified, fair, and appropriate.

Nearly four years later, intervention from the President/CEO of Northwest Airlines, a man I'd never met or seen in person, brought the two of us together. Over the next several years we shared some moving and emotional meetings in the privacy of his office. He took an enormous chance as he risked his *own* career by believing in me.

In yet another twist, the tough Federal judge I'd drawn, the man who tried, sentenced, and sent me to prison, would one day many years later become one of my strongest advocates. He would become one of the remarkable parts of my story.

Looking back at those first awful days spiraling out from March 8, 1990, it is nearly impossible for me to believe the events that followed the horror and devastation.

This is my story. It's my wish that it might bring hope to someone who has none. I have learned from others that failure often takes the path of least persistence. They taught me that life is not merely playing the hand you're dealt, it's learning to play a poor hand well.

But above all, I hope my story illustrates the beauty of a constantly unfolding universe over which some Higher Power can, and *does*, perform miracles in the face of sheer impossibility.

TABLE OF CONTENTS

Storm Clouds – Headed My Way

As my youngest child, Dawn, neared graduation from high school, I put my card in for Captain. I had to go to Chicago to take a special written exam as I aimed at the ultimate goal of every airline pilot – Captain. I passed up moving to a junior Captain position for two years so I could be home with Dawn as she approached graduation.

I completed the exam on the second day and called home from Chicago O'Hare airport. As Barbara said hello her voice immediately told me something was very wrong. Dawn had run away.

Dawn wanted to go to Florida on spring break with a number of her high school friends and her mother and I said no. I had layovers in Fort Lauderdale during spring break and watched the sheer madness of thousands of teenagers drunk, high, sprawled all over the beach, stumbling down the sidewalks, and tearing up many of the hotels. I knew sex was rampant and there was no way Barbara or I would allow Dawn to go. Although Dawn didn't openly rebel or sulk, we knew she was highly displeased with our decision.

Dawn and some of her friends waited until Barbara took me to the airport, then they went into her room, took what she wanted, and left a note for Barbara. Barbara didn't find the note until late that evening when Dawn failed to return home. Unable to call me, she spent a sleepless and tortured night alone, worrying about Dawn.

I blurted out panicked instructions as to who to call and where to look. Dawn was the center of my universe, my very sunlight, and my mind was reeling at the news of this event. I got on the Northwest plane and was home in two hours. During the flight to Atlanta something unexplainable happened within me. I don't know how, when, or why it happened nor was I conscious of anything occurring. My panic and fear turned to a white-hot level of hatred and rage. I had no conscious awareness of the transition.

Arriving in Atlanta, I got in the car and informed Barbara that regardless of what occurred from this point I would never allow Dawn back in my life. I made it clear that I *never* wanted to hear her name again as long as I lived. Once home, I told the rest of the family so everyone had the message loud and clear. I didn't care if she died in the streets, but she would never be allowed back in my home. I never hated anyone as much as I now hated the daughter who once owned my heart.

Within two days I emptied the house of all her possessions. Her furniture went to Goodwill and I destroyed everything in the home that bore her imprint. I smashed and threw away the little girl things she'd made for me as she grew up–things I had deeply treasured and cherished for many years. I went to the bank, opened our safe deposit box, and ripped up the adoption papers along with a beautiful, loving letter we had saved from the foster parents who had her the first 16 days of her life. I went to a local attorney and paid him $500 to disown her and I sought to annul the adoption, discovering it couldn't be done.

I was a boiling cauldron of hatred in the midst of all the other family chaos. The others were fearfully watching me and staying out of my way. In a way that can only appear insanely amusing, I decided Barbara needed some help dealing with this tragedy, so I called a family therapist. By the luck of the draw I plucked Dr. David Yarbrough's name from the yellow pages and made an appointment. He proved to be an invaluable resource as we struggled through this ordeal.

At our introductory meeting we briefly discussed our reason for coming, omitting any reference to my feelings about things. As we left Dr. Yarbrough said, "As long as you're coming to see me I don't want either of you drinking." There had been absolutely no mention of alcohol at that point so I thought it a strange thing to say since he didn't even know if we drank. As we got in the car I said to Barbara, "What the hell do you suppose he means by that?" When she didn't have an answer I suggested he meant we should not be drinking on the morning we were scheduled to see him. Since I rarely ever drank in the mornings that would not be a problem.

We saw Dr. Yarbrough about twice a month for nearly two years. He learned more about me than anyone except Barbara, including the fact that both my parents had died of alcoholism. Sometimes he would see each of us alone, and other times we'd go together. He even asked to see our sons, Scott and Jay, on a couple of occasions as he pieced together an accurate picture of our family and the issues involved.

Once, as he worked to get me to talk about Dawn, I made a statement that came spontaneously and with no prior thought, something I never recall ever thinking, much less saying. Forcefully I said, "I'll tell you something, doctor, I'd rather hate than hurt!" It was an astonishing and revealing statement about the way I handled emotional pain. Dr. Yarbrough knew about the alcoholic home where I grew up. He knew about the three marriages of each parent, and my travels back and forth among the families due to the conflicts I experienced. He paused, looked at me, and said, "Lyle, you survived a childhood doing that, but if you continue it will destroy you." I made no response. He was right but it took two more years before I discovered it.

One subject was never discussed – my drinking. I made no attempt to hide or avoid it because I was convinced it wasn't a problem. I didn't think I drank any more than many of my friends. I didn't drink every night, rarely *ever* drank in the morning, didn't get drunk every weekend, hadn't had a DUI since 1976, and was at the top of my game professionally. So how could alcohol possibly be a problem? However, I deliberately varied my drinking patterns and did so very consciously. Normal drinkers don't do that; they don't need to.

Unknown to me, Dawn contacted Barbara to let her know where she was and whom she was with. She hadn't chosen wisely but at least she was not out on the street and Barbara could draw some comfort from that. Barbara discreetly kept the information to herself. My anger remained at full crest, buttressed by self-pity and martyrdom as I mentally recited all I'd done for my daughter and the manner in which I was repaid.

I spent a small fortune on braces and orthodontic work, something she would never have been able to do if we hadn't adopted her and I was so glad we could do it. When she was fifteen her face began to change and suddenly her Chippewa genetics made her nose prominent and her chin appear to recede. I looked at her and I still saw my beautiful daughter; but *she* looked in the mirror and was troubled by what she saw. When Barbara talked with me about it I quickly agreed to pay for plastic surgery, and she emerged with a beautiful nose and chin. I did these things because I loved her – but in the aftermath of losing her I made myself the victim of deceit and hated her for it.

I played back her childhood, the moments of adoration for her I'd once experienced: the camping trips, the good times, and the love I had freely given that made me so vulnerable.

Referring to my childhood and the conflicts that resulted in traversing back and forth several times between families, Dr. Yarbrough made an illuminating comment. He said, "Every time you moved from one parent's home to the other as a result of conflict, you experienced a feeling of abandonment and betrayal." I had never attempted to identify or label any of those feelings but the instant he said that it struck my emotional bull's-eye. He went on to say, "Now, many years later, the person you love more than anything else in the world has abandoned and betrayed you once again and it's going to require an extremely high level of anger to overcome that." I was willing to do what was needed and I did so - to my own detriment and near demise. It was my only coping tool. The hatred was a cancer in my soul, yet I wasn't willing to give it up.

I mentally obsessed about Dawn and couldn't get her out of my mind. I had to force myself to concentrate on certain tasks that demanded total attention or thoughts of her would force themselves into my mind. There was a living torrent of hatred within me, sapping all my emotional energy and eating me alive with each passing day.

Barbara and I were no strangers to the pressures of raising teenagers. As our two sons entered that realm we became more watchful. Our older son Scott never seemed to be a problem. His friends were good kids who spent a lot of time in our home, so we got to know them well. A year younger, Jay became the rebel without a cause, hanging with kids who were troublemakers, and getting into increasing trouble. Secretly, he started smoking and before long was into drugs and alcohol. His grades plummeted and he dropped out of athletic activities. He became the center of attention within the family.

The problems continued as Jay struggled through high school. There were only brief moments of respite when we weren't in the midst of some crisis involving him. I tried dozens of heart to heart talks and when they didn't work, I turned to increasingly higher levels of discipline. I refused to allow our home and family to be hijacked by one of the children. Nothing worked. Barbara and I were a good parenting team but we were completely out of ideas - we were exhausted.

Finally, I took Jay to a licensed counselor although I held the entire concept of counseling in disdain. I was so frustrated that I was willing to try anything. I thought the only people who needed counseling were people who would not communicate and I did not believe that applied in our situation. And I expressed that to the counselor. Another of my misplaced beliefs was that one or two counseling periods should completely solve all problems and clear everything up. We did the best we could with what we had through all the ups and downs and there were many. When Jay graduated from high school I convinced him to go into the Marine Corps. He did so and I thought his path would take a turn for the better.

Barbara and I now focused on raising Dawn, who was six years younger than Jay. She was the sunlight and center of my universe, and I hoped our troubles were over.

As the years passed, alcohol slowly became more and more important to me. The event with Dawn did not push me into alcoholism; I was already well on my way, as I would learn later in treatment. Dawn bears absolutely *no* responsibility for my alcoholism, nor does Jay. But alcoholism is a progressive disease and how I dealt with Dawn's departure certainly accelerated that. After Dawn's exodus I desperately needed relief and alcohol was the only thing I knew that would answer the call. I shut everyone out. On rare occasions a friend would offer a comment in an attempt to help. Or once in a while they would attempt to persuade me to forgive Dawn and reconcile. A withering look was my response and they never approached me a second time.

Eventually, Barbara asked me not to drink at home. Once the liquor began to flow I would explode with vile comments about Dawn, even though I'd expressly forbidden anyone else to mention her name. So I drank alone and in distant places. I no longer wanted to go out with the flight crew and enjoy the evening; all I wanted to do was isolate and drink. Yet perversely, the alcohol quit working and I was unable to find relief.

Alone in a hotel room on a layover, I would open a fifth or quart of booze and pour an extremely stiff drink. I'd have to work to get the first one down. But after that they went down easily and quickly. I sat alone and drank until the bottle was empty. I longed for relief, to just drift away on a warm, mellow cloud of apathy. What I got instead was even more hatred, the stoking of an emotional blast furnace that played and re-played the past seventeen years of Dawn's life, leaving me exhausted with even more anger, self-pity, and martyrdom.

I believed that any relationship was dangerous if I was not in control of it. If the *other* person controlled the relationship I was vulnerable and in a dangerous place. Occasionally, when I was angry or felt threatened I told Barbara that I needed *no one*; that I could and would survive *alone*, if necessary. I earnestly believed I could survive alone in a cave in the mountains if I had to, giving up Barbara, my kids, and everyone else who had any sort of loving attachment to me. And that was always my emotional fallback position. But over the years I must have gotten careless. Somehow, some way, I forgot my own cardinal rule and look what happened.

I can't imagine the hurt Barbara felt when I told her I didn't need her. I can't imagine how un-needed she felt or how insecure and frightened she must have been. For her to love me as she did and receive this in return was beyond cruel. Yet there was something inside that would not allow me to become vulnerable. To make matters worse, I passed this philosophy on to my two sons, indoctrinating them with the idea that they must *always* make sure they were in control of their relationships. When I got sober, one of the first amends I made was to tell them how very wrong I had been in this regard. One of them looked at me and said, "I never thought you'd lie to us, Dad." I responded, "I didn't lie to you, son. I believed that when I said it, but I've learned it's not true. And I have a duty to tell you the truth.

One night in Seattle an unexpected thing happened as I drank deep into the bottle. I was again courting the anger and hatred, but instead I suddenly broke down and cried. The walls in the hotel were thin and our crew rooms were all in the same area. Afterwards I was tense with fear that someone heard me in the room next door. I felt ashamed because I was not one to cry; I hadn't even cried at my parents' funerals. Early the next morning I anxiously scanned the faces of the gathering crewmembers. I was looking for some telltale sign that I'd been overheard and was deeply relieved to see none. I never cried again – until treatment.

I lived like this for two years. Then one night in Fargo my world exploded into a before and after. It would never be the same again.

The End Of My Career – A Fatal Trip

For nearly twenty-two years at Northwest I enjoyed the same reputation I had in the Marine Corps. I loved what I did and the people I worked with whether they were in the cockpit or back in the cabin. I loved going to work and eagerly looked forward to my trips. I had a reputation as an excellent aviator and a good Captain. I ran a relaxed ship in that I didn't micromanage the other cockpit crewmembers. I paid attention and knew what was going on, but there was simply no need to parade my four stripes. For twenty years I watched other captains as I came up through the ranks from second officer (flight engineer) and copilot. I took from the best and learned from the worst. With extremely rare exception, everyone in the cockpit performed at a high level of competency and that was the norm at Northwest. It was routine. I thought being a captain was easy and enjoyable. The entire job of flying airplanes was fun and I loved it.

Pilots are just like other professions. Some are excellent, some are average, and some are marginal. That's also true for doctors, lawyers, electricians, plumbers, and all other callings. But the level of excellence at Northwest was routinely very high. We had an outstanding training department and the screening process for new hires was quite good. But no system is foolproof. Over the course of thirty-nine years of flying and instructing, I saw the occasional person who dearly wanted to fly but simply had no aptitude for it. Back in my cadet days, some of my friends fit that profile and my heart ached for them as I watched them depart when they washed out.

I recognize the dichotomy of talking about good flying performance on one hand while drinking alcoholically on the other. I know doctors, sports superstars, attorneys, ministers, priests, factory workers, plumbers, electricians, and myriads of others who performed brilliantly but were alcoholics. The progressive nature of this disease guarantees that excellent performance eventually deteriorates to unacceptable performance and finally the bottom falls out. The time element can vary with each alcoholic, but the end result is almost always the same. That one may perform adequately, or even excellently, while being an alcoholic does not make it okay or remotely acceptable.

The FAA had a "bottle to throttle" rule – no alcohol consumption within eight hours of flight. Northwest had a twelve hour requirement. For much of my career I played by the rules and honored the twelve hour requirement. As the years slid by and my alcoholism progressed, I found myself compromising that rule, sometimes a little and sometimes a lot. I didn't always do it and tried not to, but there were times when drinking became more important than the rule. I could always rationalize that I would be in flying condition the next day. Once I got sober I could only wonder what insanity led me to think in that manner. But as a practicing alcoholic it seemed both reasonable and logical.

There were numerous times when I was hung-over and clearly felt it. I also wondered if there was more to the twelve hour rule than the time line alone but I didn't really want to know. There was. It was a Blood Alcohol Content (BAC) limit of .04 and I seriously doubt more than a handful of pilots were aware of that at the time of my arrest.

On March 7, 1990, I and my two other cockpit crewmembers arrived in Fargo, North Dakota on Northwest flight 217. We landed on schedule at 10:05A.M. at the Hector International airport. It was a beautiful day and I flew the inbound leg, landing smoothly on runway 17 as we rolled out toward the terminal at the far end of the airport.

Three days earlier the trip began as most trips did. I had never met either of the two crewmembers and knew nothing about them. The mood was lighthearted as the trip began with the normal cockpit conversation taking place. Both of the other two pilots were from a civilian aviation background and I was the only one with military experience. We had three first-rate flight attendants who were with us the entire time. Everyone got along well as we headed out on a four day schedule.

The copilot was an excellent aviator and I knew that from the moment he flew his first leg with me. It was clear this would be one of the more enjoyable trips since he was extremely competent. The Second Officer was allegedly experienced as a flight engineer due to his previous background at Eastern Airlines, so I had every reason to believe he would do his job well. He was also on probation, which meant I would have to provide an evaluation of his performance, a practice that hadn't changed since I was a new-hire.

Typically, the setting inside the cockpit is relaxed and enjoyable. Airline training and screening is such that crewmembers routinely perform in an excellent manner – it's the expected norm. Each crewmember has a distinct area of responsibility and is interdependent upon the others. However, there is no place in the work force where errors don't occur from time to time, whether it's in the operating room, the courtroom, the cockpit or any other professional or lay endeavor.

The public has a particular sensitivity to the subject of errors, especially if they involve a doctor with a scalpel in his hand, a dentist with a drill, an attorney in a capital murder case, or a pilot in a cockpit. But the human condition is such that, like it or not, errors do occasionally occur. In nearly all cases they're quickly noticed, caught, and rectified. They generally turn out as no big deal.

Aviation has established procedures such as our "challenge and respond" checklists that tend to minimize errors, and the read back of all clearances and instructions between the pilots and Air Traffic Control is for that purpose. Additionally, each crew member monitors the others and functions as an additional safeguard. But altitudes are occasionally "busted," headings are occasionally misunderstood, radio frequency changes are sometimes missed, and other situations occur. Human beings are simply human beings and no environment is 100% error free.

Normally, these are quickly seen and corrected, usually with the help of ATC or another part of the cockpit team, and are taken in stride. Good instrument flying is merely a continuum of constant, small, corrections. For the most part, flight operations go very smoothly and professionally.

A visual approach is one that gives the pilot the authority to fly to the airport on his own, without the normal ATC procedures and instrument requirements. Obviously, the weather and other airport traffic has to be conducive to this. At one point during this trip, after being cleared for a visual approach I misidentified an airport because there were several of them between my position and point of intended landing. The first officer was not able to help since he was on the blind side and we were some distance out. The second officer was out of the loop and busy with his panel. I always set up for an instrument approach, even when I was cleared for a visual, but the angle and distance did not yet allow for an ILS lock on. I simply looked at the wrong airport.

Any error is embarrassing, whether it's a firm landing, wrong heading, or misunderstood clearance, and the correct airport was pointed out by ATC as we proceeded for the approach. I was not accustomed to making mistakes and was not pleased with this one. I always acknowledged a mistake, usually with a self-deprecating comment, because I wanted the other crew members to know that I *knew* when I erred. Conversely, when others did something, I usually just laughed it off because I knew *they* were upset with themselves and nothing more needed to be said.

Our second officer (flight engineer) was having difficulties since the first day of the trip. Since the second officer is the junior man in the crew and is sometimes fresh out of training, it's not uncommon for them to need help or assistance as they settle into the job. Most captains and first officers are glad to help. But this situation was a bit different. The second officer let us know he was very experienced so I assumed he would have no difficulty.

It became clear on our first flight segment that he did not understand the aircraft systems when I noticed a pressurization problem and drew his attention to it. I had to stop him from doing something that would have exacerbated the situation, which occurred from inattention to his panel. It was the beginning of the trip and I didn't think much about it since I had seen that situation before and we easily corrected the problem. What bothered me slightly was the fact that he seemed oblivious to what occurred.

The following day he gave us takeoff numbers that were off by ten thousand pounds and could have created a problem. I did the thumb rule math check that Captains are taught to do for a rough approximation of takeoff weight and caught the error. This was before data was furnished to the flight crews via computer. We corrected the problem, but I again observed he was not particularly concerned by what he'd done. That was bothersome and I began to pay a bit more attention to what he was doing.

The following day one of his friends rode the cockpit jump seat on his way home. It was a long segment and we had full fuel in all three tanks. In that configuration the fuel would need to be balanced between the three tanks as the flight progressed. Once in cruise flight, the second officer turned his seat completely around to talk with his friend, with his back to the flight engineer panel. It was unprofessional and I thought to myself, "I would *never* do something like that, *especially* if I was on probation!" I probably should have said something to him but my modus operandi was to avoid micro managing other crew members. The first officer was flying and as we progressed I noticed he kept adding more and more rudder trim. Finally, I looked down at the rudder indicator and was surprised to see we were *way* out of trim. I glanced back at the second officer's panel and was astounded to see that we were out of lateral balance by more than two thousand pounds of fuel. The FAA limitation was *one thousand* pounds between tanks one and three I never saw anyone get anywhere near that limitation. And we were now more than *twice* the FAA limitation for lateral unbalance. I didn't know if we had enough flight time remaining to get back within normal operating limits.

I was irritated at this point because the second officer was still engaged in conversation with his friend and completely ignoring his duties at the panel. I tersely told him to take a look at his fuel panel and get us back in balance.

The first officer was excellent, with a good personality, and I was pleased to be flying with him. We got along well and got together a couple of times on layovers during this trip. We had not included the second officer although we discussed his performance. Frankly, I found the second officer's performance puzzling. Pilots are extremely competitive and very jealous of their professional reputations. It was bewildering that he was not making more of an attempt to do the job well

– especially since he was still on probation. I believed most of his difficulty came from inattention, seemingly due to a continual need to engage in stories about himself that were meant to impress. As he did so, he ignored what was going on at his work station and *that* was causing problems. I was certainly on alert by now and under no impression that I could rely upon him to do his job.

We were approaching the end of the trip, departing Detroit at dusk. The second officer is charged with reading aloud the normal flow of checklists with a response from the two pilots up front. I called for the Before Taxi Checklist and when the second officer responded with "Before Taxi Checklist complete" I glanced at his panel over my shoulder prior to taxiing. I saw six amber lights indicating that six of the eight fuel boost pumps were off when they would normally have been on. The second officer saw me turn and look and said he was going to balance some fuel during our taxi out. After the fuel fiasco the day before, I guessed he was trying to show me he was on top of things. However, this was bizarre because no fuel will be burned and balanced at taxi power. He should have known that, but again I said nothing. My thought was to let him do whatever he wished as long as it did no damage.

As we turned onto the runway I called for the final items checklist and after the appropriate challenges and responses the second officer called "Takeoff Check Complete." Routinely, I glanced over my shoulder expecting to see no lights on his panel, which would be a normal indication prior to takeoff. Instead, I saw the same six amber lights indicating the six boost pumps were still off. The boost pumps were on the checklist he had just told me was completed. The boost pumps supply fuel under pressure to the engines and two of our three engines were currently devoid of boost pump pressure. The engines will operate normally during taxi or in cruise flight with only suction power. Indeed, we configure the fuel system using the fuel manifold with selected pumps on and off in order to balance fuel. But no one I know is sure that a flameout won't occur at maximum takeoff power and a nose high attitude with no boost pump pressure to the engines. My patience exhausted at this point, I angrily said, "Turn the f---g boost pumps on!" He did and we took off.

It's not certain and we'll never know, but we could conceivably have lost two of our three engines during takeoff, right at the most critical time. And the worst emergency a 727 can have is loss of two engines. In training we failed two engines for the Captain checkride, but those were always done in flight and never at takeoff. I fully intended to have a heart to heart discussion with the second officer after this trip was over but it ended unexpectedly and the opportunity never came.

Over the years I flew with a few second officers whose names circulated among the pilot community as having some competency problems. I found they did an acceptable job if I put them at ease and assured them there was no rush or hurry to get through anything. During my Marine Corps time I was a flight instructor in the Advanced Jet Training Command and used the same approach there when needed, although we didn't have some of the luxuries the airline environment provided. I never had an experience like the one on this flight, especially with someone who claimed to have prior airline experience. It was baffling and proved to be a once-in-a-career situation.

Several of the second officer's classmates at Northwest told me he continually interrupted the ground school instructors to explain how they did things at Eastern. He'd done that so much he was dubbed "Tom Eastern." During one of his walkarounds on our trip, he wanted to down the aircraft for something that Eastern did not consider adequate but was perfectly acceptable under Northwest Maintenance criteria. When he became insistent about it, I told him we worked for Northwest, not Eastern, and we used the Northwest criteria. Although I didn't say it, I had been a 727 second officer for over eight years and was very knowledgeable about preflighting the aircraft and the maintenance requirements.

What was normally a lighthearted, fun, and relaxed cockpit setting, became strained and required an abnormal amount of my attention toward the Second Officer's panel. The dynamics formed in the cockpit would spill over later into the courtroom.

It was the next to the last day of our trip. We would finish tomorrow and go home. I had just unpacked in my hotel room when the copilot called and asked if I would like to meet for a light lunch. I said yes and the three of us had a sandwich and some soup, talked briefly, and adjourned back to our rooms. We'd had an early launch that morning and I was going to get a short nap. Around 3:00 P.M. the copilot called, inviting me to the Speak Easy Restaurant and Lounge to have a couple of beers and some hors d'oeuvres. The Second officer was also going. Typically, I was a loner on layovers but for whatever reason I decided to join them. We talked as we walked the several blocks to the Speak Easy, a place I'd never been before, and I paid little attention as we made our way there.

A pitcher of beer was ordered, but I ordered a rum and coke, which was one of my preferred drinks. I had no intention of staying and getting drunk, nor did they, as far as I knew. Several hours passed, pitchers of beer were consumed, and I kept the waitress busy bringing rum and cokes. The second officer was strongly showing the effects of the beer while the copilot showed no sign of intoxication. The second officer suddenly appeared at our table with a guy named "Charlie," whom he met at the urinal. Charlie was purportedly a Vietnam vet. He began helping himself to the beer and I quickly pegged him as a phony as I listened to some of his comments and exploits.

I never talked about Vietnam unless it was with close friends who also served there. I was not interested in chatting with Charlie about Vietnam and it was clear to me he was never there and was an imposter. A short while later I politely asked Charlie to leave, but he ignored me. I asked again, this time a bit firmer and less politely. Again he ignored me. Finally I told him to "get the f—k back to the bar and leave our table," and he left because I was now angry. Although I thought I was low key and discrete, several nearby patrons overheard me and they later testified in court about this incident.

We continued to drink. I came back from the restroom to find the second officer involved in a verbal clash with two men sitting nearby. As I approached our table and heard the comments, I told him he was out of line and to be quiet. Then I apologized to the two patrons and offered to buy them a drink, which they declined.

If I went anywhere on layovers I normally went by myself and the primary reason for doing so was to remain anonymous from a professional standpoint. I didn't want to be identified as an airline pilot. In the midst of crew gatherings in public conversations by flight attendants complaining about a passenger or talking about flights made it too easy to be overheard. Flight crews who were identified while out drinking were on dangerous ground.

To my dismay, the second officer had openly bragged to these two men that we were airline pilots. It was a reckless disclosure. I was extremely angry because he put all of us in serious jeopardy. He appeared intoxicated at this point and I told the copilot to get him out of the bar and back to the hotel. They left with the copilot assisting the second officer out. The second officer paused long enough to declare that he could beat their ass, and the copilot hustled him on out of the bar.

I knew this was a bad situation and I tried to smooth things over with the two men. They were pleasant enough and asked if I knew a certain Northwest pilot who lived in Fargo, Captain George Lund. I said I did and that he was a good friend. It was too late to try to deny who we were. I was hoping our mutual association with George might provide us a pass on possible adverse consequences.

Although the second officer's behavior was reckless, my own was not good either. I was drinking at a time and place forbidden by regulations. I have no idea how much longer I stayed after the other two pilots left, but it was at least several hours more. Although I didn't feel drunk, I lost my balance as I stood to leave and fell, the chair skittering across the floor as people turned to look. I drew more unwanted attention. I left the bar and returned a few moments later, asking directions back to the hotel.

Since I'd left my watch in my hotel room and had not seen a clock in the bar I was unaware of the time. I believed it was still fairly early in the evening and I would get a decent night's sleep.

Pick up had originally been set for 5:00AM. We needed to be at the Fargo airport one hour before our departure time. The flight attendants asked if we could slide it fifteen minutes and get a few minutes more sleep. I said okay since it would be very early, traffic wouldn't be a factor, and it was an easy ride to the airport. I stressed that no one should be late as we'd be cutting it close and could not afford to wait on someone. The next morning all of us showed up ready to go except the second officer. We tried to rouse him twice, waiting as long as we could, then left instructions that he would have to catch a cab to the airport. The morning was not off to a good start.

We arrived at the airport and a Northwest agent told me the FAA was waiting for us. I assumed it was merely an FAA inspector going on an observation ride with us and I was okay with that. Some pilots didn't particularly like FAA observation rides but I never had a problem with it. It was just part of the job and I was simply never concerned about it.

The FAA inspector was Verle Addison, but he wasn't interested in an observation ride. He immediately told me he had a report about a Northwest crew who were drunk at the Speak Easy. I responded that we had been there but I didn't think anyone was drunk. At the time I actually believed that. But all the nerve endings in my body came to full alert because alcohol issues at Northwest Airlines were deadly.

At that time, Northwest Airlines was the only major carrier with no alcohol program for its pilots. Decades earlier, a former CEO, Donald Nyrop, was approached by representatives of other airlines in an attempt to get Northwest to join the rest of the industry by implementing a program. Nyrop, angrily responded that "Northwest didn't have any alcoholic pilots, and if they did they'd fire them." Then he showed them out of his office. One of the four pilots present related that story to me.

The idea that there were no alcoholics pilots at NWA was beyond absurd. Alcoholism is an equal-opportunity disease and there is no vocation or profession, no line of work *anywhere* that is free of alcoholism. Northwest policy was to fire anyone who came into the public eye or drew any attention because of alcohol. Over the years, I saw a number of people terminated due to drinking situations. Those situations were rare and infrequent, but when they occurred they ripped through the airline like wildfire. The people involved left a legacy of disgrace and their names were permanently etched on our individual walls of shame. None ever returned; termination was swift and irrevocable.

We were in deep trouble and I knew it. I was hung-over but felt sure I was up to the task. Verle Addison checked my licenses, as well as the copilot's, and talked to us about the eight-hour rule. He did not appear concerned about our appearance and never suggested we were not in fit condition to fly. I took that as a good sign. I was sure we were okay on the FAA eight-hour rule but I *knew* I had violated the NWA twelve-hour policy. As it turned out I violated both, but the other crewmembers had only violated the twelve hour rule; still, enough for termination.

Addison left the operations office and I completed the paperwork for the flight. I called and asked flight dispatch to put on more fuel due to the weather.

The copilot had gone to the aircraft to perform his preflight duties. I joined him and asked what he thought we should do. We were both uncertain. I was not at all sure what Addison's position was. He was not telling us not to fly and never suggested anything in that regard. Addison was nowhere to be seen and I had no idea what he was doing.

Our second officer was still a no-show, so I told the copilot to do the walk around, the exterior preflight, once he had completed his cockpit checks. I completed my own checks, preflighted the second officer's panel, and configured it for engine start.

The aircraft was facing the terminal and we could see the gate area through the large glass windows. The second officer finally arrived in the gate area and we could see him talking with Addison. Addison departed once again and the second officer made his way to the cockpit. I told him we'd done his walk around and that I had set his panel up. I told him to check what I had done, then get the checklist out so we could accomplish the "before engine start" procedures.

It was push back time and Addison was nowhere to be seen. Since he was not specifically preventing us from flying I assumed he was tacitly giving us the okay to go. It appeared his only concern was the eight-hour rule. I responded to the push back crew, released the brakes, and began the push back. When cleared, we started the engines. The push back crew disconnected and we called for taxi. I tensed and waited for ground control to tell us to return to the gate. At that point we had fully operated the aircraft and if Addison was setting us up, then we had completed the process. Nothing came.

We were told to taxi to runway 17, a long distance away, and I kept waiting for a radio call instructing us to return to the gate. There was nothing. The Fargo tower then cleared us for takeoff and the copilot took the controls, since it was his turn to fly. It had taken seventeen minutes from push back to the takeoff point and we'd heard nothing from Addison. Later, Addison and the prosecution would claim we pushed back and immediately got airborne which was untrue. We were scheduled to land at Minneapolis, change airplanes, go to Newark, and return to Minneapolis. It would be a long day. I felt sure there would be no alcohol in our systems by the end of it.

But what was going to happen in the meantime? I desperately hoped this would somehow drop through the cracks. It was delusional thinking, but my mind was racing. Perhaps we would be called in some days later, after Addison's report reached the company, and we could come up with some story that would prevent termination. Unlikely, but I was hoping with the desperation of a dying man.

I make no excuses for what took place. It was wrong and I was wrong, period. As all of this was occurring, I was reacting as any alcoholic would and was willing to do anything to avoid the consequences – and escape the situation. Once, I lived by a code of honor but my alcoholism slowly sabotaged my values and I was willing to do anything to avoid what was in front of me. I will say it again – what I did was *wrong* and there is no excuse for it, period. Alcoholism does not give me or any other alcoholic a free pass for anything we do.

As we climbed through 20,000 feet the second officer tapped me on the shoulder and motioned to the radio panel. I switched to the frequency he used for company reports and heard the radio operator instructing us to report to the Vice President of Flight Operations when we landed. We were dead in the water. My mind raced. The general offices were a few miles from the airport. I didn't care if I had to invent a story saying Martians kidnapped us, but we *had* to buy enough time to let the alcohol metabolize out of us. As it turned out, we wouldn't need the Martians.

We landed at approximately 7:00 A.M., on runway 11 Right at Minneapolis. The copilot did his usual good job of flying. Since the steering tiller was on the Captain's side I took the airplane, exited the runway, and began taxiing to gate 21. The weather was not good, there was ice on the ramp area, and gate 21 was the most difficult gate on the airport to park at. It angled in and there were crowded parking spots on either side, making it dicey when aircraft were at those other gates. As luck would have it, both gates were occupied as I headed into gate 21.

I managed to get us in, stopping precisely on the centerline and right on the spot where the nose wheel was supposed to rest. Perhaps God actually *does* watch over fools and drunks.

The fifty-eight passengers deplaned and I walked off the airplane. Coming out of the jet way, my heart stopped as I saw Northwest company officials, FAA personnel, and two uniformed airport police. An overweight FAA agent with a pockmarked face approached me and asked if I was Captain Prouse. I said yes, and he asked me to step over to the side. His ID badge identified him as Doug Solseth. The copilot and second officer followed, and were also asked to step over to the side. Passengers were starting to notice the unusual activity so we were taken to a room on the second floor.

There, Mr. Solseth informed me I was under arrest and presented me with an arrest document, which I signed. The copilot and second officer repeated the process. It was early morning, March 8, 1990. It was to become a twelve-hour ordeal unlike any I had ever experienced.

Of all the feelings that overwhelmed me that day, shame was the greatest. Although I experienced a surreal sense of fear and dread, shame and humiliation surged through my very marrow. During that day I had many moments of sheer out of body experience. There were times I was *sure* this couldn't be happening to me and I was suspended high in the room watching it occur to someone else. Then I would suddenly be transported back to reality and the gut-grinding impact that this *was* happening to *me*.

It was a twelve-hour day of blurred events. At one point, the head of our Air Line Pilot Association, Captain Pete Dodge, was called and his face was lined with deep concern when he arrived. I always liked Pete and had great respect for him. I could hardly meet his eyes as he spoke with us. An ALPA attorney talked with us but I have no memory of what was said. We went to two different medical facilities, escorted by two uniformed police officers, and submitted blood samples both times.

At one of those facilities a reporter saw three uniformed airline pilots escorted by police officers and that was our entry into what would soon become a media blitzkrieg. Finally, Northwest Airline attorneys deposed us. I drew Mr. Doug McKeen, known to be a brutal interrogator.

Strangely, my recollection of him was a gentle one. He did his job, was thorough, prodding, and methodical. But his demeanor was calm and he appeared sorry that he had to question me. I was defeated, completely broken. I never experienced such humiliation and with it, humility. My body language echoed my disgrace and I sat as if compressed, seemingly much smaller than my normal size.

I only remember one specific question Mr. McKeen asked, "Captain Prouse, do you think you abuse alcohol?" I had never been asked that before. My head was down and I slowly looked up, pausing as I considered the question. I replied quietly, "I don't know." And I didn't. In the aftermath, how could I *not* know? But at that moment, I truly didn't know the answer to that question.

Later, I saw Mr. McKeen in court and approached him. I wanted him to know I held no hard feelings and truly understood he had a job to do. I really wanted to tell him I appreciated how kindly he treated me that day, but I didn't have the words.

After the deposition we were driven back to the airport. It had been an interminably long day and was finally over. The three of us sat in a car driven by the assistant chief pilot, Captain Gene Frampton. No one spoke. I looked out the window and it was pitch black. It was almost dark when we landed a thousand years earlier. A thought seeped through my mind "All the light in my life has gone out. It's been forever extinguished and I will live in this darkness forever."

The shame was overwhelming and it was only just beginning. In the days, weeks, and months ahead it would become exponentially worse. It was exacerbated by the fact that I had not lived my life doing shameful things. To the contrary, I was the standard bearer in my family for duty, honor, country. To my children I espoused honesty, character, and integrity. I grew up trying *always* to bring honor, pride, and dignity to all my endeavors. That was true whether I was donning a Marine Corps uniform, representing my heritage, my family, my profession, or my airline. And now I brought shame and disgrace to my entire life – everything I treasured and valued. I was having a difficult time dealing with what had just occurred.

I went to my commuter apartment, a nice place near the airport. Fortunately, none of my other three pilot roommates were there. For the first time that day I thought about calling Barbara. Suddenly, it dawned on me that I was supposed to be home that night; I should have landed in Atlanta by now. I phoned home and the answering machine picked up. Barbara spent four hours at the Atlanta airport waiting for me before finally heading home. I listened to my voice on the answering machine, and when it stopped for the incoming message I didn't know what to say. I managed a mumbled message to Barbara that a disaster had taken place that day and I thought I had lost my job. I said I would be in on the first flight in the morning and hung up. Thankfully, she didn't return my call and I will never understand why. It was the biggest gift she could have given me. I was sick and didn't want to talk.

I spent a sleepless night tossing about while reliving the day's events. There was no way to escape the relentless torture. The next morning I donned my uniform and walked through the Minneapolis-St. Paul terminal for the flight to Atlanta. Every time someone glanced my way I flinched and felt the blow of shame. Soon they would all know. *Everyone* would know.

How had my life come to this? I worked hard to establish and achieve an honorable trajectory through life. Suddenly my life had been hijacked and I found myself in a smoking crater with wreckage all around me. I came a long way in life, through many struggles, and thought I had emerged victorious. A lifetime of effort was gone and all I could feel was shame, disgrace, and dishonor.

Devastation

I sat on the DC-9 the morning after the arrest. I spoke to no one and realized this would be the last time I ever wore my uniform. Upon landing, I quickly exited the gate area. I knew all the agents and used to laugh and joke with the mechanics, baggage handlers, and groomers. I wanted no one to see me or speak to me. I got to the front of the terminal and saw Barbara parked nearby. I dreaded the walk to the car, and felt like I had to climb over the curb to get inside with her.

Unable to even look her way, all I could do was quietly struggle with the words, "Honey, I'm so sorry." She pulled away from the curb and in her soft voice and south Texas accent, she said, "Who, better than I, can possibly understand how you feel?" We drove home in silence; I simply couldn't speak about the events of a few hours ago.

I expected her to have an angry reaction and she had every right. Certainly, it seemed she would have a number of questions at the very least. Yet Barbara's soft voice and brief comment was all that fell on my ears that morning. It was another huge gift from her.

I walked in the house and Barbara went to work. It was deathly quiet, tomb-like. Every nerve ending in my body seemed to be shorting out. I wanted out of my skin. I walked to the phone and called Dr. Yarbrough. I said I needed to declare an emergency and had to see him immediately. He cleared his calendar and I drove to his office. I was emotionally and mentally shredded.

I walked into Dr. Yarbrough's office and told him what happened. His face registered shock and surprise as he took in the news. Shaking his head in disbelief, he walked around the side of his desk saying, "God, Lyle, this is horrible. This is just terrible." Then he paused thoughtfully, looked up at me, and made a statement that went beyond my limited ability to understand. He said, "But maybe this is what had to happen." I had no idea why he'd say that to me. I couldn't even begin to struggle with it and I didn't even try. He worked intimately with me for two years, learning all there was to know about me – almost.

He left the office and came back a few moments later. He said, "You have an appointment tonight at 6:00 P.M. with Dr. Uzee. He's a very prominent psychiatrist on the other side of Atlanta. He is a recovering alcoholic and cocaine addict, and is also certified in Addiction Medicine." I never *heard* of addiction medicine.

It was Friday, March 9th, 1990. I knew of no doctors who saw patients at 6 o'clock on Friday nights. The timing of the appointment conveyed a certain sense of urgency and I knew there was deep concern from both doctors. Much later, I was told they wanted to head off a suicide. My emotional condition and appearance prompted that concern.

Barbara came home and we headed across Atlanta to Dr. Uzee's office. I hadn't eaten for two days so we stopped and I tried to get a hamburger down but one bite was all I could manage. We made our way to Dr. Uzee's office and went in. Barbara waited in the reception area as the doctor and I moved to another room. I have no memory of what took place, what was said, what questions were asked, or how long he and I talked. The whole event was very much like an alcoholic blackout but I was sober. I don't know if we talked for ten minutes or an hour. What I *do* recall is such total defeat that I didn't try to hedge answers or cut corners; I did my best to answer as honestly as I was capable of at that moment.

At some point Dr. Uzee looked at me and said, "Lyle, you're an alcoholic and you need to get into treatment tonight." All my life I hated alcoholics. They were the losers, the dregs of society, and the non-hackers. I felt nothing but disgust and repugnancy toward them. I watched my parents and swore *never* to be an alcoholic. I remembered small Oklahoma towns on the weekends during the powwows, when I saw drunken Indians on the streets. Again, I said, "I will *never* be like that!"

And now, after being told I was an alcoholic I didn't react. I simply felt numb. In the twenty-four hours since my arrest I suspect somewhere deep inside me I connected the dots. I think I made the connection at some level that my life was completely destroyed because I drank alcohol in a bar when I wasn't supposed to. I realized that I'd lost the ability to control my drinking; that I was no longer able to "just have a few" and leave. I think I *knew* I was an alcoholic. In the past, other alcohol-related incidents were written off to bad luck, circumstances, coincidence, and I dismissed them accordingly. "That could happen to *anyone*," had been a favorite theory. Not now, not anymore.

I paused, looked at Dr. Uzee, and said, "I thought you'd probably tell me that. I have no problem going into treatment but I just got home today. I'd like to go home, have Barbara pull the drapes, and just hang onto me. *Please*, just let her hold onto me until I can absorb what's happened and my mind can uncoil. Then I'll go in first thing Monday morning." He looked at me and said once more, "You need to get into treatment – *tonight*."

I paused and thought to myself, "Why did I come here tonight if I'm not going to follow this doctor's directions?" so I said, "Okay." It was my first lesson in willingness.

Dr. Uzee drew a map to Anchor Hospital. Barbara and I made our way back across Atlanta to the facility and it was dark as we made our final turn. The headlights hit a sign and I came to a stop with the lights directly on it. The sign is no longer there, but at the time it said: *Anchor Hospital: A Hospital for Alcoholism and Other Chemical Dependencies.*

As I sat with the sign in front of me, I felt as though I had been kicked in the stomach. I sat and looked at the sign and wondered how my life could have come to this. I was fifty-one years old and my life was to end in a treatment center for alcoholics. I had microseconds of recall, flashing back to the high points in my life, defining moments of pride and accomplishment that made me who I was and gave me an identity. I measured my success by them and each allowed me to slowly rise from the rubble and become someone. But in *that moment* it was as though a giant eraser swept everything away and it was all gone. In the seconds that followed I counted for nothing. I had no self-worth and no value as a human being.

Later, I would read a doctor's report with the summarizing paragraph stating, "Given the history and background of this man, it was unlikely to believe he would ever be a productive member of society." Yet I had come far and accomplished much – and now I had lost it *all*.

Treatment

S lowly, I began the drive down the winding hill into the treatment center. As the car crept forward, for the first time that day it occurred to me that it was March 9th – our 27th wedding anniversary. Beaten and ashamed I muttered to Barbara, "Helluva' way to spend an anniversary, huh?" She responded softly and quietly, "It might be the best one we've ever had." As with Dr. Yarbrough's statement earlier, I was at a loss for words. *Who* could possibly think something like that at a moment like this?

The answer lay in the heart of a wife who loved me unconditionally and would stay with me no matter what happened or what I became. Barbara stopped drinking three months before my arrest and she had no intention of abandoning me now. We had traveled far together, but I could not remotely comprehend what she was saying.

Our family was slowly torn apart and she had watched it disintegrate. Mere hours before, our entire lives were irrevocably changed by my arrest and this was the final blow. Or so we thought.

As I made my way down the winding hill to the treatment center my mind raced through imaginary pictures of what I would encounter. The movie, "One Flew Over the Cuckoo's Nest," flashed into my mind. I could not have been more wrong.

An African-American nurse named Joanne admitted me at 8:00 P.M. that Friday night. She was bright and attractive, but more than anything else she had a soft and serene manner, which helped settle me a tiny bit. She is still a good friend today, many years later. Once I was signed in and all the paperwork completed, Barbara kissed me, gave me a hug, and left. I was alone in this foreign place, a place I *never* thought I would see.

Joanne took me to the Adult Unit, where I would spend the next twenty-eight days. A clinical assistant (CA) named Don finished my processing. His appearance yelled "ex con," which he was. He was balding with a fringe of white hair. Prison tattoos covered both arms and his long white unkempt beard frizzled outwards and down toward his chest.

Don took me by the arm and apologetically said, "I have to strip search you." This was the final degradation in the midst of all I had already heaped upon myself and my face must have registered it. He said, "I don't want to do this, but I'm supposed to. Do you have anything on you?" I shook my head no. Don looked at me, paused, and said, "Okay, I'm not going to search you." I breathed a sigh of relief and he took me to my room. The omission of the strip search was a huge gift and I was deeply appreciative. Already I was gaining a new perspective on life and foregoing a strip search was a gift I would never forget.

I was also learning not to be so quick to judge people by their appearances. Don was a kind and considerate man, a recovering alcoholic and addict, as was nearly the entire hospital staff. In the days to follow I learned much from Don as he generously helped me settle in. A few days later, as the media blitz about me began, Don looked at me and quietly said, "When ya' do whatcha' did...ya' get whatcha' got." The meaning was clear. I did what I did and I must now accept the consequences. This was not a new concept; I'd always done that. But I had never done anything so catastrophically serious and I was dreading the outcome.

The night I arrived most of the patients were attending an outside recovery meeting, so the hospital appeared almost empty. An hour later they all came pouring back in. Many were laughing and all appeared friendly. However, I wanted nothing to do with anyone. Even in this setting, a treatment center for alcoholics and addicts, I felt completely inferior because of the shame I was carrying. I couldn't meet anyone's eyes and I certainly didn't want to speak with anyone. In spite of that, many introduced themselves. They were from everywhere: Utah, Arizona,

Alabama, Louisiana, Kentucky, and a host of other states. I wondered what sort of place I was in. Finally, I met some people from Georgia, but the mix of people from all around the country puzzled me.

I spent a restless night and awakened early the next morning. I arrived the night before with only the clothes on my back. The staff gave me a toothbrush and some toiletries. I had to sign out an electric razor since sharp objects weren't permitted. I cleaned up the best I could. It was Saturday morning and the weekend routine was in place, suspending the busy activities and daily events in the normal treatment schedule.

I walked outside to the back of the hospital where the recreation area was. Unbeknown to me, the hospital was barely three miles south of the Atlanta International airport. Suddenly, I heard the unmistakable roar of a jet taking off and I instinctively turned to look, as I always have and always will. It was a U.S. Airways 727 and it was close. It was the same type of plane I'd been flying. Steep in the climb profile, the landing gear was just coming up as I watched it accelerate skyward. Within seconds I was hit with the realization that I would never again fly or see the inside of a cockpit. I began to get sick. Swallowing hard and choking it down, I turned my back and walked away.

A row of chairs lined the recreation area next to the hospital. I walked over and sat down. The chairs were about three feet apart and I saw someone in my periphery sitting in the chair on my left. I didn't look at the person and I didn't want to talk. A voice said, "You know, if I only had a month to live, this is where I'd want to be." Having only been there one night it seemed a bewildering comment. I had no idea if they were talking to me, the birds, the trees, or someone on *their* left. A second passed and I felt compelled to respond. Without turning my head, I uttered a somewhat non-committal, "Really...?" The voice replied in an angry manner, "Yeah! 'Cause every god damned day here seems like a year!" I never turned to see who owned the voice and I still didn't know when I left the hospital twenty-eight days later.

Although I was in a place I never expected to be, the kind of a place that previously conjured up all sort of negative images, it later became my cocoon, the place of a rebirth. I discovered people who cared deeply about me even though they didn't know me. These strangers huddled around me as the days passed. Through countless encounters and end-less hours, they patiently worked to piece me back together.

In those early days I felt as though I had landed on Mars, on a totally foreign and desolate planet. As I lay in bed at night I could only wonder what happened to me and what brought me to this place. I never experienced such a feeling of total isolation. Consciously, I knew Barbara was still with me, but I felt so alone. I could not have been more emotionally isolated if I was alone on a small island. People moved around me and I was aware of them, yet I was absolutely isolated.

As a patient I was not allowed phone calls or visitors. A few days into treatment I received a composition notebook sent by Barbara. She quit answering the phone due to the incessant barrage of calls from scores of reporters all over the United States. We had an unlisted phone number but the reporters had no trouble getting it. So she listened to messages on the answering machine and returned the calls of friends. There was no one who hadn't called, it seemed. All the talk shows called, from quality shows like Oprah's to Inside Edition, Current Affair, and Geraldo.

The first several pages of the spiral notebook listed names and messages from friends who called. They wanted to know if we were okay and if they could help in any way. I was touched as I read the long list of names – yet I still felt completely alone. At the end of the names was a message from Barbara. She said, "Keep your spirits up, concentrate on your recovery, forget the outside world, and come home to me. We will get through this. God has a plan in mind for us. Love, Barb." My mind rebelled against the idea that anything good could come from this horrible nightmare.

I received a Bible from Mike Cunningham, an Ex-Marine friend of mine who had a meat cutting business in Conyers. He was devoutly religious and was affected by what happened to me. He circled a verse and put the ribbon at that point. I opened it to Jeremiah 29: 11-13, and read:

> "For I know the plans that I have for you," declares the Lord, "Plans for welfare and not for calamity, to give you a future and a hope. Then you will call upon Me and come and pray to Me, and I will listen to you. And you will seek Me and find Me, when you search for Me with all your heart."

How could these things be true? How could anyone *possibly* think such things? I could more easily understand Einstein's theory of relativity than grasp Mike and Barbara's comments.

In the near future I would spend a day in federal prison simply trying to *imagine* having a good day once more. I didn't ask for much, just a fleeting image of someday smiling, laughing, and enjoying a "good day." It was important to imagine, yet it was beyond my reach. I quit trying. It was impossible to see there could be any positive outcome from this nightmare.

As I began the first week of treatment that Monday morning, I looked at the busy schedule of events. There was precious little time during the day when I wasn't involved in a group or lecture activity. And the day didn't end until we completed the simulated recovery meeting at 8:00 P.M. The meeting was conducted by the patients and overseen by the staff. Anchor Hospital followed a 12-step protocol for recovery, as do most treatment centers I'm familiar with.

In the early days of my treatment I was so fractured that I could hardly dress myself and find my way to the various functions. Robotically, I sat, listened, and attempted to absorb information. My head was always down, eyes averted, and I never took them off my shoe tops. I wanted no one to know who or what I was. The media soon took care of that.

Within a day or so of my entry every lead news story on television had to do with the three Northwest Airline pilots arrested for flying drunk. Time, Newsweek, People, and other magazines pushed the story and published photos of me. Jay Leno had a field day with me in his nightly monologue. Leno told his audience, "So...if you're flying Northwest and can't find the beverage cart...check the cockpit!"

Lewis Grizzard was a local humorist who carried some public baggage of his own involving alcohol-related incidents. But a few days into treatment I read a newspaper column in which he parodied a make-believe conversation between the copilot and me prior to flight. It was particularly hurtful.

Suffering more than I thought was humanly possible, the publicity firestorm pushed me toward the dark abyss of suicide. I never thought myself capable of such thoughts. In Vietnam I wrestled with the idea of suicide versus capture should I be shot down. I never resolved that internal struggle, resting first on one side of the question then the other. I had a reputation of being durable and I'd survived many difficult experiences. In a brief time I moved beyond the point of thinking about suicide to actively planning it. I had reached the point of unbearable suffering. It had to end and any means to accomplish that was acceptable.

My physician was Doctor Philip Wilson, the medical director for Anchor Hospital. He put me on medication, something he hated doing when dealing with someone who already had an alcoholism problem. But I was so shredded and destroyed that my vital signs were off the page. The tiny yellow pills did nothing to grant me sleep at night. I lay awake night after night, unable to sleep as my mind played and replayed the arrest and the horror that followed. I wished, over and over, that I could rewind the tape and do things differently. There was no way out and I just wanted to die.

Several days later, Dr. Wilson examined me again. When he asked if I was having any problems, I told him I was unable to sleep. He smiled and replied, "We've never lost a patient due to lack of sleep." I got the message. I would sleep when it was time, so I accepted that premise. Later, I became aware that many patients would do anything to get drugs of *any* sort and I wondered if he thought that was what I wanted. It wasn't.

Although it felt like I never slept, I somehow managed a few moments of sleep. For nearly the first week, I had a recurring dream each night. In the dream, I would awaken to discover I had not actually done these things. I would gulp in huge amounts of air as my spirits soared with indescribable relief and I would rejoice with incredible gratitude that none of it was real!

Then...my eyes would open and I would see the walls of my hospital room. My spirits would plummet as I sank into a blackness of despair. This was a daily occurrence for the first week. I thought to myself there could be no crueler hoax, yet I never found myself angry with God for the dreams; I never attempted to blame Him.

As I planned my suicide, I had a breakthrough moment where I knew it would be the *only thing* worse than what already occurred. My family could not survive the scarring and stigma of my suicide in a treatment center. I can only ascribe that insight as a God-given moment of clarity in the midst of my devastated emotional condition. Reluctantly, I pulled back from the idea of killing myself. Perhaps it was a throwback to my Native roots, but I believed I might be able to will myself to die and that was acceptable. As long as I didn't dishonor myself more than I already had by slashing my wrists or hanging myself, death would not only be acceptable, but welcome. So I devoted endless amounts of emotional energy trying to make my heart stop beating. If there had been a switch in my mind to stop my heart, I would have flipped it without a second thought.

The treatment process was subtle and I was not able to see the changes occurring. In the midst of all I was learning, I slowly began thinking more about living than dying. I owe that to the love and dedication of my counselors, the doctors, and fellow patients. I would have been lost without them.

On March 16, 1990, one week after my entry into treatment, patients watching TV notified me that Northwest Airlines fired me. Furthermore, the FAA issued an emergency revocation of all my flight licenses, something rarely done at that time. Pat Brennaman, an Air Line Pilot Association attorney at Northwest, asked Barbara to send in my licenses. Pat was a superb attorney with unquestioned integrity and I had nothing but respect for him. He had talked with me the day I was arrested. Barbara feared my reaction when I discovered she surrendered my licenses, but Pat assured her it had to be done. It was an unfounded fear because I accepted, even that early in recovery, complete responsibility for all that took place. I always accepted responsibility for my actions, in the Marine Corps, and at the airline. This, however, was a bitter pill to swallow due to the extreme consequences involved. I already lost my FAA medical certificate due to the diagnosis of alcoholism, so I was now completely stripped of everything involving my flying career. There were, however, more losses headed my way.

The hospital had two TV sets and I stayed clear of both. There were times I would walk out a door and go completely around the hospital to avoid passing by a TV set. However, certain patients felt compelled to bring me all the bad news and jokes, so I was constantly informed.

A few days into treatment I was taken outside the hospital to a meeting of Birds of a Feather, a group of recovering pilots worldwide.

Ashamed and humiliated, I dreaded walking into a room of pilots with my story so freshly before the public. I expected to be spat upon by my peers. I would not have gone if I had not been forced to.

Perhaps one of the most profound truths I learned was that we need love *most* – when we deserve it the *least*. I received it that night. There were thirty-six pilots in the room that evening and each one looked directly at me and told me how they got there.

That night I experienced love, kindness, and understanding, the very opposite of what I was expecting and deserved. Several meetings later I asked a gent named Charlie if he would mentor me. He agreed and was there for sixteen years until his death. He went down the recovery road ahead of me and knew where the bumps and ruts were. He knew how to stay out of the ditch and steered me away. In the intervening years I have tried to pass that along to others behind me. So it goes, with one alcoholic helping another.

Nearing the end of the first week I began to get word of legal consequences. Although hospital policy dictated no visitors or phone calls, grim things were happening on the legal front that my counselor was forced to tell me. First, Minnesota was going to charge me with a state misdemeanor resulting in a 90-day jail period. This news was a crushing blow. I expected FAA action, and expected to be fired by Northwest. However, *no one* anticipated legal action, neither the ALPA attorneys nor the Northwest attorneys. No one knew of any laws on the books that applied to this event. North Dakota also filed charges and finally the federal government followed suit. Over the next two weeks I received five more debilitating pieces of news, each one escalating the penalties and charges.

I would be in a group of patients and the door would open. A staff member would step inside and began to scan the faces as I held my breath and watched. As they looked at me, they would motion me out and my heart would sink. Each time the news was worse, the penalties increased, or in some cases doubled, and I would have to struggle to breathe. I felt as though the air was sucked out of the room and I couldn't get any oxygen. I began to feel as though this would never end. I was introduced to the concept of acceptance, a process *much* more involved than I ever imagined. I worked hard to grasp this idea and employ it. Yet each time I was given the latest bad news I seemed to start over from zero.

I asked my counselor, Robin, about acceptance and explained my failure and frustration. I thought acceptance was some form of absolute. That once obtained, I would be invulnerable to the fear and panic that disabled me with each new, escalating legal event. No, Robin explained, acceptance is a constantly ongoing process, and I would have to rise to a new level of acceptance with each new and bigger challenge. I left his office feeling that I *might* be making progress, and starting to gain *some* understanding. But I was not looking forward to the continuing climb up the mountain ahead. It was getting steeper and steeper and the challenges were formidable.

As all this was occurring, I experienced what was probably my greatest breakthrough in treatment. It came unexpectedly. Wednesday of my first week I walked into room 358 of the hospital, the room where my group therapy was held. I was still tucked up inside myself, could not look at anyone, and was struggling with my shame. As the door closed, I neither intended to talk nor did I intend *not* to talk; I was simply there. Eight or ten of us took our seats as Robin began the group session.

Shortly into the group I began to talk. I have no idea why as it was totally counterintuitive to all I felt. For some reason I began to speak of Dawn and all my defenses came down in a choking, sobbing rush of tears. I didn't feel it coming or I would have headed it off. Perhaps it was the very first time in my life I looked pain in the face and simply accepted it for what it was. Anger was my coping tool and I could either avoid or override pain by calling up more anger. But not this time – I simply allowed the pain to come – and felt my heart break.

As I sat there sobbing, my body racked with uncontrollable pain, I surrendered my vulnerability in front of all the others. For the first time ever, I acknowledged my helplessness and my hopelessness, and accepted the pain for what it was. A few moments later, as I collected myself, I immediately regretted what I had done. I felt naked, as though I was sitting in the group with no clothes on. I dreaded the walk back into the hospital population when the door to the room opened. However, as the group ended, I was surprised as each of them came and held me in a hug, expressing a heartfelt gesture of support for what I just managed to do.

I began my healing that day. Only by becoming weak could I become strong again. Only by making myself open and vulnerable to others could I inspire or gain their trust, thus allowing them to do the same with me. Only by acknowledging my powerlessness could I begin to gain power. I was caught in a turmoil of paradoxes, all of which could easily confuse me. On that day I learned it *was* okay for men to cry, that it had absolutely <u>nothing</u> to do with my toughness or my manhood. I lived under that myth for a lifetime. God granted me the ability to recover the full range of feeling every human being is entitled to. Mine was shut off for a long time. I rejoined the human race that day, as a full-fledged member, but it would take a while before I could see that.

I wrote Barbara that I wanted to see Dawn again. When the staff discovered this they said they would waive the no-visitor rule because this was such an impossible breakthrough. It was time to put our family back together. I asked Barbara to get in touch with our youngest son, Jay, and bring him also. Of course, Scott would also come. I was gaining new insight, not only into myself but into others as well. I was able to understand that Jay did not wish to be an alcoholic or addict anymore than I did. I understood that my parents had not willingly chosen that either. *I made no excuses for any of us*, but I gained an understanding of what we were suffering from. But most of all, I could forgive and move on.

The staff allowed our family to meet in a hospital dayroom. Both Dr. Yarbrough and Dr. Uzee asked if they could be present at the reunion. They added that they would stay out of the way, but each genuinely wanted to see our family come back together again.

So, in my second week of treatment I walked into a dayroom and saw Dawn for the first time in two years. She knew about my hatred, had seen me angry before, and was fearful of coming up from Tampa, where she now lived. She was married now and I didn't even know her last name. As I looked at her for the first time in two years she appeared smaller than I remembered.

No words can describe the feeling I had when I put my arms around her and told her how much I loved her – instead of how much I hated her. In her arms was Lauren, my five-month old granddaughter I knew little about. Barbara leaked the information to me and I shut her off because I didn't want to hear it. I took my little granddaughter in my arms and she stole my heart as quickly as Dawn had the first time I held her. I walked to Jay and hugged him also. He was still drinking and drugging and, while I made no excuses or allowances for him, I was able to love him as he was, something I was unable to do mere days earlier.

I saw the two doctors standing off to the side – I glanced over at Barbara. She was experiencing a moment of great joy as she watched her family reunite in one place, pulled back together by love, and becoming a whole family once again. We were so splintered and so fractured for so long.

Once the excitement died down I turned to matters I did not want to discuss. I told my kids they should prepare themselves to see me hand-cuffed and led into custody on television. Yet, even at that point, the worst was yet to come.

Barbara was standing to my left and I saw her extend her arms outward, palms up, and she softly said, "I feel as though the sky is falling down all around us...but I'm catching the stars." I couldn't speak. Tears welled up in my eyes as I looked at the beautiful girl I had married who, in the midst of total disaster, was managing to catch the stars.

As I sat in group a few days later, the door opened and a CA stepped in and began searching the group. I kept my eyes on him, hoping against hope he was looking for someone else. He wasn't. I stepped outside and saw Robin. This time Doctor Gallegos, a staff doctor, accompanied him. My mouth went dry because a doctor had never been present before. We walked to Dr. Gallegos' office and he told me to sit down – another bad sign. He said, "Lyle, I have to tell you a federal grand jury has just indicted you and you're looking at 15 years in prison and a $250,000 fine. And an attorney is coming in to see you on Sunday and wants $50,000." I was staggered. Every nerve in my body shut down and I went numb.

I sat in stunned silence as Dr. Gallegos said, "I have to ask you if you're going to hurt yourself." I shook my head no. I walked back to my room in a daze. Inside my room I sat and looked out the window. Unable to remain still, I got up, went to the bathroom, and splashed water on my face. Then I attempted to take a drink of water. I walked to the main part of my room and collapsed. I do not remember falling but I remember my face against the carpet, and I was crying for the second time in treatment. I said out loud through the tears, "God, I can't do this anymore. I just don't have anything left – not even one more time. Please help me."

I got to my feet and something strange occurred. Out of nowhere I remembered a patient who had recently left AMA (against medical advice). She just walked out. Her name was Lilly and we had been close friends. She was a hard looking hairdresser who smoked like a chimney. Normally, I would never have spoken to her, but for whatever reason she and I used to stay up late at night and talk. I grew fond of her and was sad when she left.

Word filtered back to the patient group that she went home, relapsed, nearly died from alcohol poisoning, and was beaten by her husband. Reportedly, she went to a local hospital and spent time in the ICU. I remembered that Lilly had written in my textbook, as many other patients did, and I had her mailing address.

I don't know why, but I sat down at my desk and wrote Lilly a letter. I never alluded to what we heard in the patient group, but I expressed concern and encouraged her to return to us if things got bad. I was absorbed in the letter for twenty minutes. When finished, I addressed it and took it to the nurse's station to be mailed. I returned to my room and was suddenly aware that for the period of time I had been concerned about Lilly and engaged in writing her, I was at peace. I was free of the fear that choked me. Gone were the mental pictures of prison and the hopelessness that had marked so much of my journey thus far.

Later, I would learn about "getting out of self" when overwhelmed with fear, doubt, and what the future held; that becoming "others centered" instead of "self centered," was the secret for finding peace in times of turmoil. So simple, yet not something I would instinctively know. Even today I still need to be reminded. But my experience with Lilly's letter reinforced all I would later be told. Ironically, it was the day I received the most horrific news of all. I had never known such terror, yet I slept that night and awoke the next morning rested.

The policy of no visitors or phone calls was designed so we would focus on our recovery full time, with no outside distractions; yet I was given outside news every two to three days that was paralyzing in nature.

So I had to double and redouble my efforts inside the hospital. Because there was a television in the recreation room, I spent evenings in my room reading as much as I could about alcoholism and recovery. I read and reread the primary text for alcoholics, along with a second book. I did every exercise in the thick workbook we'd been given although most patients opted not to do them and the staff didn't insist. Everyone had to do a lengthy writing on the first Step, then submit a life story.

I watched as counselors exhorted patients to get their assignments completed in the waning days of their treatment. They *had* to be done before discharge. I completed both before I was halfway through the twenty-eight days.

Robin knew I had issues with my parents, both of whom had taken this disease to their graves many years earlier. He suggested I write a farewell letter to my father, since I'd had more difficulty with him than my mom. I spent hours writing the letter, then rewriting it. Finally, I took it to Robin and announced I was ready to read it to him. Robin informed me I would read it in front of the entire patient group. I turned white, "Oh no, Robin, I can't do that! There's just no way I could do that." He leaned back, looked at me, and replied, "The power is in the group. If you want the healing, you need to do it there. But," he continued, "If you absolutely cannot do that, I'll listen to it and we'll do it that way."

I went back to my room. I never took the easy way out. Not here in treatment, not as a Marine or in any of my other roles in life. I took my treatment seriously and tried to do everything I was asked to do. But I didn't know about this. I wanted no shortcuts but I had written an intensely personal and lengthy letter to my father. I thought I could figure out a way to do it in front of the group, so I began reading the letter out loud in my room. Over and over, I read it aloud and knew it took exactly seventeen minutes to conclude. I repeated this exercise at least twenty times. I thought I could inure myself to the emotional parts by exposing myself to them again and again so they became routine and meaningless. Finally, I told Robin I was ready.

The large patient group gathered and I nervously pulled out the letter and began to read. It was if I had just written it and every ounce of pain hit me in the heart as I struggled over and over to get through it. I had to stop, take some deep breaths, and wipe away my tears so I could see the paper.

Many years later I traveled to the small Kansas town of Eureka. I sat at my father's graveside and read the letter out loud. It had the same impact as it did that day in treatment. I let my tears fall on his grave, and when it was over, I stood and walked away in peace.

Looking Back At The
Beginning – Wichita - 1938

T
he September 26, 1938, edition of *Life* magazine has a lengthy black and white photo layout of Adolf Hitler and Neville Chamberlain meeting at Berchtesgarden. A few pages later there is a series of eight dreamy and palatial homes that "anyone can afford if they make $5,000 to $6,000 a year." The top home, priced at $10,000, was designed by Frank Lloyd Wright, the leading architect of the day. It could be had for $58.82 per month, according to the FHA and a 20 year mortgage.

I pushed my way into the world three days after the magazine came out. My sister would follow twenty-three months later. I was born in Wichita, Kansas, a town that sprang from the Kansas prairies in 1863 when peaceful Wichita Indians built a settlement of grass huts there. The area had long been neutral ground for many tribes who came there to trade. Wichita evolved into a rough and tumble cow town, then eventually became known as "The Air Capital of the World" due to Boeing, Beech, and Cessna aircraft plants.

My parents, Vernon and Louise Prouse, were both native Kansans. They were good people and extraordinarily hard-workers, but they were also alcoholics. Life was never easy and the day-to-day environment was challenging. Our economic situation was like elastic stretched to the limit, always ready to snap. Owning a home was out of the question and most of my childhood was spent in rentals. Old autos with faded paint were the norm for us. Make-do repairs, windows that didn't work, and second hand tires or retreads kept us going.

Before I entered seventh grade we moved like gypsies, living first in Oak Ridge, Tennessee, during the war years of WWII. Then it was on to Jacksonville, Little Rock, and Fayetteville, Arkansas, before returning home to Wichita. In Fayetteville, the city condemned the home we lived in at 10 Northeast Street. We moved into a converted chicken shack a few miles away on Mount Sequoyah.

I constantly changed schools and dreaded the routine of making new friends. Playing baseball eased my constant reentry into strange and unfamiliar situations and became my social lubricant. I was somewhat shy, even though some of my early report cards commented that I was a natural leader.

Fayetteville was a town of 13,000 in the late 40s and early 50s, nestled in the northwest corner of the state and home to the University of Arkansas. It was a beautiful rural area of hills and countryside near the Ozark Mountains, a peaceful place where life seemed to go by slowly.

I had my first job at the age of nine or so as I took a morning paper route for $5 a week and sold newspapers on the town square in the afternoons for a nickel each. I made two cents per paper and became the top businessman among us newsboys, selling thirty papers a day when twenty was considered high success. That first summer I paid for my own bicycle, a brand new $39 red Western Flyer, at the rate of $3 a week.

I wanted a .22 rifle so I answered a magazine ad and sold enough skin salve to win a cheap single shot .22 rifle that still resides in my gun safe. Alone with my faithful dog, Mac, I spent many afternoons hunting squirrels and rabbits as I roamed the hills and woods. Mac was a terrier mix, rather stocky, with the most expressive eyes I ever saw on a dog. He possessed amazing intelligence and his expressions seemed almost human.

My parents started a diaper service business that failed after many months of backbreaking work. The equipment was primitive, with two old fashioned tub washers with wringer attachments and two dryers.

They worked long hours each day, their hands red and raw from soap and bleach. Their faces mirrored their exhaustion. They never complained and as I watched them I unconsciously absorbed their work ethic. They were unable to sustain the business so they closed it and we moved back to Wichita. Unknown to me at the time, trouble was brewing between my parents and bad things lay ahead.

As I entered my early teens the alcohol finally tore the family apart. For most of my childhood I don't recall alcohol being a problem. Suddenly, it loomed larger than anything I ever saw or experienced and it dwarfed everything around me. It was an alien presence, turning my parents into strangers and creating a constant sense of uncertainty in our home.

We attempted to break out of our social and economic strata by moving into a nice area of Wichita, and for the first time I glimpsed the surroundings of comfortable middle-class America. The almost new duplex at 535 Rutan Street was nicer than any place we ever lived and I enrolled at Roosevelt Junior High. Immediately, I felt out of place and knew I didn't belong. Perhaps I sensed the more affluent atmosphere and decided I wasn't accepted; I was very uneasy.

I became the target of a cliquish group of boys, led by a very popular and large boy who was on the junior high wrestling team. Although Gary never came after me, nearly all his followers did, and I engaged in fights with most of them. I was always the outsider, the underdog, and always the one no one was yelling or cheering for. I remember the frightened and desperate loneliness and the cotton-mouthed fear of each fight. I heard the sound of my voice an octave higher, felt the blood pounding in my heart and head. I could hardly breathe. Somehow I always managed to prevail, but each time it was over I always walked away alone, with no friends and no supporters, wondering when the next situation was going to come.

There seemed to be no end to the conflicts and my school days were tense as the weeks and months dragged by. There was no easy way to do it other than one day at a time.

As I made my way to class one day, I climbed the stairs into a mezzanine area of the school. There was a large glass window area overlooking the front entrance of the school. Gary and some of his friends had cornered a student who was mentally handicapped. They were telling him to take his pants off or they were going to throw him from the window. I saw the crowd and the fear on this boy's face. Although I didn't know him personally, I was angered at how he was being bullied and intimidated. My anger overrode my fear of the crowd and I walked over to him and then turned and confronted the group. They dispersed and that was the end of it.

I hadn't been at Roosevelt long when my parents announced we were moving again but this time I welcomed the news. We were in serious financial trouble and needed to exit quickly. My parents headed for a WWII housing project on the southeast edge of Wichita called Planeview, located near the Boeing aircraft plant and McConnell Air Force Base. It was an economically depressed area and was where we needed to be.

Planeview consisted of very small single unit homes mixed with equally small two, three, and four plex single-story homes built during WWII. Construction had been hurried and the dwellings were not intended to last, nor did they hold up particularly well. They were all simple structures without garages and were cheap to buy or rent. They had asbestos exteriors which was easily chipped and broken, and often had splotchy areas of missing siding.

The only available housing was in the all-black section so we moved into a small single unit at 2565 Holyoke Lane. I hadn't led a sheltered life but I'd never been around many black people. It was a depressed and squalid area. We settled in and I felt okay. I made many black friends but it was a tough neighborhood and I remained watchful. Although my bicycle was chained to the outside gas meter, the handlebars, seat, and carriage rack were stolen. I came home one afternoon and found someone trying to crawl into my bedroom window after taking the screen off.

Both my parents worked and my sister and I were alone much of the time. She was never to go anywhere unescorted, so I went wherever she went. I grew to resent that responsibility even though I understood it. I settled in comfortably and enjoyed my school time at Planeview. There were none of the problems that plagued me at Roosevelt and I felt at home in my new surroundings. Planeview was not a pretty place but I was at ease and life seemed good.

It was a homogenous and diverse area. Blacks, Whites, Hispanics, and Native Americans all lived there. The overwhelming majority of the time everyone got along and there was very little trouble. It was before gangs and drive-by shootings, and the only vice any of us sought was alcohol. Street drugs were scant and were deemed deplorable. It was the 50s, a time when girls were not ashamed of their virginity and a promiscuous girl was whispered about.

Two unmarried people living together was unheard of, and a single girl who became pregnant usually went away to have her baby and tried to hide the event. There was a totally different moral compass in the 50s notwithstanding the advent of Rock 'n Roll, Elvis Presley, The Big Bopper, Jerry Lee Lewis, and all the rest.

I met Truman Ware in the 7th grade and we quickly became friends. Truman was a Kiowa Indian. I became close to him and his family. He and I were about the same size and our personalities meshed. We both had a good sense of humor and laughed a lot. We shared many classes together and were teammates on the high school baseball team. Truman was outgoing and friendly, yet there was a quiet toughness about him no one ever questioned or challenged.

The Indian blood in my family was rarely discussed. Although it was stronger on my mom's side, dad allegedly had some too. I knew nothing about my mother's family, and have no recollection of ever meeting any relative from her side. I never considered it abnormal to only have one set of grandparents, cousins, aunts, and uncles. Years later I realized that half of my family tree was a mystery.

As I approached my teens I began to get brief snippets of information from my mom about her family. The graphic nature of those revelations was such I'm almost sure she was drinking when they were revealed. She was grimly abused in her family; and her stepfather raped her repeatedly. She disclosed no specific details but her eyes left no doubt as to the horror and pain. My father mentioned the abuse and the fact that my mother married him primarily to get away from her family. That was confusing and troubling news to a young teenager.

I learned that a backstreet doctor also raped my mother while she was a teenager. It was the 1920's and the doctor refused to perform an illegal abortion on her older sister unless my mother had sex with him. To someone my age these were monstrous revelations and I was ill prepared.

As time passed I pieced together many things, including the native blood, or as much as could be gleaned. From what I learned, we were Comanche and whatever other tribe may have been on my father's side, plus English, Irish, and Swedish. I do not recall a specific moment of discovery and the vagueness about my mother's family clouded the matter. In spite of the missing pieces I began to have a gnawing awareness of my Native ancestry.

My sister and I both had dark complexions, turning even browner in the summer. I had coarse coal black hair and hazel eyes; my sister had dark brown hair and hazel eyes. We did not look distinctly Indian, but it wasn't hard for someone to identify us as such.

Contrary to the Hollywood image and stereotype of the American Indian, many of mixed blood had their own defining set of physical characteristics. Dark genes did not always predominate and in the surrounding native communities of Kansas and Oklahoma, I saw many whose physical appearances belied their Indian ancestry.

As Truman and I became closer friends, I spent more time with him and his family. That increased even more as events in my family added to the disintegration. The Wares welcomed me to the summer pow-wows and most weekends found us in small towns and campgrounds in Oklahoma for the native gatherings. I grew to love the Wares and envied their closeness with each other. There was laughter everywhere, an almost universal joy I missed along the way, and I was grateful they included me.

I had an aptitude for bead and feather work and spent countless hours assembling my dance regalia until I could enter the arena and dance. Truman's mother, Priscilla, supplemented what I was missing with her beautiful craftsmanship.

Among the Wares, I was exposed to native culture although I was learning more about Kiowa things than Comanche. Truman's grandmother lived with them and spoke only Kiowa. I marveled at the difficult sounds of the language. Their home was a peaceful refuge and they came to refer to me as "their Comanche son" while I unconsciously began to think of them as my adopted family.

My home life was rapidly coming apart and my parents were each drinking more. There was never any domestic violence, nor was there open fighting and shouting. But there were more and more embarrassing incidents involving my parents' intoxication, and tension in the home was palpably high. There was a strong undercurrent of uncertainty, so common in alcoholic homes, and an ominous fear of what might be next.

Our house was small and crowded. I walked into the tiny bathroom one morning as my father was shaving. He said, "You'd better prepare yourself for some bad news." I was shaken by his tone and expression and immediately thought he or my mom was going to die. Shortly after I was told they were divorcing.

My mother was seeing a Wichita psychiatrist after she was diagnosed with a nervous breakdown. The medical fees were staggering and my father struggled to pay them. In an effort to stem the problem, and at the suggestion of the doctor, we moved out of Planeview and into a small, new home at 5927 Bunting Drive on the outskirts of Wichita. The home was beyond our financial means but was a desperate attempt to change my mother's surroundings. The house appeared large, mostly due to the treeless expanse of bare dirt. As I sprigged it with tiny grass shoots, working long hours in the hot Kansas sun, the yard seemed immense. Many years later, I returned and was dismayed at how tiny the house and yard were. Prior to this we never had anything new but we were now in a new home in a nice neighborhood. My father replaced our old car with a newer one. He was doing everything he possibly could.

The change in living conditions appeared to work for six months and then the marriage collapsed. I just turned fourteen; my sister was twelve. My mother met with my sister and me before she left and tearfully told us she could not take us with her. It was an emotionally wrenching experience for all three of us. I fought back the tears. I adjusted to life without my mom and tried to move on. My father managed to hang onto our new home for a short while before we had to move back to Planeview. It was the only time we ever owned a home, even for a brief period.

My father was deep in debt and was working a second job most nights and a third when he wasn't working the second. He put in eight hours every day at Beech Aircraft, working overtime when he could get it. He came home, changed clothes, and worked in a service station until near midnight. He ate, he slept, and he worked.

My sister and I were on our own. I always worked and since the 9th grade my paychecks from the Wynn-Warren IGA store went to help with the family finances. My sister did the same with much of her babysitting money. I would like to think I was altruistic about my contributions but I resented it after a while. My friends were acquiring cars for their high school days and I wanted one more than anything. I would occasionally keep enough money to buy some beads or leather for my craftwork.

The three of us did the best we could without my mom. Then my father decided to marry an overbearing woman named Eleanor. She had a daughter slightly older than I. I disliked them both.

It wasn't long before I clashed with the new stepmother and step-sister, so I moved in with my mom and Marvin, her second husband. Marvin was a skinny, cadaver appearing man with a chicken chest and an Errol Flynn-like moustache. He held himself out as a tough WWII Marine but I later learned was a clerk-typist and never saw action. I considered him a blowhard and a phony.

I finally managed to buy a '41 Chevy for $100, which I traded for a '46 Buick that seemed a city block long. Marvin and my mom then co-signed a loan for me so I could buy the car of my dreams, a black and white '51 Ford Victoria.

A few months later I clashed with Marvin as he was upholstering a kitchen chair. He came at me with a hammer in his hand. I told him to put it down or I'd take it away and show him how to use it. He stopped in his tracks, paused, and ordered me out of his house. I was going back to my dad's but as I picked up my car keys he told me to leave the car or he would report it stolen. It broke my heart to part with my dream car but I refused to show any emotion. I turned on my heel and walked across most of Wichita to my dad's home. As I left, I told Marvin he was inheriting the payments along with the car. Hitting him in his pocket-book was effective and a week later I was summoned over to a police car as I left school.

Bud Wallace was a large middle-aged Wichita cop whom I liked. He was also Marvin's friend. I sat in Bud's patrol car and he informed me that Marvin was offering to return my car if I would assume the payments. I was overjoyed at the offer but maintained a reluctant demeanor before agreeing. I made it clear I would have nothing more to do with Marvin. I got my car back the next day.

My father divorced Eleanor and a short time later married a very attractive lady named Marcine. She had two children, a boy and a girl, but by this time I was almost ready to graduate from high school and had little contact with any of them. That marriage was also short-lived and they simply moved away from each other without the benefit of divorce.

The booze had long since swallowed up both my parents. There were many embarrassing episodes in front of my friends when one parent or the other did something that mortified me. I never wanted friends around if there was a chance one of my parents might show up; I just never knew if they would be sober. But my sister experienced dramatically worse things.

On one occasion, after I graduated and moved out of the home, my father and Virgil, one of his alcoholic boyhood friends, brought a cheap, floozy woman to our home. I first met Virgil when I was very small and I *never* saw him sober; he was always reeking of booze, his speech slurred, with a leering, drunken grin across his face. They picked the woman up in a local skid row bar and all of them were drunk. My sister came home after school and walked into the house seeing only the weaving, slurring Virgil. She asked where my father was and he put his finger to his lips, shhhh'ing my sister to be quiet. She then saw my father in the bedroom with the woman.

A short while later this experience was repeated. My sister came home from school and thought no one was home. But this time she encountered two total strangers, both naked, and my father had allowed them to use our home. Both of these experiences were incredibly shocking for my sister, who was a sophomore or junior in high school at the time. I learned about these events months later and I was so angry I wanted to physically confront my father. My sister talked me out of it.

Connie moved out and, following my example, became another family nomad. She lived with my mother and Marvin for a year. My father was a good and decent man but his alcoholism destroyed any semblance of a moral compass. There was a time when he could _never_ have allowed these things to occur.

For the sake of my mother I maintained an uneasy truce with Marvin, being superficially polite and courteous while trying to keep my distance. That marriage only lasted a short while and ended in another divorce.

There were many drunken situations with my mother that broke my heart. Seeing my father drunk was one thing, but seeing my mom drunk was entirely different. I never knew if she would be drunk or sober when I saw her; or if she would be able to answer the door if I came for a visit.

There was something so sad and heart breaking about it all. I would be disgusted and infuriated as I watched the woman who gave birth to me stumbling, slurring, and hopelessly drunk. It was an inconsolable mix of sadness, anger, embarrassment, shame, and frustration. Those feelings were all in a blender and I couldn't separate one from the other.

It's odd that when I was living the experience of my parent's alcoholism, I could easily see the damage being done, not only to themselves, but to us. Later, faced with my own alcoholism, it was amazing that I couldn't see it in me. After the miracle of recovery began to grow, I could look back at my mother and father, and see they were following the normal path of untreated alcoholism, each getting progressively worse.

Marine - 1956

I graduated high school at seventeen, turned eighteen in September, and went to work for Boeing Aircraft Company, where my father worked. I moved into my own place and was free of my parents, the alcoholism, and the chaos. I went into the Data Processing Department and began learning about IBM data processing equipment. I found it challenging and intellectually stimulating although my interest was limited.

I considered joining the service upon graduation but remained undecided. Wichita's economy had always been boom or bust depending upon the state of aircraft manufacturing but that line of work was not for me.

Very few graduates left Planeview for college. Many married their high school sweethearts, hired on with Boeing, Beech, or Cessna, and settled into life routines. I had crushes on girls but was shy and dated very little. There were no romantic connections to hold me. Several older friends were ex-Marines and I was fascinated with their stories of the Marine Corps. A high school acquaintance returned home from Marine boot camp and we spent an evening drinking in a local tavern. He regaled me for hours about his boot camp experiences, many of which involved seemingly brutal stories of recruit training.

I immediately sought out a Marine recruiter and signed up. Since I was now eighteen I needed no parental permission and I wanted to find out if I was up to such a challenge. I truly didn't know. I was an average student, unremarkable in academics and sports, never the most popular guy, and never a standout anywhere. As I prepared for departure my only goal was to successfully complete the 13-week Marine Corps boot camp program.

I left Planeview on December 5, 1956. I went to the barbershop the day before and walked out with my Elvis style pompadour and semi-ducktail hairstyle on the floor. My ex-Marine friends advised me to do this so I wouldn't draw any immediate and unwanted attention from the Drill Instructors (DI's). I boarded a Lockheed Constellation aircraft, my first commercial flight, and headed for the Marine Corp Recruit Depot in San Diego.

As I viewed the enormous airplane, I was nervous with anticipation. I had never been far from home and all my life experiences seemed minimal. I knew the Marines reputation. The adventure before me held many unanswered questions and I was not at all sure I could measure up. I landed a few hours later in San Diego. I deplaned with my orders in my hand and was directed to the pickup point for new recruits. As I exited the airplane a slight breeze carried the scent of eucalyptus trees my way. California was a stark contrast to the Kansas prairies a few hours distant.

A DI met us at the assembly point; a hard-looking man, trim and muscular in an impeccable uniform, his Smoky Bear hat tilted low over his eyes. Five other recruits also arrived and we were told to line up. The intimidation began immediately and I had serious concerns about this decision. After all the stories from my friends, I was sure I would have a psychological edge but being face-to-face with the DI changed everything.

The ride to the Marine Corps Recruit Depot (MCRD) was short since it bordered the San Diego airport. Upon arrival we reaped the whirlwind as DIs shouted and pointed, running us from place to place as we were processed in. I was part of a frenetic herd of stampeding bodies, my brain tumbling as I tried to figure out what to do next. We received our herring-bone utility uniforms, bucket issue (miscellaneous items), and were marched to the receiving barracks where we would remain until enough recruits arrived to form a new boot camp class.

Within three days a collage of American youth trickled in from all parts of the country and we began our training. There were ex-gang members, well-educated college students, gregarious and outgoing individuals, a former Army sergeant, and young men from every segment of our social fabric.

Our class of 70 recruits was designated Platoon 1080 of 1956. Staff Sergeant Parsons was our senior DI with Sergeants Haughton and Mitchell as junior DIs. They would take us through 13 weeks of training. Parsons had a hint of a smile as he watched us bumble our way through precision close order drill and maneuvers. Haughton was reputedly an ex-British Marine with a bit of an accent. He was short and must have challenged the minimum height requirements for the Marine Corps, but he could run forever. Mitchell was an Indian from Oklahoma. I held out hope that I might get a slight break from him. It was not to happen.

All three drill instructors were superb. Parsons was completely unflappable, save for the slight hint of a smile he often struggled to hide. In the mornings Haughton often looked and smelled hung-over but he always performed brilliantly, if somewhat short-tempered. Mitchell was sharp as a knife, the epitome of military countenance. He spoke with the verbal inflection I immediately recognized as a "reservation accent". All three made the most physically demanding task look ridiculously easy. Later, I would learn they changed uniforms as many as three or four times daily so they always appeared fresh and immaculate. They led by example, always *demonstrating* what we were to do, and automatically taking away any excuse for poor performance. I wanted to remain completely unnoticed by the drill instructors, but was immediately assigned as the squad leader for the fifth squad comprised of eight men. I had never led anyone anywhere and was deeply uncomfortable with this assignment.

Squads were assigned various duties in their platoon area and squad leaders were held accountable for their squad's performance. During the first few days no one came anywhere close to satisfying the drill instructors. I was summoned to the Duty Hut where the DIs resided. A call to appear was cause for immediate terror, equivalent to being ordered into the lion's den. An entry ritual had to be performed, usually many times, before entrance was permitted. Finally, I was told to enter. Fearfully, I opened the door and stepped inside.

I was pounced upon by all three drill instructors, each yelling at me from different angles, as I stood and braced myself at attention. I took some blows, designed more to get my attention and frighten me than to cause physical damage. The effect was instantly successful. Once away from the duty hut I vowed never to repeat the experience. I never considered myself tough but I called my squad together and told them I would take each of them on to avoid another trip to the Duty Hut. I was making the overnight transition from a carefree teenager to a young Marine forced into becoming a leader. This was lesson number one.

My squad came together quickly and became a team. We experienced the esprit de corps the Marine Corps is renowned for and it grew stronger daily as we faced more adversity and challenges. Misfits didn't last long. By the time graduation day arrived nearly half of our original group washed out of training.

I was summoned to battalion headquarters in my first week and interviewed by a baldheaded mustang officer (ex-enlisted man). Captain Burnett commented that I had an extraordinarily high General Classification Test score (GCT), which came from a series of tests given prior to actual induction into the Marine Corps. I stood at attention as he looked at my service record book (SRB) and asked me a series of questions. I had no idea where the questions were leading but I remained braced, eyes straight ahead, giving him the answers to each inquiry. Finally, he asked if I would be interested in attending the United States Naval Academy at Annapolis. My heart jumped and I enthusiastically said I would. After passing a special physical exam for the academy, I was told to stand by for orders to the Bainbridge Maryland Prep School where I would train for nine-months prior to entering Annapolis. I was elated.

As I stood there I could not know I would spend three years chasing this dream trying to correct bureaucratic bungling. It would turn out to be a heartbreaking and disappointing experience.

In the meantime, I adjusted to the new boot camp routine. I learned that getting set back was every recruit's worst nightmare. It meant repositioning to a platoon behind and losing time toward graduation. Going to a strange platoon also meant re-acclimating to new DIs, a disturbing thought in addition to the time lost.

I worked hard and pushed new envelopes for personal endurance. I continued running when I thought my lungs were bursting and my heart would explode. I gave myself no permission to quit as long as one other man in the platoon was still on his feet. I would rather die than give up. That attitude was precisely what the DIs were molding in each of us as part of the Marine legacy.

With each passing day we slowly morphed into Marines. The days were crammed with demanding activity from reveille to lights out. We were given a few hours each Sunday to rest, relax, and write letters. We ran everywhere and were given half the normal time to do what needed to be done. As the weeks passed and our utility uniforms became more worn and faded our status among the other recruits climbed.

We had become inextricably interdependent upon each other and that was the lesson to be learned. In combat one man's lapse or failure to perform could kill or wound many others. Our entire platoon was a team. When one man failed we all felt it one way or the other.

If there was any special and single emphasis on training it was at the Camp Matthews rifle range. The Marine Corps prided itself on marksmanship and this phase was critical. In three weeks our bodies and muscles adapted to the torturous firing positions as we worked toward qualification day. That day came and we awoke to rain and strong wind, nullifying all our previous sighting in work. Only three out of seventy earned the coveted Expert badge that day. I was out shot by two points, coming in second highest in the platoon.

In my final week at the range I sustained a painful and debilitating foot injury that made it impossible for me to walk. My DIs could easily have discarded me due to the injury but they chose to keep me as I gritted my way back to full duty.

In our final week of boot camp, our DIs announced that the top three recruits would receive PFC stripes (Private First Class). My only hope had been to survive the 13-week ordeal so I was stunned when my name was announced as the number two man. I never excelled at anything before. The competition was extreme; the ordeal long and grueling. Graduation day arrived at last. The thirteen weeks seemed like thirteen years or some point in time that could not be measured. On "The Grinder," the parade grounds, a half-mile long, I stood at attention wearing dress greens for the first time, with the prized Eagle, Globe and Anchor, pinned proudly on each lapel.

The reviewing stands were filled with family members and friends of those graduating from all the recruit platoons. None of my family or friends were able to attend but that did not dampen my spirits.

The band struck up the Marine Corps hymn, and it was difficult to keep my emotions in check as indescribable feelings reverberated throughout me. Many, many years later, that same experience returns each time I hear "From the halls of Montezuma, to the shores of Tripoli…". Once a Marine, always a Marine, and I knew I belonged to an elite group of men I would be forever bonded with, the United States Marine Corps. All the pain, exertion, and physical torture of the past thirteen weeks were worth the feeling of that moment. I couldn't help but glance down every now and then at the red-bordered PFC stripe on each sleeve.

Semper Fi - Camp Pendleton

We arrived on military busses and I gazed at Camp Pendleton's rugged terrain for the first time, the tops of the peaks shrouded in fog. The place looked formidable indeed.

We were met by a Gunnery Sergeant who could have been a recruiting poster. He had tan skin and a blonde crew cut, and told us we were going for "a little walk up to the shelf," whatever *that* was. Although trim and muscular, he declared that he "was a 40 year old physical wreck" and we should have no trouble keeping up. Half a day later we dragged ourselves back into our Quonset huts – dead-tired, sweating, and sore.

I was disappointed when I drew a duty assignment for our first weekend of liberty. I had big plans for Tijuana liberty. I was going to get a small USMC tattoo high on my shoulder, drink some Cerveza beer, and check out the pretty senoritas. A week later when my comrades were scratching at scabby tattoos and some were exhibiting symptoms of gonorrhea, I was glad I missed all the action.

We attended classes on every weapon an infantry Marine could expect to encounter, and all of them required exhausting hikes up into the hills to each classroom setting. There were endless exercises in squad, platoon, and company tactics. We spent a full day watching firing exercises in one of the immense and flat valleys near Cone Hill. We saw everything from tanks to artillery but when a flight of four AD Skyraiders came roaring overhead at tree top level for napalm and strafing attacks, my eyes followed until they disappeared over the horizon.

Much of our work was done at night. We snaked our way high up into the hills and set up night defenses; digging in, setting fields of fire, and opening up with tracers that lit up the night. It seemed impossible that any living thing could penetrate that wall of fire yet I knew it had been done before and would be done again in the nightmare of actual combat.

Finally it was over and time for me to go home. I originally signed up for a new enlistment called the "Six Month Reserve" program, and I had completed my six months. At Camp Pendleton I changed my mind and wanted to enlist for a three-year tour but the Annapolis appointment was pending and I was sent home to await orders to Bainbridge Prep School.

As mentioned earlier, the appointment never came. In the interim I went back to Boeing Aircraft while making reserve drills and waiting things out. At Boeing I encountered a beautiful young woman my age named Connie (ironically, she had the same name as my sister). Her dark hair and eyes, combined with a stunning figure, was a visual magnet every time she entered the room. Perhaps it was my new level of confidence gained from recent experiences in the Marine Corps, but I approached her and we began to date. As we dated she became more serious about our relationship. I didn't want to lose her so I gave her an engagement ring even though I wasn't ready to get married.

Suddenly, seemingly overnight, she and her mother became immersed in the Jehovah Witness church. At her request, I spent some time looking into the church doctrine and gave it a good effort. However, I was unable to make the religious transition so we parted. A beautiful and shapely woman, she was my first love and permanently etched in my memory. My time with her was an entirely new experience, contrasted by what I had seen in my family. I loved being with her. Connie soon married someone else and I moved to Kansas City, Missouri, where I finally exhausted my attempts to get into the Naval Academy.

My mom's life was coming apart. One gray and frozen wintry day in 1960, my sister and I drove three hours in a Kansas snow storm to take her to the State Mental Hospital in Larned, Kansas. As we drove into the complex I immediately noticed a nearby building with high fences and a sign indicating it housed the criminally insane. Amidst the depressing gray winter backdrop we had to leave her. Every mile there and back echoed a grim and sad reminder of our family demise. My mother spent a year at Larned, undergoing electric shock treatments, adding another harsh chapter to her already tortured life.

My sister was happily married and pregnant; but my father had left his last marriage and was drinking heavily again. Eventually, my mother was released from the state mental hospital and remarried again, this time to a man by the name of Ralph Lavelle. I never met him but he owned a bar in St. Paul, Minnesota and that's where she moved. It seemed a deadly combination – an alcoholic married to a bar owner.

By this time I was emotionally blunted; I just took things as they came and moved on. I turned my attention to what lay ahead; there was nothing I could do for anyone in my family. It was 1960. I was twenty-two but felt much older.

My mother's marriage soon evaporated and she disappeared from my life. Ten years would pass and I would be in my early thirties before she surfaced and we would have any contact again. I got word at one point that she was somewhere in the New Orleans area and had been injured in a fire. Later, I heard that she was beaten and raped again. I suspected alcohol was involved in her difficulties but I never really knew.

I believe all suffering should have a purpose. What I saw and experienced did not prevent me from becoming an alcoholic; these things rarely do. But recovery has allowed me to look back and remember without bitterness, understanding that nothing my parents did was by design and intent. I have been able to extract gratitude for the good things they gave me while they were sober, choosing to focus on the good versus the painful experiences. I have the power of choice...

Dreams of Flying - 1961

It was April of 1961. As I stood at attention before my commanding officer, he informed me I was the only Marine in the unit who qualified for the new Marine Aviation Cadet (MarCad) flight-training program. Although I had always dreamed of flying, the disappointing attempt to enter the Naval Academy was still fresh and I was fearful of another repeat experience.

Still, I thought about the possibility of flying. It was a boyhood dream and even during our lean years I managed to build many inexpensive model airplanes. My commanding officer informed me that roughly 50% of the applicants would wash out during the eighteen month program. He said nearly all the applicants were coming in from the civilian world and would have a minimum of two years college; many would have much more than that. I was being given an opportunity to come in the back door, sans college, since I was an enlisted Marine. I had to spend a day taking a battery of tests and if successful would undergo a special flight physical.

Failure has always been unacceptable for me. My parents never foisted this upon me but it's always been there and I wrestled with this decision due to the high potential for failure.

Flying was always a dream, but I thought it was for the rich and privileged, the college-educated, and those above me in the stations of life. It was difficult to imagine someone with my background as a pilot, but I continued to mentally romance this opportunity. The statistical probability of washing out due to my educational deficit was not lost on me and it dogged my decision.

Finally, I decided to make the attempt. I went home to Wichita and told my friends I was leaving for Pensacola to start my flight career. I attended a powwow and was surprised when Truman's family requested a "special" for me since I was going away. As I danced at the head of the procession, with friends and supporters tailing in behind me after shaking my hand, I was deeply affected by the moment and the occasion.

On the long drive to Pensacola I thought about the unacceptability of defeat in this endeavor. If *successful*, I would wear those prized wings of gold, designating me as a Naval Aviator, and beyond that would be the gold bars of a commissioned Marine Corps officer. It was almost too much to dream. The thought of returning to my Native community as a failure was abhorrent; I simply could never face them if that occurred.

I reported to Naval Air Station (NAS) Pensacola on June 3rd, 1961 at the age of twenty-two. Pensacola was a beautiful city, nestled in the Florida panhandle, with vestiges of the old Spanish influence. Its flavor was unlike any other Florida city and it was the home of the world famous Blue Angels. Every Marine and Navy pilot began his flying career in Pensacola.

I was processed into the Indoctrination Battalion where cadets from all over the United States reported in and formed the next class. Preflight was a 16-week initial training phase run by Marine DIs. This was the first of four phases in the eighteen-month program. During the final week of Preflight, cadet officers ran the various incoming cadet battalions. They relished their positions as upperclassmen and pounced on the newcomers.

We were issued baggy, ill-fitting coveralls known as poopy suits, which marked us as newly arriving cadets. We visited the barber and received a thirty second haircut that left all our hair on the floor (now called the "deck"). There was little about our immediate appearance to hint that we might someday be dashing fighter pilots.

One week later forty cadets gathered and became class 21-61. We were given a math screening test to see if remedial work would be needed. Although I could reason out many of the answers, I left the answers blank if I couldn't apply sound math principles. A number of us were taken out of the class and sent to a two-week pre-math class. Later, when our academics moved into trigonometry and physics problems, I was glad I had spent the time in pre-math.

I re-started my cadet life in class 23-61 with thirty-three other prospective aviators. Thirteen of these would not make it through the eighteen month process. Our assigned DI was Marine Staff Sergeant Larvie, a Lakota Indian and the uncle of Pete Larvie from my boot camp platoon. Pete didn't make it through boot camp with us and although I recognized the name and tribe, I said nothing.

Most of my classmates were from colleges all over the United States. Their sudden introduction to Marine DI's was an eye-opening experience. I smiled at their reactions. Having been through boot camp and several years of military training I was comfortable and did not have any mental or emotional surges at my new environment.

Preflight focused on physical, academic, and military training. We never got close to an airplane during this time. A white badge was awarded to those who excelled in any area. I quickly received a white badge in Military. Physical training was difficult but doable. Academics proved to be my primary area of challenge. My peers said we were covering a college semester in three weeks and I felt like I was in the midst of an academic whirlwind. One of my roommates was Gene Dietz from Ohio, who had a degree in electrical engineering. Gene was a good guy, witty, and very bright. He tutored me each night during study hours. In turn, I helped him and my other roommate with military subjects, which came easily to me.

Staff Sergeant Larvie was a typical Marine DI, sharp, smooth, and professional. I liked him. I had to smile as others chafed at the deprecating aspects of our training. The worst form of address in Preflight was "Mister!" although it was usually said in an unflattering way. In boot camp it had been "Shit coolee, Maggot, Numb nuts," and other colorful forms of address and I chuckled at the contrast.

Preflight was intense and rapidly paced. I found myself inwardly surprised and amazed as academic test scores were posted. I consistently underestimated my academic effort and was surprised to be doing so well but I continually had to work harder than my peers.

Navy flight training demanded a lot of time in the water and I was not a particularly good swimmer. Weeks later, we faced a stringent series of graduation exercises in the large training pool. One was an underwater swim of fifty feet on one breath, twice any distance I felt capable of swimming. I psyched myself up that morning, telling myself repeatedly that I could do it. I was astonished when I pulled myself out of the water at the fifty foot mark.

Other requirements were equally daunting and one was the Dilbert Dunker. It was a cockpit mockup mounted high on a steep rail that plunged into the deep end of the swimming pool. The angle was approximately 30 degrees although it looked nearly straight down. The mockup jarred heavily when it impacted the water and slowly pivoted upside down. Panic and bubbles swirled about the strapped in cadet as it sank deeper into the pool.

Our instructions were to take a deep breath when we hit the water and wait out the bubbles until we could see. We were to slowly and deliberately release ourselves from the four harness connectors and pull ourselves out of the canopy, exiting on a particular side. I climbed to the top of the rail, stepped into the cockpit, and strapped in, trying to maintain a passive demeanor to disguise the fear inside me.

My heart was pounding. I came down fast and hit hard, going upside down as I fought to stay calm while the bubbles swirled and disorientation set in. I felt the device sinking as I concentrated on following all the directions. There were divers to assist those who panicked and were unable to get out. I looked at one and saw his eyes in the facemask watching me. I came out on the wrong side and had to repeat the exercise. But this time there was no fear of the unknown; I had experienced it and knew I could do it again. It was a valuable lesson, that most of my fears were much worse in my imagination than in actual reality. The second time was easy and I was completely calm and successful.

In our final week we were to receive our cadet officer assignments based on class standing. We had just completed a lengthy "peer review" where each of us confidentially rated our classmates from top to bottom. The peer review, combined with a composite score from all three phases of our training, would determine our class ranking. We gathered in a large squad bay while Staff Sergeant Larvie began calling names beginning at the bottom of the class.

When the first five or six names were called I began to breathe easier. At least I wasn't on the very bottom. My group continued to grow smaller as the names were called off and I became uneasy. I was *sure* my name should have been called before now.

Finally, there were only two of us and my name was called. Frank Harrington was number one and I was number two. I always thought Frank would garner the number one slot, but there was no way I expected to be number two. Frank died later in an F-8 Crusader crash in the Philippines.

Unbelievable. I was Regimental Sub-Commander. I was in charge of the Indoctrination Battalion and my classmates were clamoring to come over and harass the new guys just as we were harassed fifteen weeks earlier. Each morning, as I pinned a row of four gold bars on each collar, I stared at them in disbelief.

On the final evening many of us gathered in the AcRac Club, the lesser version of an officer's club, as we celebrated this successful phase of training. Staff Sergeant Larvie was there with his wife and he summoned me over. After introducing me to his wife, he told me how proud he was that I did so well. It was an unexpected gesture and comment and I was touched by his directness. I knew his remarks were due to the culture we shared since so few of us managed to hit the high water marks in life.

My Alcoholism

For most of my life I never thought much about alcoholism because I was never going to be an alcoholic. I *thought* I knew a lot about alcoholism after having lived in the midst of it with my parents. There was also a lot of it in the Indian community. I knew about alcoholic *behavior*, but that is *vastly different* from knowing about the disease itself. As I continued to drink, I occasionally became mildly concerned and I would devise tests to see if I was an alcoholic. I would quit drinking a month ahead of a scheduled FAA physical. That proved that I had no problem because I was convinced no alcoholic could go a month without a drink. It was a false premise, but one I accepted as credible at the time.

I had many arguments as to why I wasn't an alcoholic. I didn't drink every night and I was sure most alcoholics did. But I also varied my drinking patterns on purpose so I would *never* fit a certain profile, something most normal drinkers never even consider. I rarely drank in the mornings, perhaps three times a year, and I was convinced alkies consistently had to do that to smooth out. I couldn't stay drunk for three days or three weeks and often heard stories of alcoholics doing that. I didn't get drunk every weekend; didn't beat or abuse my wife and kids. Most importantly, I was too successful. I was at the top of my game, an airline Captain, and alcoholics were found in the alleys drinking out of brown paper bags.

I had all the other collateral denial arguments, as well. I didn't drink as much as many I knew, never had a divorce, hadn't had another DUI for nearly fifteen years, wasn't having job problems, and thought life was good. So how could I be an alcoholic?

Once I was in treatment and got honest with myself, I identified with almost every symptom of alcoholism. I didn't want to…but there was no way around it if I was honest. There were many symptoms, but most notable for me was loss of control. I found it more accurate to call it "loss of predictability," which meant I could not predict what I was going to do once I took the first drink. Maybe I would have two drinks and go home. More likely and almost certainly near the end, I would *intend* to go home, but I'd stay and close the bar–or finish the bottle. That was *never* my intent when I planned to just have one or two. I learned it wasn't the tenth drink I had to worry about; it was the *first*. It was the first one that impacts the area of my brain that is affected by this disease. It's the part of my brain that controls eye blink, heart rate, blood pressure and all the involuntary functions of my body. Thus, I have *no* control over it.

As to alcoholism actually being a disease, I doubted it was really a bona fide illness. I assumed the American Medical Association must have had a show of hands on the disease issue at one of their conventions and voted it in. I was consistently ignorant and factually wrong about alcoholism.

Anchor hospital had a full medical staff of counselors, doctors, psychiatrists, and a Ph.D. psychologist. All but a couple were recovering, and all the doctors were certified in Addiction Medicine. Ninety percent of the entire hospital staff, including cleaning crews, kitchen, and security personnel was recovering. *No one* can approach an alcoholic like another alcoholic. When I looked in the eyes of the counselors and doctors, I saw the truth. I *knew* they were once where I was now. Their current lives validated what they were telling me.

Doctors, all of them certified in Addiction Medicine, usually handled the disease lectures and films and they knew their subject intimately. There is something so unique and complex about the disease of alcoholism that someone not afflicted simply cannot understand the nature of the process. Over the years I have seen a handful of exceptions, but they were all professionals in the field. There's a good reason why alcoholism is often called "the disease of a thousand faces". It is often confused with other medical conditions, always belying the fact that it is a standalone *primary disease* and is not secondary to other conditions. Because we do not all progress at the same rate and due to the early, middle, and late stage symptoms, it is easy to deny this disease and look elsewhere.

I learned that half a century ago, in 1956, the American Medical Association declared alcoholism a disease because it met specific scientific criteria. And since that time it can be found in the doctors' diagnostic manual, the DSM-IV, where every disease is listed along with its symptoms. Alcoholism has a clear biological base, with identifiable signs and symptoms, and has a predictable course and outcome. The actual cause is still being studied but we know it is not caused by intentional acts or choice. The "choice argument" has some phenomenal brain studies that are educational and enlightening.

It is a three-axes disease, acting in a physiological, mental, and emotional realm. While it's true that the disease begins with a conscious decision to drink, once the brain becomes locked in the addictive process, a person will continue to seek the substance. At that point, without some form of intervention or treatment, the person will become the chief aider and abettor in their own demise.

I also learned that alcoholism and drug dependence are America's number one health problem, cutting across all social boundaries and affecting both genders and every ethnic group. The National Council on Alcoholism and Drug Dependence (NCADD) says nearly eighteen million Americans have alcohol problems and another five to six million Americans have drug problems. More than half of all adults have a family history of alcoholism or problem drinking. Tragically, more than nine million children live with a parent who is dependent on either alcohol or drugs.

One-fourth of all emergency room admissions, one-third of all suicides, and more than half of all homicides and incidents of domestic violence are alcohol related. And almost half of all traffic fatalities are alcohol related. Heavy drinking contributes to each of the top three causes of death: heart disease, cancer, and stroke. Sadly, Fetal Alcohol Syndrome

(FAS) is the leading known cause of mental retardation. When I testified in Washington, D.C. regarding my experiences with alcohol, I listened to a Native American representative state that 75% of all babies born on the Wind River reservation were afflicted with FAS. A whole generation of Shoshones and Arapahos were being wiped out by alcohol because alcoholic mothers were drinking during pregnancy.

As a taxpayer and consumer, I was staggered by the high price of alcoholism. Alcohol and drug abuse costs the American economy approximately $276 billion per year in lost productivity, health care expenditures, crime, and automobile crashes. The NCADD estimates that these damages trickle down to individuals to the tune of $1,000 per year.

I learned that genetics play a strong role in alcoholism. With one alcoholic parent, my chances were four times greater that I would become alcoholic compared to someone from a normal family. With two alcoholic parents, I had little chance of not becoming alcoholic, once I chose to drink. In addition to my parents, I had an uncle who was an alcoholic and a cousin who was an addict. Both committed suicide. Even with a genetic predisposition, I could have avoided becoming alcoholic if I simply never picked up a drink.

Both chronic and progressive, alcoholism is a disease capable of being arrested but is never cured once in place. Some mistakenly believe they can stay sober for twenty years and then start over with their drinking. It's an oft-fatal error. Statistically, they end up drinking as much or more within a month as when they first sought recovery, with the same consequences returning as before.

Occasionally, the active alcoholic will appear to be doing better as they try to manage their drinking, but it's only a brief illusion and is *always* followed by still worse progression and downward slide. The most vivid example is one very close to me. Pat and Bill were neighbors, who lived across the street, and our families had grown up together. Before I ever considered that I might have a drinking problem, I was quite sure Bill did. One Sunday in church, several years after I got sober, Bill approached me with blood shot eyes and whiskey breath. He asked if we might speak afterwards.

I introduced Bill to some other recovering alcoholics and he became involved in a recovery effort. Several weeks later, Pat called and excitedly told me how much better things were. Bill was now only drinking a twelve-pack a night instead of a full case of beer. I explained that as long as Bill was drinking *anything* he could *not* recover from the disease; that any alcohol at all was enough to keep the disease active. Pat brushed me off and again expressed her gratitude.

Within the next year things got predictably worse and Pat divorced Bill. Bill moved several counties away and continued to drink. One night he returned to Rockdale county, parked on a country road, and shot himself to death. The first bullet didn't do it and he had to shoot himself a second time. It was several days before he was found. Although there was nothing Pat could do to force Bill to recover, she couldn't hear what I was telling her. She continued to believe that Bill's decrease in drinking volume indicated he was getting better.

I continued to learn about alcoholism. As I saw it from the inside out it was easier to understand why non-alcoholics are so baffled. Alcoholism is a lengthy process, not an overnight event. There is an early, middle, and late stage to the disease with different markers along the way. I visualized a fifty mile stretch of highway, straight as an arrow, with the white centerline precisely in the middle at the beginning. With the slow progression of alcoholism, I curved the centerline one inch to the right at each mile point, slowly veering it slightly out of kilter. Mile by mile the centerline subtly eased off center one inch at a time. It was impossible to stand at mile one, peer down the line, and determine when or where it began to go astray. At the fifty mile mark it's clear something is amiss. But traveling down the line, mile by mile, it's difficult to detect. And so it is with the alcoholic. Adding to the confusion, some become alcoholic in a short period while others take decades. Women tend to become alcoholic quicker than men due to certain biological differences.

As an alcoholic lay person who has studied the disease, I have a nodding acquaintance with the brain chemistry involved, with words such as neurotransmitters, synapse, dopamine, serotonin and many more. I've learned about the mid-brain functions and such things as the hedonic set point. I know about the metabolic process of alcoholics versus non-alcoholics, the formation of THIQ and what it does. I've seen the recent technology that shows actual pictures of live alcoholic brains as they react to alcohol. There's a virtual plethora of data that is indisputable.

I want to know *why* an airplane flew, not merely that it does. I wanted to know about this disease so I might live with it, or I would surely die from it. As I remained sober over the years, it became clear that what I *knew* about my alcoholism was *not* what kept me sober. What kept me sober was what I *did* about my alcoholism. Knowledge is fine, but staying sober is an action program, not an intellectual exercise.

We did painful work in our hospital groups as we exerted "rigorous honesty" to recover. To me, rigorous was synonymous with painful. I had to disassemble myself, put all the parts out on the table for all to see. Then I had to discard the parts that no longer worked and implement new parts in the hope I could build a newer and better model. This process is inherently abhorrent to most of us. It takes great courage to do the required work day after day.

I think nothing is more instinctively frightening than change. Each time I heard the word *change,* I thought of it in terms of cost. I was going to have to give something up, lose something, or abandon something. Never once, *not ever*, did I consider that I might gain something. Yet, everything I was asked to change, everything I gave up, resulted in large net gains and incredible benefits. Nothing can exist in a vacuum, and recovery taught me how to fill the void with something positive each time a change from something negative was required.

In my world, alcohol was the solution, *not* the problem. Alcohol released me from torment and torture, allowed me a blessed escape, and even though it was only temporary it was worth it. Non-alcoholics cannot imagine this. Even when consequences occurred, the relief granted overrode the consequences. I wrecked my car once but the phenomenon of euphoric recall soon dispelled the damage done and it just didn't seem so bad. The event in Fargo had a price tag too expensive and I finally sought recovery. It was my bottom – the ultimate event that finally forces the alcoholic to seek help. Every alcoholic who recovers eventually experiences such a moment. For many, however, the bottom is death.

Alcohol was a symptom of the disease and not the cause. My problem was life itself, how I saw it and how I reacted to it. I had to learn how to approach *everything* in life anew. Nothing changed in my outside world; the changes all took place *within* me. The twelve step model employed by my treatment center was designed precisely for that. There is no way to describe the power of that process. But it's been the primary means of recovery for seventy-five years, in the US and in 180 countries worldwide; I have found it to be the most consistent, rewarding, and enriching way to a happy life. It works.

I could not go back to the way I once lived; I had to go above and beyond anything I had previously experienced – *if* I was to stay sober. I had to give back more than I took, make amends and repair damage wherever I could, and strive to leave this world a better place because of that effort. And I could only keep what I had by giving it away to others less fortunate. It is a lifelong task for those who recover and I know of none who complain or are unwilling to do what's asked of them. There is no search for sainthood as we do these things; we do not look for recognition. But we *must* do these things if we're to stay sober and enjoy our recovery. Those who fail to recover end up dead, insane, or locked up in prisons and jails. Perhaps the worst fate is reserved for those who escape the above, but live out their days alone in a facility having their diapers changed while someone wipes the drool from their chin.

I believe recovery is much more a gift than an accomplishment and those of us who receive it are in the very small minority, percentage-wise, within the alcoholic community. So it is to be treasured and guarded at all costs. It is a national tragedy that so few recover, because alcoholism and addiction are highly treatable diseases. And while the disease of alcoholism is progressive, so is recovery.

One industry study wanted to know what could be gained by treating alcoholics and returning them to the workplace. The results were startling. Absenteeism dropped by 89%, tardiness decreased by 92%, problems with supervisors decreased by 56%, production errors decreased by 70%, and hospitalization costs dropped by 36%.

Consistently, studies have shown that recovering employees are more productive, more loyal, and become better workers than their non-recovering counterparts. Few who successfully recover from this disease can do so without an immense sense of gratitude, a new joy in living, and a dedicated desire to be an honorable, positive, and stalwart citizen of the universe. It's what recovery is about.

Preparing for the Darkness - 1990

I concluded my twenty-eight-day stay at Anchor Hospital on April 6, 1990. It was time to go to Minneapolis and be arraigned. The other two pilots had already appeared before a Magistrate but I'd been allowed to complete my hospital stay. Although we'd tried to keep my treatment quiet, the media had guessed where I was and published the information that I was an alcoholic. The general media seemed to require no confirmation of anything; if they thought it they published it. I read articles where the writer told his readers precisely what I'd been thinking as I did this or that, as if they had access to my innermost thoughts. I still see that done today with others and I'm astounded that the public never seems to question or challenge *how* any reporter or journalist is gifted with the ability to *know* what a complete stranger is thinking.

I never enjoyed any anonymity as an alcoholic because the entire public was let in on it. Initially, it fell as a curse, adding to the mountain of shame and humiliation, but as time passed it became a blessing in ways only God can orchestrate.

One reporter from Minnesota, using guile and masquerading as someone else, called Barbara at her job and tried to get information over the phone. Barbara immediately sensed the deception and refused to answer his questions. However, he reported that Barbara had "confirmed" I was in a treatment center. She'd done no such thing. Reporters also called our neighbors but they were our friends and were incensed at such calls. There were no lengths to which the reporters wouldn't go. Later, this same reporter attempted to force my attorney to grant him an "exclusive" interview with me after the trial and I refused.

I had only two more days left in treatment when one of the CAs excitedly came and got me. "Go to your room," he said, "and look at the door next to yours!" I did and as I stopped at the room adjacent to mine I looked at the nametag on it. My heart jumped because it said "Lilly M." My friend Lilly had come back to us. I knocked on the door and she answered. We hugged and I had tears in my eyes. I was so glad she came back for help. Lilly is still sober today, as far as I know.

At one point in my treatment I was told the federal marshals were coming to take me back to Minneapolis to be arraigned. I desperately needed an attorney to prevent that but I was confined and restricted inside a hospital for alcoholics. Every phone call by a patient required an individually approved and signed order from a doctor. My situation became so dire that they put me in a room with a phone, gave me a phone book, and said, "Make all the calls you need and take all the time necessary."

I found and then lost two attorneys before finding Peter Wold in Minneapolis. Each time I thought I had an attorney the desperation would lift and I would slide into relief. Then, a day or so later, I would receive a call saying they couldn't represent me for one reason or another. My heart would race and I would again be back in the room with the phone desperately trying to find someone to help me.

The Air Line Pilots Association was trying to help although I'd put them in a horribly bad spot. While many pilots had individually come to my aid and assistance, many others thought I should be publicly shot for foisting such a black eye on the profession, and I completely understood their feelings. The Air Line Pilots Association was between a rock and a hard place, yet they attempted to help as much as they could.

I was briefed on three attorneys in the Minneapolis area. One was a well-known but extremely expensive trial lawyer I couldn't afford. Another was the Minneapolis version of Gerry Spence, the flamboyant, fringe-jacketed attorney from Wyoming, and I was told his style of lawyering might be helpful or it might be extremely damaging. The third lawyer was described as quiet and methodical, a deep researcher, but he had never tried a federal case before, and he was my choice. Peter Wold came to visit me in the treatment center shortly thereafter. I was in a foyer and I saw him coming down the walkway. He was a handsome gent of medium height and weight, but I thought, "My God! I have kids who look older than him!"

I never knew an attorney like Peter Wold. We quickly became friends, and he became devoted to my case. However, I knew he was riding a dead horse; the only conceivable outcome would be a guilty verdict. Peter didn't share my view, and he spared no effort in my defense. His integrity was unquestionable and his character was superb. I could not have made a better choice in spite of his inexperience in a federal courtroom.

Initially, I told Peter I just wanted to plead guilty and get it over. In fact, I *was* guilty, if not strictly in the legal sense, then certainly in the moral sense. I had never tried to dodge responsibility in my life. Peter wanted to plead not guilty. He told me the media had whipped up such a firestorm that a public execution probably wouldn't satisfy them. Then he quietly said, "Lyle, when you plead not guilty you are not saying, 'I didn't do it.' You're simply exercising your constitutional right to have your accuser prove the accusation." So I listened to Peter and accepted his advice.

In treatment I had finally learned to listen. Many times I had sat in a group, head down, eyes down, with my counselor's words bouncing off the top of my head as he said, "Lyle, you are going to *have* to learn to accept help." I had a long way to go but I had made some progress learning to trust, listen, and accept help.

On April 9, 1990, I appeared in Minneapolis before Magistrate Judge Earl Cudd. The trial date was set for June 27, 1990. It was later moved to July 25th so the prosecutor could go on her family vacation. Unlike my two codefendants who had appeared a week or two prior to me, I was not handcuffed before being taken in. The media had loved and exploited that with my fellow crewmembers. After entering our plea, a U.S. Marshal fingerprinted me and said some kind words to me as he was rolling my fingers. His kindness was completely unexpected and I was touched by it. Standing next to him was another U.S. Marshal whom I would meet once again twenty years later when he was seventeen months sober. He tracked me down to thank me for helping him get sober after reading an account of my own journey into recovery. I was then released. Throughout it all, reporters yelled at me, stuck microphones and cameras in my face, and tried to evoke a comment or reaction. I maintained my calm as best I could, and tried to ignore them, which was impossible.

I returned to Atlanta and asked to go through thirty more days of treatment at the facility next door, Talbott-Marsh Recovery Center (TMRC). They were joined at the hip with Anchor Hospital. TMRC was originally founded to treat medical professionals such as doctors, dentists, and nurses, but had branched into other areas. I'd heard it was a more intense and advanced treatment although it was difficult to imagine how anything could be more intense than what I'd just completed.

It was a long-term treatment facility and they wanted a ninety-day minimum commitment. I knew I would be in a courtroom before then, so they accepted a thirty-day promise from me. I asked for this additional treatment time because I wanted a rock solid foundation beneath me for what lay ahead – mandatory prison time. I was already well invested in my recovery; I knew the routine and I'd read all the literature numerous times. But I also knew recovery was not an intellectual process. It had to be absorbed and experienced first-hand and I needed to be solidly immersed in that process. It was a good decision and it served me well in the days that followed.

As the days passed my expanding sense of recovery helped me feel slightly more peaceful about what lay ahead. Progress was slow, coming in tiny, nearly imperceptible slivers, but it came. If it was fifty miles into the woods, it was fifty miles out and I knew that. I worked to strengthen my recovery, and I focused daily on the acceptance aspect. But each night, as I saw the day end, I was aware that I was one day closer to facing the inevitable. It was a haunting thought at the end of each day.

Ed Youmans was assigned as my counselor. The first time I was summoned to his office I glanced at a large, framed document on his wall. It said, "There are only two things you need to know about God. First, that there *is* one; and second, that it's not *you!*" Ed was an extraordinary counselor. He had incredible insight and I marveled at his gift for approaching so many different people in *just* the right way.

As the years have passed, Ed and I have become close friends. Today, he runs a small treatment center in Griffin, Georgia, and I go there regularly to participate in his patient groups and have lunch with him. I never leave without recognizing that I've once again received more than I could possibly give. One day I commented about that and Ed smiled and said, "Do you know why that is?" I said no, and Ed said, "Because you can't out give God." Ed always kept it simple.

At TMRC Ed took over where Robin had left off. I liked Ed immensely and knew I'd lucked out once more. Everyone was aware of the firestorm I was operating in. Once he looked at me and said, "If you can stay sober through all of this it's gonna' make one helluva' book!" This comment did nothing to ease my worries. I spent thirty days at TMRC, soaking up recovery like a sponge, living in a halfway house, and adding to my foundation of sobriety. As at Anchor, I had many intense and heartwarming experiences with my fellow patients. Many were suffering as deeply as I was and I didn't have a monopoly on misery. I tried to help them, and in the doing of that I helped myself. The days and nights passed, and then it was time to go home and prepare for trial.

The Trial

Back home for the first time in two months I had very little time to prepare for the trial. I bridged the gap from the safety of the treatment center to the outside world of recovery. The staff at Anchor and TMRC told me, "Treatment is discovery, and once you leave here you enter the world of recovery." I was discharged at 10 AM and was in a meeting with other alcoholics by noon; I wasted no time.

Conyers had very few meetings at that time and most were cloudy with cigarette smoke. I told Barbara I thought my liver was going to make it but my lungs were going to go. I never smoked and never did drugs, not even experimentally. I was a true-blue alcoholic. I traveled ten miles down I-20 east to Covington, and became part of the noon group there. The ventilation system seemed better and I could at least see the front of the room through the smoke.

Jack and Jerry were two attorneys who lived in Covington, both with many years of sobriety. They took me under their wing and eased my way into the group. We would often go to lunch after a meeting but I would usually have coffee while they ate. I was broke and still had too much false pride to let them buy me something to eat. As time went on, those walls began to come down and once in a while I would eat a sandwich with them. I was still struggling with accepting help, but I was working on it.

One day, as we approached the restaurant, a drunk came up and asked for a handout. Jack quickly handed him five dollars. The man turned and headed for a nearby liquor store. Shocked, I said to Jack, "What are you doing! Can't you see he's just going to use it for booze?!" Jack looked at me, and with all the compassion one alcoholic can have for another he said, "Lyle, that man doesn't have a choice. He *has* to drink right now, and a drink may be the only thing that saves his life today." It was an insight I never had and one I've never forgotten. The three of us were given the power of choice through recovery and the freedom to walk away from the bottle. Jack has since passed away and the loss was a blow to our group.

So today, when I see a homeless person holding up a sign that says, "I'm homeless and need money," or "I'll work for food," I just give the five dollars and don't worry about how it will be spent. I try to give from my heart, and what that person does with the gift is none of my business. I've done *my* part, and my part is all I can control. I think God wants it that way.

I was worried about money, but there was no way anyone was going to hire me. In the small area where I lived, all the local papers carried my story, the TV saturated the populace, and everyone knew about me. Since getting a job of any sort was out of the question the next best thing was to focus entirely on my recovery.

I followed directions and found a mentor. Matter of fact, I got two since one was a pilot for Delta and would be gone a lot. The other was Bob, a wonderful and kind man I looked up to, but he was a heavy smoker and died a few years later of lung cancer.

As the trial approached, Bob stopped by my house. He asked how long we would be gone and I said I was told to expect up to six weeks. Bob said he and some other recovery folks would take care of my yard and keep an eye on the house. I was still not good at accepting help and said, "No, Bob, don't worry about it. I'll take care of it." I had *no* idea how I was going accomplish that since we were broke and I certainly couldn't afford to pay someone to do it. It was an instinctive reaction to someone wanting to help me.

Then Bob said something that struck me. He put his hand on my shoulder and said, "Lyle, please don't cheat us out of an opportunity to help you." I let go of my old thinking and I said okay. They took immaculate care of our home while we were gone. Each week another sober member of my group came and lifted one more thing from the list of problems I was dealing with. They did it because they cared about me; because I was one more recovering alcoholic.

Before we left I brought the mail in one morning and glanced through the items, almost tossing one letter that appeared to be junk mail but I opened it anyway. I glanced at it and took a second look. It was a cashier's check for $10,000 made out to me! I looked away and then looked back, unable to believe the number of zero's. I counted them once more. I couldn't believe my eyes.

Then I noticed a name down low in a corner. The check was from Charlie Young, a Captain I'd flown with a long time ago. Charlie and I had not gotten along when we flew together. As we taxied in on the final segment of our month together, I said to him, "You know, Charlie, it doesn't take any talent to be an asshole." That's how we ended the month. Yet here was a gesture that went magnanimously beyond the word *generous,* an act of kindness that defied description. For the longest time, I sat and looked at the check. As I absorbed it, my eyes became moist. It was yet another act of kindness that came from a most unexpected place.

I taped the check to the kitchen cabinet and when Barbara came in from work I told her to go look. Like me, she had trouble believing what she was seeing. We were financially strapped. While this would not get us out of the hole, it was an incredibly huge move in that direction and allowed us to take a deep breath of relief.

I sat down and wrote Charlie a long letter. Many years later, when I had a chance to personally thank him, he pulled it out of his flight bag and told me he saved the letter.

Captain Frank Taylor and his wife Mary had been the first to shock me in such a way. Frank and I had been cadets at Pensacola decades earlier. Within mere days of our story making headlines, I opened a letter from Frank. He had carefully wrapped $2,000 in cash and sent it. A week later, he sent more, but this time it was $5,000, again wrapped in a sheet of paper.

I have never known such kindness and generosity. I was completely disarmed and immensely touched by these events. Part of it was due to the severity of what happened and my resulting desperation and weakness. Part of it was the untapped area of my heart that *never* expected such help from my friends.

As time went on, dozens of Northwest pilots and flight attendants chipped in and helped us. Many times it was all we had, yet we could scrape by because of their generosity. Several pilots began sending us small amounts each month, which was a huge help. Each gesture of help was a special event and each person carved out a special place in our hearts. No words will ever be able to express our gratitude, nor will we ever forget it.

On July 22, 1990, Barbara and I headed for Minneapolis to face the trial. I used a calculator to compute gas, lodging, and food expenses. I thought we might make it if we could buy bread and sandwich meat and sought the cheapest motels. It would be a two-day trip and the trial would begin on July 25th. It was a remarkable journey.

I had learned to live one day at a time, focusing on the present moment, and would not allow the fear of tomorrow to destroy that. As we drove the twelve hundred miles to Minnesota, Barbara and I talked and even laughed from time to time. The face of America slowly changed as we drove closer to the most difficult challenge we ever faced. I asked Barbara to read to me from a text on recovery; there was nothing new in what I was hearing, but I was somehow renewed each time I heard the words again. We did this for two days. No doctor could have prescribed a better regimen than Barbara's soft, south Texas voice, as she read the words I would desperately need to remember in the coming days.

We crossed the St. Croix River on I-94, from Hudson, Wisconsin, into Minnesota. The large monument welcoming us to Minnesota was directly in front of us and I pulled over and stopped. We were now in the land where everything was going to happen. I looked at Barbara, leaned over, and kissed her. I took a deep breath, realizing how close we now were to the disaster ahead of us. I reached over and slowly took her hand; she smiled at me and squeezed my hand as if to indicate she knew what I was thinking, and we drove into Minneapolis.

Barbara continually reassured me we would survive this. I wondered where her confidence came from. Something inside her never wavered.

While I was grateful for her and the attitude she maintained, I could not share it.

My attorney, Peter Wold, knew we were broke and he offered his home to us. I was no longer so proud I could afford to refuse, so we moved into Peter's home on Medicine Lake. We stayed with him a short while as things got under way. Then his brother and sister-in-law, Jeff and Becky, offered to let us move across Medicine Lake into their finished basement apartment. They were gracious and kind and we were deeply appreciative.

Peter Wold and the other two attorneys moved for separate trials but were denied. He thought our chances of success would be better if we could present our own case individually and the other two attorneys felt the same about their clients. The motion was denied; it would be a joint trial.

It was difficult for all three attorneys to coordinate their defense attempts. I was not having any contact with the other two defendants except when we were together with our attorneys. At some point during the trial the first officer told me the second officer was calling him repeatedly. Finally, he told the second officer to quit calling. At the time I gave it no thought since we were all up to our eyes in difficulties.

Years later, in a phone conversation on August 22nd, 2009, the first officer told me the purpose of the calls. Allegedly, the second officer wanted to concoct a story at my expense and offer it to the prosecutor in exchange for the two of them escaping prosecution. The first officer told me he was already in dire straits and did not want to add to that by getting caught in a lie; so he told the second officer to quit calling. I also learned later that the second officer allegedly commented to one of our expert witnesses that he would testify against either of us in exchange for immunity.

We were the first to be tried under this law. As the statute was worded there was a presumption of impairment for any blood alcohol content above .10. Both the first and second officer's BAC had been below that. Because of the presumption clause, the law created a presumption of guilt and negated a presumption of innocence. Had the wording simply made it *illegal* to fly with a BAC of .10 or more it would have been a different matter. In addition to the problem the wording created, the prosecutor wanted all three of us, so she struck the wording relating to the .10 presumption when the indictment was made.

The trial commenced with jury selection on July 25, 1990. Judge James M. Rosenbaum was assigned as the trial judge. None of the three defense attorneys considered this a good thing. Judge Rosenbaum was known to be fair, but he was also no nonsense and tough. I would receive no sympathy, but then I didn't expect any.

The media overwhelmed us everywhere we went. To avoid them, we began leaving from back doors and traveled the short distance to the courtroom via back streets. Then we would alter our routes. The reporters quickly split their forces and covered all avenues of approach. I will never forget the terror of walking into a mass of reporters, fighting like a pack of dogs to get near me, thrusting cameras and microphones in my face and yelling questions at me. It never ceased and I never became accustomed to it. I attempted to mask my fear with a neutral expression and can only wonder how successful I was. Barbara was always at my side and her presence was comforting. But even as I felt comforted, there was also the deep guilt that she was exposed to all of this.

As I approached the crowd I would silently mantra the Serenity Prayer, until it began to take effect: "God, grant me the serenity to accept the things I cannot change, the courage to change the things I can, and the wisdom to know the difference." As I did so, I could feel an ever so slight lessening within me.

I was cautioned to say nothing in the elevators as we rode to the sixth floor of the U.S. Courthouse because reporters were planted to catch anything we said.

The prosecutor was Betsy de la Vega, an Assistant U.S. Attorney reputed to be a formidable prosecutor. Since this was such a high profile case, I knew they would pick someone who would win without question. I learned that ninety-eight percent of all federal prosecutions end in convictions, so there was little doubt what the outcome would be. In later years, I would look more closely at this percentage and question our judicial system's authenticity. The near automatic conviction rate seemed worthy of suspicion. Fortunately, I knew I was guilty so it wouldn't be a factor.

I was a public pariah, held in angry contempt and scorned by many. While that devastated me, I understood and accepted it. Yet, there were touching experiences that came unexpectedly and caught me by surprise each time. During the lunch breaks we tried to find small, nearly uninhabited places free of reporters and local people. Several times we were recognized as we walked down the busy and crowded streets going to lunch. Once, a horn honked and I glanced at a car stopped at a traffic light. The driver sat at attention and rendered me a hand salute. Perhaps he'd been a Marine, or maybe a Vietnam vet, but I was moved and my eyes moistened. I looked directly at him, nodded back as I acknowledged his salute, and his hand came down. Several times people called out, "Good luck, Captain," and I was again taken by surprise. Once I heard someone yell, "Semper Fi," the Latin Marine Corps motto of "Semper Fidelis," meaning "Always Faithful." I expected to be spat on, and these moments touched my heart.

Shortly after Peter took the case, and before the trial, he was involved in an incident that shook him to his core. On June 10th, he was returning home after a golf tournament and party when he was stopped by a state trooper. The trooper recognized him as one of the lawyers for the three pilots. Peter was cited for DWI. He was shaken and mortified at what this was going to do to our case. He called me and I could tell he was suffering badly as he struggled to tell me what happened. Having gone through my own experience, I had nothing but empathy for him. He offered to withdraw from the case, but he had become my friend and I wanted him to continue. Regardless of what took place, whether the media reported this or not, we would press on to the end.

The days passed and nothing appeared in the papers so we began to breathe easier. However, the afternoon before I was to testify, Jerry Tosch, a local reporter approached Peter and asked if he would like to comment on his DWI. Peter stiffened with terror. Tosch was the same person who'd phoned Barbara and masqueraded as someone else in an attempt to get information from her while she was at work. It was abundantly clear that integrity and ethics didn't get in his way when it came to his brand of journalism. Tosch said he was going to run the story the following morning, just as I was taking the stand. Peter pleaded with Tosch not to run the story. Tosch agreed to hold the story in exchange for an exclusive interview after the trial. I don't know if Peter ever granted him an interview, but I refused to speak with him.

Tosch typified most of my early experiences with reporters. Most were less concerned about facts and truth than scooping their competitors and getting something into print or on TV. There were precious few I trusted and none with whom I wished to speak. Eventually I came to know several who were bright and shining beacons of their profession. Laura Palmer, Diane Sawyer, Ted Koppel, and Pam Martin represented the finest within the field of journalism; capable, gifted reporters who went after the story but never compromised their integrity or journalistic ethics. In the years that followed, more made their way into my acquaintance and it was gratifying to sit down and trust those journalists who possessed a sense of honor and integrity. It's not unreasonable to suppose every profession is plagued with similar problems.

I was guilty. And although that was true, I became disabused of the picture I'd once held of our legal system. Watching TV shows such as *Perry Mason, LA Law* or *Judd for the Defense*, along with what I learned in high school, created an image of a pristine procedure. I thought there was a purity attached to the determination of guilt or innocence and rules to be played by.

During my trial I saw a police officer blatantly lie under oath and get away with it. I watched the prosecutor repeatedly misstate facts and evidence, and I came away with a completely different idea about our system. One of our blood tests got "lost," and the prosecutor made some claims in her closing argument that were clearly wrong and inaccurate. She referenced rules pertaining to alcohol and truck drivers that were incorrect. Bill Mauzy, the attorney for the copilot, objected to the statements but was rebuked by Judge Rosenbaum. Then she completely invented *new* evidence. She made a statement that the oxygen bottles in the cockpit were empty when we landed, implying we were all on oxygen due to our intoxication. It was just plain wrong – it never happened. As a defendant I was powerless to interrupt the proceedings. After Judge Rosenbaum allowed the statement about truck drivers, the attorneys let her get away with the statement about the oxygen bottles. No longer did I believe in the blindfolded lady holding the scales of justice in her hand; *that* was a farce and a charade.

Repeatedly, I watched the jury foreperson play to the reporters and cameras. Each time the jury came back from a break, she was loud and obnoxious, openly drawing attention to herself. After the verdict, she was the first person on TV, with reporters sitting in her kitchen as she held forth to the cameras. I could only wonder how she'd performed in the jury room. All of it was appalling, and I was completely unprepared for what I observed.

One juror, an old man, slept through much of the proceedings.

It was not the system I once believed in. As the years passed, I have repeatedly said *Thank God I was guilty* and not an innocent person trapped in our judicial system. We have the finest system of jurisprudence in the world, but it is flawed and errors *do occur* much more than we often acknowledge. With every single high publicity case that's come on the scene since my experience, I said to Barbara, "I *hope* he or she is guilty because they *are* going to be convicted!" The O.J. Simpson case was a clear exception, and I was surprised by that outcome.

When Johnny Cochran theatrically declared in the O.J. courtroom that a trial was "the search for the truth," I turned to Barbara and said, "No, it *isn't*. It's a contest to be won at any cost. And hiding witnesses and evidence, secreting reports and documents, misstating evidence, manipulating lab results, DNA tests, or anything else is okay – *as long as you win.*"

Thank God I was guilty. But I felt as though I'd gone through the experience in a sewer instead of a courtroom. And always, I was aware of a voice inside me that said, "*None of this* could have happened – if *you* had not done what *you* did." I was not a victim; I put myself here. I was grateful for Peter Wold and others like him who take on the cases of the despised, the desperate, and the forlorn. I do not believe the guilty should go free. I am a hardcore believer in acceptance of personal responsibility. I subscribe to the old adage I first heard in treatment that, "When you do what you did, you get what you got." But without people like Peter, we would be at the mercy of a very one-sided system. Guilty or not, each of us deserves an honest and fair proceeding.

The jury convened to deliberate my case at 11:30 A.M. on the morning of August 16, 1990, a Thursday. They were released at 5:00 P.M. They deliberated until noon the next day and were then released for the weekend. On Monday morning, August 20th, they deliberated about 90 minutes and came in with a verdict at 10:30 A.M. I knew what it would be.

Although I knew all along what the verdict would be, the case took a twist after the prosecution presented its case. Surprisingly, many in the legal community began to comment that absolutely no direct evidence had been presented that showed any of us were impaired. And impairment was the legal issue, specifically, whether we were able to perform in a normal manner. Although the prosecution meticulously dissected the flight, listened to all the radio communications, and plotted the progress of what we did and how we did it, they could find no flaws or errors. It was pointed out that I had called Flight Dispatch and requested extra fuel due to the weather conditions. Additionally, no one could testify that anyone stumbled, exhibited slurred speech, or anything else to indicate an impaired condition. The government witnesses all parroted the same exact phrase when they said we "had the stale smell of alcohol and blood shot eyes." It almost sounded as though they had been rehearsed. The sole evidence presented was the Blood Alcohol Content on each of us, and on *that* rested the entire case.

Observers in the legal community thought an acquittal might result, and this possibility was reported in the media. I tried hard to ignore it but in spite of myself, and even though I wanted to suppress all whispers of hope, the thought began to develop – *Was it possible we might be found not guilty?!*

When all this began, I told Peter I knew he would do his best but he was riding a dead horse and I would be found guilty. I told him it would be okay and for him not to worry about my reaction. As we took our seats and the jury came in, Peter sat to my right and I knew he was tense. The jury immediately announced a verdict of guilty as it applied to me and I saw Peter stiffen. I reached over, patted him gently on the knee, and whispered, "It's okay, Peter...it's okay." Peter took it hard.

I never toyed with the issue of legal guilt versus moral guilt. Regardless of how one might split hairs on the legal issue, I knew I violated all the rules and deserved what came my way. I refused to become immersed in the disparities of the trial, refused to be a victim in *any sense*, and have steadfastly said that everything was fair and appropriate; that I deserved it all.

Up to this time I had not spoken to the press. We left the courtroom and I decided to make a statement on the steps of the courthouse. I said I respected the decision of the jury and bore no one ill will. I refuted the idea that Northwest bore any responsibility for this incident by their refusal to join the other airlines with an alcohol program. I then said, "This trial has brought a lot of negative publicity to Northwest Airlines. Northwest is a *good* airline and I would ask the public to appreciate that there are 40,000 good employees at Northwest; and only three are on trial here today." I ended my statement and walked away.

As with virtually all cases, appeals were going to be filed. Later, a reporter pointedly asked me, "If you believe so strongly in acceptance of responsibility, why are you filing an appeal?" I replied, "Because there are rules that each side is supposed to play by. And when those rules are disregarded, something needs to be done and that's what an appeal is about. The rules apply to all of us under the constitution and they need to be respected by *all* parties." I knew only five percent of all appeals were successful. Even if an appeal was successful, it only meant another trial, so I was not going to just walk away free. I was not attaching any realistic hope or optimism to an appeal. I was going to prison.

Sentencing

Judge Rosenbaum set the date for sentencing as October 26, 1990. I returned home and resumed my recovery activities, building on what was now a certain outcome. Barbara and I did all we could to prepare for my departure.

I went through the entire house and made detailed instruction lists on how to do all the things I normally handled, things Barbara was totally unfamiliar with. I put all these in a notebook and organized them for her. I labeled pieces of equipment and referenced where the instructions could be found. Barbara was going to be alone, with no one to help her, and I wanted to make it as doable as possible.

We had an attorney change the house from joint ownership to her name alone, in the event something happened to me in prison. We did likewise with other items; I wanted everything to be as clean as possible, with no possible legal problems if I didn't come back.

I went to the Russell Building, the large federal building in downtown Atlanta, to surrender my passport and arrange for bond. I was fearful I would have to sign the house over and it was a *huge* relief when they accepted my signature alone. Once again, I left with a sense of gratitude over something I once would never have considered a gift.

Barbara and I went to Minnesota on October 24, 1990, for the sentencing. Jim O'Rourke, a Northwest Captain, paid our airfare to and from Atlanta. Jim would later visit me in prison. He was a good and supportive friend who later died of cancer. Two other Northwest pilots picked us up at the terminal curb. They whisked us to a parking lot where Jim gave us a new Oldsmobile to use while we were there. Throughout everything, we experienced one kindness after another as friends gathered around us.

We drove straight to Peter's office, said our hellos, and I instantly sensed something was wrong. Peter sighed and said he just received a letter from Judge Rosenbaum two hours earlier. The letter said the judge was going to depart from the sentencing guidelines and stiffen the sentence. The guidelines involved numerical designations of offense levels and an algebraic method of arriving at a sentence. Mine had been set at level thirteen which required a minimum of twelve months in prison and a maximum of eighteen months. There was no provision for a suspended sentence. Prison was mandatory. As the Captain, I knew I was going to get eighteen months, and I had worked hard to accept that.

Now the sky was the limit and I could be sentenced to a maximum of fifteen years. What doubled my terror was the prosecutor had not asked for an increase in the sentence; this was something the *judge* wanted to do. An extra month or so may have placated Ms. de la Vega, but this was going to be big. The media was notified about this latest development, and public anticipation began building.

In the weeks prior to sentencing, I had two identical dreams where I stood before Judge Rosenbaum expecting an 18-month sentence. Instead, he gave me five years and I awoke when the gavel slammed down on the bench. Each time, I came to cold and sweaty. I told Barbara about the dreams and said I thought they were visions; that I was being told what to expect.

We left Peter's office and I retreated back into what always worked before–what I had learned in treatment. I was powerless over what was going to occur, just as I was powerless over alcohol. Acceptance became my only avenue to peace. Again I recited the Serenity Prayer, and the grim tightness inside me began to ease. I didn't have the power to handle this or affect the outcome, so I turned to a Power greater than myself.

On the morning of October 26, 1990, I walked into Judge Rosenbaum's courtroom for the final time. Standing outside, I told Barbara I thought she would be returning home alone, and that I would be led away in handcuffs after the sentencing. We entered the courtroom, I hugged and kissed her, gave her my personal effects, and turned and walked through the small swinging doors to the defendant area.

I thought to myself, "This is the final bludgeoning I'll have to take. After this, it's all over. It's done." I found a semblance of peace in that.

I was in treatment with a federal judge who cornered me at every opportunity to explain how things were done. Frankly, he gave me some information I could have done without. He told me the sentencing procedure was a charade. The sentence was carefully and methodically researched and determined ahead of time. Even though I was expected to speak, as was my attorney and any witnesses who appeared, he told me the sentence was set the moment the judge walks in the room. Nothing changes, he told me, regardless of what's said or done by others. All the letters from friends and family had been read and considered. There would be no last minute sway of emotional appeal to change anything. *It just didn't happen*, and he was firm about that.

So I knew my words would have no effect on the sentence, yet for two days I tried desperately to compose something to say but was unable. I was just too scared. Judge Rosenbaum asked if I had anything to say before he sentenced me, and I stood to speak.

Even as I stood I didn't know what to say. My quiet prayer was simply, "God, please let me get this out. Please let me speak from my heart. Please help me get past the tightness in my chest and the choking in my throat." I spoke for several minutes and still wonder how I was able to do so. I've read the transcript of what I said and don't remember most of it.

I said in part, "I accept full responsibility for this incident. And if anyone bears the brunt of it, I do as the captain, and I acknowledge it. I have never done anything other than that. I cannot change what happened seven months ago and I cannot change what happened yesterday. I regret it and if I could change it I would; but I can't. So I accept it."

"I don't want to go to prison but I know I must, and I intend to find something positive in every day that I'm there. I intend to come out of that institution much farther ahead than I was when I went into it. I'm bound and determined to make the time serve me and not just serve the time."

"Positive things that have come out of this. The terrible trauma we had in our family two and a half years ago has been resolved. I've regained two of my children and for that I am profusely thankful."

I was grateful for my sobriety, for without that none of the good things could have occurred and I absolutely knew that. The other two defendants said very little, both of them apparently as scared as I was. Then it was time for Judge Rosenbaum. He delivered an eloquent and searing address to us and I agreed with most of what he said.

Judge Rosenbaum said, "I have had many letters written on each of your behalf, and they talk about your respect for your job and your training. Your failure to live up to your commitment to the safety of your passengers is a tragedy [for you] and a tragedy for your profession.

"On a personal level, the fact of this crime and the pain of its punishment is heartbreaking. The pain and ultimate punishment always falls on the families. I do not have the power to ease the pain of your families, of your spouses, of your brothers, your sisters, your parents, and your friends. The greatest heartbreak is reserved for the children."

The judge continued, "There has been noted each of your personal fine characteristics, and you have them. Defendant Prouse is a decorated Marine. Your acts of heroism speak for themselves and are well recognized. I received a letter from a Marine Brigadier General who took you as his aide. I do not just lightly read a letter like that."

Referring to my remarks on the courthouse steps, immediately after my conviction, he said, "And I tell you that I found both chivalrous and proper your statements, Mr. Prouse, after the trial, that these acts were not those of the airline for which you worked or about all airline pilots in general. That's true, but it's not acceptance of responsibility. Even your decision to accept treatment and counseling for your alcoholism is not acceptance of responsibility."

The judge concluded, "The hand that will punish you is mine, but the hand that strikes you is your own. And I do so with no joy."

I sat and listened and it was the lowest moment of my life. Everything he said penetrated my soul. He pointed out that each of us had achieved the American dream, but now forfeited it. I painfully played and replayed that many times in my sleepless nights, but hearing the words from him, delivered from the bench, made them iron-steel hard as they pierced my heart.

As he delivered his lengthy statement, it was clear he was setting the stage for the stiff sentence he was about to deliver. He said he never received as many letters on behalf of a defendant as he had on me. All that aside, he said, he had little choice but to do what was required. He was correct and I completely accepted that. Then, it was time for me to stand and face him. I took a deep breath and stood up expecting five years or more.

I was sentenced to sixteen months in federal prison and three years of supervised release afterwards. The sentence was a stunning shock in light of what I was expecting. I truly experienced one of the first miracles in my journey that morning. Peter was incredulous at the sentence, at first believing the judge must have said *sixty* months instead of sixteen! Why the judge ratcheted the sentence down from the bench would remain a mystery for two years.

As Judge Rosenbaum met with Peter in his chambers two years later, he told Peter that he changed the sentence from the bench, something I was told *never* occurred in the judicial process. He said he looked at me, thought about my time as a Marine, a Vietnam veteran, and a human being, and came down from the four years he intended to impose. When I heard this from Peter, I was deeply affected. If a miracle is an event that occurs against near impossible odds, this certainly was one.

Over the years, I have spoken in hundreds of places around the country and to thousands of people. Occasionally, I would be approached by recovering lawyers and judges after an event. Each has corroborated that what took place that morning simply never happens. A miracle occurred the morning of October 26, 1990, as I stood and looked in the eyes of Judge Rosenbaum.

The other two pilots were sentenced to twelve months. To this day they are unaware of what occurred and that they were headed for three years in prison until the judge came down on my sentence, giving me 25% more than they received. Afterwards, I was asked if I was angry about getting the longer sentence. I replied that I was the Captain, and as such the sentence was appropriate. I blamed no one but myself – and I never had from the onset.

Judge Rosenbaum then put sanctions on me that effectively ended my flying career forever. I was forbidden to fly an airplane for the first year of my supervised release, and I could not fly with any passengers for the remaining two years. When added together, the prison time plus the three years of supervised release, would end when I was nearly fifty-seven years of age. With mandatory retirement at the airlines of age sixty, I could not possibly go through all the re-licensing requirements. Even assuming I could, there would be no time left for me to actually fly. So, it was over. I would never fly again. Or so everyone thought at that moment.

The judge did something else that surprised everyone. I expected to be led away into custody for the benefit of the TV cameras. But the judge noted that this case was a first of its kind and there were complex legal questions to be resolved. He would allow us to remain free until all the appeals were exhausted. The other two pilots chose to remain free, but I declined.

I told the judge I had been convicted and would enter prison *now*. I asked for a couple of weeks to say my goodbyes and get things in order; I asked to enter prison the Monday after Thanksgiving. It would be my last holiday meal with my family before going away.

The judge was taken by surprise and later told my attorney he was lost for words at my response. He said to this day no defendant who has stood before him has chosen to go into prison with an appeal pending.

But I had learned to live life on life's terms and not my own. It was one of the criteria for recovery; and pressed home repeatedly. No amount of wishful thinking was going to keep me from going to prison. I told my kids that I was terrified of going in, but the reality was I could never walk out the back door until I first walked in the front.

I wanted no more countdowns. I had gone through enough of them already. I remembered a day in a high school English class when my teacher, Miss Ramona Martin, read a poem. Miss Martin was an aging teacher who never married. She loved poetry and sometimes cried when she read it, while I paid little attention. But I remembered an excerpt she'd read, "A coward dies a thousand deaths; a brave man only one." Strange, how that came back to me. I was not going to die a thousand deaths as I awaited entry into prison.

Everyone was clamoring to talk with us. There was no TV show I was aware of who hadn't called. Oprah Winfrey was the only television personality I considered. I respected her, but I wouldn't risk it. Going on television was a paralyzing thought, and I didn't know if I had the courage even if I trusted a particular media person.

While I was in treatment, there was a person with connections to Diane Sawyer, another lady I admired and trusted. A short time later I received a call from Janet Tobias, a producer for Diane Sawyer's "Prime Time Live" show, and I spoke with her briefly. I felt I could trust Diane Sawyer but I was having a difficult time deciding to go on TV. Over the course of the next several months Janet Tobias called several times. We had conversations but I remained noncommittal.

Finally, I agreed to meet with Janet and she flew in from New York. Barbara and I met her at a nearby restaurant because I didn't want a reporter in my home. We sat and talked for more than two hours. The lighting in the restaurant was dim, but at one point Janet turned and I saw tears in her eyes. That struck me, and it appeared that she was a person who truly felt something about the story. I agreed to speak with Diane Sawyer, but wanted her to call me personally because I had some boundaries as to what we would discuss. I would talk only about my own personal situation. I would not talk about Northwest Airlines or the other two pilots.

Diane Sawyer called and she was as decent on the phone as I thought she would be. She accepted my terms and wanted Barbara and me to come to New York. We were broke and even though the network would pay our travel costs, I knew there would be small miscellaneous expenses we simply couldn't afford. Diane agreed to come to Atlanta and we held the interview in the downtown Ritz Carlton hotel.

Peter wanted to be in on the interview so he came down. I don't think he had any legal concerns, but he wanted to meet Diane Sawyer. She was a professional journalist and didn't throw me soft questions, but I saw compassion in her face. It was just days before I was to enter prison and Diane asked if I was angry about it. I replied, "No, I'm not. I don't think I'm being sent to prison to prevent me from flying again drunk. And I'm not sure what purpose it's going to serve. But if society says I need to go, then I'll go, and I won't complain about it." When the interview was over, Diane got up and came around the table. She gave me a hug, and then she hugged Barbara.

One of the lighting staff said he had been part of many of her interviews, but this was one of the best. I was glad it was over. It aired a few weeks into my prison time. I was unable to see it.

As I readied myself to go into prison, I recalled a saying from my Marine Corps days. "Courage is not the absence of fear. It's the ability to continue in the face of it." So now it was time to summon all the courage I could and walk into the federal penitentiary. I did so on December 5, 1990 – exactly thirty-four years to the day I entered Marine Corps Boot Camp.

Prison

A few days before I had to report to prison, Barbara and I went to the north Georgia mountains, a place that became our refuge. We had no money but could travel there and back for just over a tank of gas. We would walk the quiet, beautiful area, sit on huge rocks in the rushing whitewater of the Tallulah River, hold hands and be at peace. Strangely, it seemed as if God reserved it for us during our visits because we seemed to have the entire area almost to ourselves each time we went. I was always aware of that.

We went there many times, but this would be our last day for a long while. As we first entered the area there was a large pool at the bottom of the mountains. It appeared calm and placid. A mile higher up, the river was wild and rushing, roaring as it passed by. It was "our place." We sat on the huge rocks in the river and looked at the beauty of the fall colors.

The fall leaves floated down, falling into the rushing river around us and were immediately swept away. As one fell beside me and disappeared, I looked at Barbara and said, "This is how our lives are right now. Out of control, and like the leaf that just fell and was swept away, so are we. But one of these days, when the turbulent ride is over, we'll come out the other end and emerge into that pool at the bottom. It will be calm and peaceful, and we can stop and rest when we get there."

Barbara kissed me on my cheek, took my hand and said, "We'll come back here someday, and when we do it will be better." It was an unforgettable moment frozen in time. So*meday* seemed an eternity away. I leaned over and kissed this beautiful woman who began life with me so many years ago and had chosen to stay on this journey.

Barbara and I drove to the Atlanta Federal Prison on December 5, 1990, arriving at 1:00 P.M. No one who has walked through the doors of a prison will ever again glimpse the world as it existed before that moment.

The day before, I sat in a noon recovery meeting. The man sitting next to me talked about problems with boredom and how it was affecting his sobriety. A legitimate topic, since boredom could easily be the persuader to head for a bar. As the topic reached me, I said, "I would give anything to be bored right now. I have to report to the Atlanta Federal prison in twenty-four hours and I'm terrified. I would give anything to be bored, to have nothing going on, and to just be sitting still wondering what I could do."

We drove into the prison Receiving and Discharge (R & D) area and Barb kissed me goodbye. I kissed her – then kissed her again. Nothing felt right about saying goodbye and I didn't want the moment to end. She was trying to be brave, but she clung to me as tears rolled down her cheeks. I didn't want to let her go but knew I must. She told me she loved me as I turned to leave. It was a tearful and wrenching farewell. It was an incredibly low moment in my life, but I learned to just pick up my pack and march.

Barb's boss accompanied us to the prison. Barbara was afraid she might be too upset to drive home after leaving me there. I learned later that she wept uncontrollably on the way home.

An almost exclusively African-American staff ran the Atlanta Federal Prison, from the warden on down. My estimate was approximately ninety percent of the staff was African-American, with a few white and Hispanic guards and personnel. That is not intended as a racial comment; merely a statement of fact to provide a picture of the facility. Racial prejudice was the order of the day and it was openly practiced with no attempt at disguise or subtlety.

I will never excuse the type of behavior and the racial prejudice I saw in prison. But generations suffered at the hands of white police, white judges, and white prison guards, so when the opportunity presented itself, as it did in the Atlanta prison system, it came as no surprise. I was an avowed anti-racist, and was angry to find myself the victim of something I so hated. I spent a month in Rapid City just prior to going into flight training in 1961. It was the first time I ever saw open prejudice against Indians and I rebelled against that as well.

I received a list of items acceptable in federal prisons and carefully tailored what I was bringing to comply with that list. Apparently, the list did not apply at Atlanta. They confiscated nearly everything I had brought, including my beadwork materials. I hoped to renew my skills with something that took up a lot of time.

A guard named Hurlman processed me into the prison along with a female guard named Jacobson. Hurlman was overweight, seemingly illiterate, and had a two or three day growth of beard. He told an old inmate named Winchester to go get my uniforms. Winchester had a skullcap of short white hair. His eyes were red and rheumy and he shuffled when he walked. He seemed as old as the prison. He soon came back with some khaki trousers and shirts. I was directed to change into them, which I did.

They took all my belongings, along with my clothes, and I was not to see them until I got out. They photographed me for my prison records and ID card. Afterwards, I spent an hour in a chair waiting while they did whatever they were doing. I didn't care if I sat for ten hours. I wasn't going anywhere and time was only time now.

Hurlman brought my prison ID card, with a forlorn-looking photo of me on the front and my inmate number, 04478-041, across my chest. The name read, "Norman Lynn Prouse," an error, but I wasn't sure if I should bring it to their attention. I was in a strange, foreign place, and was unaware of what was supposed to happen or what I was supposed to do. Finally, I got up and walked a few feet over to where Hurlman was sitting. He turned, looked at me and said, "Yeh, wha' yew want?" I pointed to my ID and said, "My name is wrong here. It says Norman

Lynn and my name is Norman Lyle." Hurlman leaned back, pausing as he attempted to process what I'd said, looked at me again, and said, "If the computah say yo' name is Lynn, and thuh judge say yo' name is Lynn...then yo' name is Lynn!" It was an early introduction to prison guard mentality.

I shrugged and said, "Okay by me. I'll be whoever you say." I turned and walked back to my chair. For just a fleeting moment I entertained the hope that my felony conviction would go to Norman Lynn instead of Norman Lyle, but that was not to be.

I was taken to my cubicle in G Building. I put my bedding down in G-4 and looked up as Carlos Duarte stood up from the cubicle next to me. I didn't notice he was there. With a Hispanic accent he said, "Hi, my name is Carlos and I'll help you if I can." I nodded but said nothing. Carlos was a handsome Colombian in his early thirties with a dazzling smile. He was from an aristocratic family who raised Paso Fino horses, but Carlos got sidetracked in drug trafficking. I didn't know much about prison yet and trusted no one. I wasn't about to become someone's girl-friend, so I remained distant and alone.

The cubicles were built from cinder block, measuring eight feet by twelve, with two small beds in each. The walls were five feet high so everyone could be seen as they stood when the counts took place. Each building housed around seventy inmates and there were eight such areas. The floors were concrete and there was a heavy buildup of polished wax, added to daily as an endless parade of inmates waxed and buffed the floors.

The windows were small bricks of diffused glass that let in some light, but were impossible to clearly see through. The area between the two beds was approximately twenty-four inches and each cubicle had two small lockers for individual articles. Combination locks secured them but each lock had a key slot in the back and could be opened by the guards. When two inmates were in the cubicle, one had to sit on a bed because there was not room enough for both to move in the area between. There was approximately five feet or so at the end of the beds where the lockers were.

I spent my first night in prison and awakened early the next morning, getting up in the dark so I could get in and out of the large bathroom area before the other convicts mobbed it. I brought two pair of shoes with me; one pair of black steel-toed Nike's and a pair of white jogging shoes. In the dark I managed to put one of each on. As I returned from the bathroom area, the lights came on and the inmates began stirring.

I noticed an inmate staring at my feet as I came up the long corridor. He was "Country Billy" Cummins and he said, "I lak yore shoes," and I looked down and saw that I was wearing one black shoe and one white shoe. Embarrassed, I looked at Billy but said nothing. Country Billy smiled and said, "I'll bet yew've got 'nother pair jus' lak 'em," and I started laughing. Billy was a good guy, quiet and minded his own business. I had the impression he was hard as nails.

Carlos had a cube-mate named Eddie, a hard case from Kentucky who spent most of his life in prison. Eddie took it upon himself to find me a blanket my first night so I could sleep warmly. I was taken aback by his thoughtfulness, but really appreciated it. Another unexpected act of kindness came from Matt Dorsey, a handsome, clean-cut college kid in his twenties who was mixed up with drugs. The prison beds were instruments of torture and the springs in mine sagged like a hammock. I wondered how long it would be before my back came apart. Within the first few days, Matt came into my cubicle carrying a large piece of plywood, which was exactly the size of my bed. I saw a number of these but had no idea how to obtain one. He placed the board between the springs and mattress, and my sleeping situation improved one hundred percent. I didn't even know Matt and he chose to extend this act of kindness. I soon learned that the plywood boards were highly valued within the prison system.

As time went on, I got to know Carlos, Eddie, and the other inmates. Some I liked and most I didn't. One inmate told me, "The test here is would you invite the person to your home once you're out." The almost unanimous answer for me was a resounding no.

I liked Carlos because he had some legitimate remorse at what he had done. Rarely did I encounter an inmate who didn't claim to be innocent. A scant few seemed remorseful but most contended they were only in prison because of bad lawyers. Carlos told me he wanted to spend time in schools once he got out, so he could talk to kids about drugs. Prison was a world of deception and delusion, but I believed Carlos.

He also had a great sense of humor. In prison some jobs were better than others. Carlos had latched onto a good one, cleaning the warden's office at night. There he could work unsupervised, at his own pace, and no one bothered him. It was a two or three hour job, leaving Carlos free to work out during the day. Carlos was hoping to eventually get into the boot camp program. He was in superb physical shape.

The warden's name was Jackson and he was practically indistinguishable from the rank and file guards. The lieutenant told Carlos that Jackson always placed a small black hair on the backside of the toilet, down low, and would check each morning to see if it had been properly cleaned. Carlos told me that he always got the hair – and while he was down there next to the toilet bowl he rinsed Jackson's coffee cup in it. Jackson drank from that cup each morning.

I laughed every time I thought about Jackson's coffee cup. Occasionally, I would ask, "Hey, Carlos, you still taking good care of Jackson's coffee cup?" He would grin and say, "Hey, mon, I sure am!"

There were five hundred inmates at FPC Atlanta, a Federal Prison Camp. Most FPCs are designated minimum-security stand-alone facilities. The Atlanta FPC butted directly up against the main Atlanta prison and was simply an extension of it. The guards rotated quarterly to the camp but were incapable of making the mental shift between the camp and the main prison. The camp was run in the same manner as the main facility. We had fences, razor wire, counts, and lockdowns.

In treatment I heard many stories from patients who had been in different treatment facilities. I was only in one and had no comparable frame of reference. In prison, it was the same but this time I heard from inmates who spent lifetimes in prisons all over the country. They served time in Lewisburg, Lexington, Tallahassee, El Reno, Sandstone, Marion, and a dozen others. Some inmates eventually matriculated from maximum-security places to the camp after fifteen or twenty years. Two or three in the Atlanta FPC were reputedly Mafioso, and only ten to twenty were actually white-collar criminals. The vast majority were drug dealers, some minor and some big time. The rest comprised the full gamut of criminal activity.

Atlanta was a different sort of prison. Because it was a minimum security facility there were no gang rapes, violence, or other activities often depicted on TV. An occasional fight broke out but that was rare and most of the conflicts involved yelling, name calling, and chest bumping. No one wanted to go to the hole or back behind the walls. According to the well-traveled cons, it was run more like an FCI, a medium security facility, and some thought even more restrictive than that. There was homosexual activity but it was generally known to occur within a small ring of inmates, all of them Hispanic except for one African-American inmate known as Butterfly.

The prison administration did all they could to prevent the inmates from knowing anything that affected prison operation. The reason was simple. They did everything they could to ignore directives and were reluctant to meet even the most minimal requirements. Apathy and incompetence ruled the day and ran the prison. Yet when exposed for one situation or another, I admired the prison's flawless ability to cover up and avoid public exposure.

The FPC was structured in a curious way. All the muscle areas involved male guards, but there were women in various positions of power. I did not expect to see women working anywhere in a men's prison.

Although not meant for my eyes, I accidentally saw a document that said seventy- seven percent of our prison population was in for alcohol and drug offenses. Yet they had no alcohol or drug program. When I asked if they had one they said yes. I quickly learned that the truth in prison was one of the earliest fatalities and the staff would lie for abso-lutely no reason.

I asked to go to the program. It consisted of a once-a-week video with twenty-six inmates attending. No groups, no meetings, no recov-ery, no nothing. We walked in, saw the video, and walked out. I did the math. Seventy-seven percent of five hundred inmates amounted to three hundred and eighty-five. But only twenty-six attended the weekly video, which was a farce. I attended since it was the only game in town. I hoped to see something I could use in my recovery. The other twenty-five inmates convened outside each week after the film, and laughingly planned their next drug deal. They attended because they got a certificate for every ten films and it went in their case files. If they got enough of them their chances improved for increased halfway house upon release or a furlough while they were still locked up.

In my second week I walked in and saw a video entitled "For The Honour Of All." It was about the Alkali Lake band of Indians in British Columbia who had gone from 90% alcoholic to 90% sober in approximately fifteen years. It was an astonishing and heartwarming experience as I sat and watched. The people in the film were the same persons who'd lived out the story and I was deeply impacted by their amazing odyssey. At that moment in time, It would not have been possible for me to believe that nineteen years later I would get to meet all of them, spend a week on their Reserve, sweat with them, and speak at their annual sobriety celebration.

As part of my intake process I met with a prison psychologist after I'd been there a short while. He worked for the prison part time while working on his doctorate. As we talked, he learned I was recovering. I talked about the pathetic situation inside and the lack of a program. He asked if I would be willing to start and lead one. I said I would.

With his help, the two of us fought the prison administration and finally got a program in place. It took two months. The program was fragile and sketchy, hard to establish, and even harder to maintain due to resistance from the staff. The camp administrator was a man named Gibbs. Gibbs wore garish suits and outrageous sunglasses as he strolled the prison grounds. I glimpsed him for the first time and thought, "In another setting I could easily mistake him for a pimp." He insisted a guard sit in on our meetings, but no inmate was going to open up with a guard sitting there. As I suspected, after a few minutes the guard wandered away to do other things, so we could actually hold the meeting.

The first meeting was large, with probably twenty or more inmates attending. But once they discovered there was no prison advantage to be gained the number quickly dropped to between four and seven. These meetings were for the inmates and nothing else.

We needed a text for the readings and I asked Barbara to send my book in. Prison rules forbade any type of hard cover book unless it came from a bookstore. Ostensibly, drugs could be smuggled within the hard covers. Before I left for prison, I went to Tattersall's, a local bookstore, and asked if they would be willing to send me books. They knew my situation and the owner kindly agreed. Barbara took the book there and Tattersall's sent it in.

R & D, who handled incoming mail, saw the highlighted parts of my book and the writing in the front, so they knew it was not a new book. A short, heavyset, square woman guard by the name of Ms. Ndebe was in charge of the mail. She had a long, rectangular face and her chin appeared to touch the front of her chest.

She called me to come get the book and then wouldn't give it to me. She made me return night after night for a week as she, or one of her helpers, teased and taunted me with the book. I refused to react. I stood and looked directly at them, remaining silent until she decided she wouldn't give me the book that particular night. After a week of this she finally handed me the book and we had what we needed to conduct a meeting.

We held a meeting once a week. I would make the announcement from the duty officer's PA system in his office and then walk through the rest of the inmates with the book in hand, drawing looks and stares along the way. One of the hard cases approached me once and I wondered if there was going to be trouble. Instead, he said, "Prouse, you got balls. That takes some balls," and he walked away.

The prison staff did everything they could to sabotage and undercut our meetings. We held the meeting in a room in an old trailer, and I would have to track down the guard with the key. Sometimes I spent the whole hour looking for him, and at times he wouldn't even be in the camp. Once, the guard refused to open the trailer, telling us to "go find a park bench and hold your meeting there."

Still, we persevered and did what we could. For those of us seeking recovery these meetings were lifesavers, like an oasis in a desert.

I truly believe the eyes are the windows to our soul. I became accustomed to the dull, glazed look in the eyes of the prison staff. There was an uncomprehending, slow motion aspect to any request I made or any exchange I was forced into. In truth, that same condition existed within some of the inmate population as well.

I met Wilson, who was assigned as the primary staff person in charge of me. Wilson was one of the few white guards I would encounter. He had a potbelly hanging over his belt, white hair, and a manner of speech that reminded me of the movie actor, Chill Wills. He was in charge of job assignments in the camp. He decided if I would work on the land-scaping crew, go to the powerhouse, sort mailbags, or whatever. In the horribly distorted prison environment, Wilson was on the same level as the CEO of Ford or General Motors, albeit on a miniscule scale.

Guards in the prison had various job titles and I never knew how they got them. It was obvious they had received no special training and the titles were simply awarded with an appropriate pay grade. The prison chaplain, for example, appeared to have little, if any, clergy training. He spent a brief stint as the chaplain then moved on to the parole board where he would receive higher pay. He went from being known as Chaplain Cook to "Throw-The-Book Cook" on the parole board.

Wilson had "Counselor" next to his name, as did several others. Yet never, not *once*, was I ever aware of any counseling that took place with any inmate. Wilson approached me during one of my first days. I was outdoors in the prison compound as he walked up to me. Pointing to a large, muscular black inmate named Roy Holliman, he said, "See that guy over there?" and I nodded yes. He said in his Chill Wills voice and accent, "Took me two weeks to break him." That was my introduction to Wilson and his "counseling."

I took a breath and considered my response. Prison was a no-win situation and I knew it. It was pointless to say or do something that could prove harmful to Barbara in the long term. I looked at Wilson and attempted to maintain a neutral, quiet composure. I said, "Mr. Wilson, I'm going to be here for sixteen months. In that time you can pretty much do with me whatever you wish. But the *only* way you will ever take my dignity is if I choose to give it to you. And I will never do that." I said it quietly, so it did not come as a threat. Wilson stood and looked at me. A long pause ensued as he worked to process what I'd said, and I turned and walked away. It would be the first of many encounters with Wilson.

In my first few days, an inmate who worked in the warden's office came to me and said there had been considerable activity about my admission to prison. He saw a special notice on Warden Jackson's desk notifying the staff I was there. Because of all the publicity I was assigned a special inmate designation known as CIM, Central Inmate Monitoring. CIM status was reserved for criminals with high profile, high-publicity cases, crimes involving a million or more dollars, and situations where one inmate had testified against another. CIM inmates were more closely monitored. Supposedly, more people in the chain of command would have to be involved if any changes to my incarceration were considered.

I spent the first week in an indoctrination phase, known as A & O, admissions and orientation. I reported each morning to the corrections duty office and was assigned jobs for the day. Generally, I cleaned floors, washed windows, and did whatever else needed to be done.

Lieutenant Stokes was the first duty officer I met. Of all the guards I met during my experience, he was the most harmless. And he was even decent, a statement rarely made about a guard. Medium height and slim build, he was the ultimate Barney Fife and I found him comical, although I could never openly laugh at his expense. He walked like he was always going to a fire, but often didn't know where he was going or why. He would issue orders that made no sense, but they were always issued assertively as people looked at each other with puzzled expressions.

He loved hearing himself talk on the PA but would often forget what he was supposed to say in the midst of an announcement. Certain announcements, such as the one for each of the prison counts, had a prescribed verbatim format. Stokes would get part of the way through, sounding very officious, then forget what came next, and end the PA sputtering something like, "Okay ...everyone...just stand still where you are...." Lieutenant Stokes treated me decently and I appreciated that.

"Bullet Head" was an obese guard who tipped the scales at 350 pounds or more. He belonged to the minority of white guards. Rolls of fat began under his chin and made their way all the way down to his posterior, which was much wider than his shoulders. He was sadistic and many feared him. He was even unpopular among the other guards.

I heard of Bullet Head well before I met him. As I stood in line one morning at 5:00 A.M. to sign up for my daily collect phone call, one of the inmates came out of the office and announced that Bullet Head was in there. As people signed up, Bullet Head was confiscating their rings, he said, no matter what they were. The line moved slowly as I stood and considered this, pondering what I was going to do. The easy solution was to take my wedding ring off and put it in my pocket. But I had a thing about that and hadn't taken it off in many years. I decided against it. Furthermore, I was not parting with my wedding ring, regardless of what Bullet Head said. So that meant going to The Hole if it came to that.

I entered the room when it was my time to go in. I bent over to sign the phone roster and put my left hand on the desk, where the clipboard was, and Bullet Head saw my ring. I was astonished that nothing was said and I walked out without a problem.

Bullet Head was conducting mail call one day and began bragging about his time in Vietnam as he tossed letters to inmates. I stood quietly, waiting for my mail, listening as he bragged about how fierce he had been. He said that he enjoyed *wounding* men. Then, he said, he would masturbate in their face and after he climaxed, he would kill them. This phraseology is much more refined than the words Bullet Head used. As I watched and listened, I was willing to bet anything I owned that he never saw combat, much less the four back-to-back tours he bragged about.

Nowhere else except prison could he do the things he did and say the things he said. In that environment, he could thrive because nobody could confront him. He favored abortion, he said, because his fifteen-year-old daughter had one. Prison was a sick place.

There are two severely sick groups of people in prison. Each group comprises the dregs of society: the inmates, the leeches who suck it dry, and the guards who prey on others. The worst of the two groups went home each night. It was a sick and obscene place, designed to emotionally castrate and permanently scar those inside while ensuring that inmates return again and again. And they do, with a recidivism rate in the 86-88 percent range.

Taken at Camp Pendleton, California early 1957

Barb and me after our return to Northwest

Feb 25, 1963 Barb pins my gold wings and 2nd Lt bars on

Barb and me after I'd been returned to the left seat as Capt

Dawn in her senior high school year – my favorite photo of her

Family photo soon after returning from Vietnam

1956 I'm a senior and Connie is a sophomore

Nov 1, 1993 Capt O.C. Miller watches as I sign my
back to work agreement

Chu Lai, RVN, 1965 I'm in A4 Skyhawk aircraft #8
with my name on it

Age 9, Fayetteville, AR, with the rifle I won by selling salve from a magazine, in "back yard" of home that was condemned

Approx 1972, me in regalia with Dawn

Prison Potpourri

P rison is also an ideal place for outside people to conduct studies as the inmates are literally a captive audience. At one point, inmates were solicited to participate in a lengthy and involved test known as "The CRIS Test," Coping Resources Inventory for Stress. The test was an elaborate device designed by five doctors, the most notable of whom was Dr. Kenneth Matheny from Georgia State University, a man with international credentials. It was designed to cover fifteen areas of stress coping skills: self-disclosure, self-directedness, confidence, acceptance, social support, financial freedom, physical health, physical fitness, stress monitoring, tension control, structuring, problem solving, cognitive restructuring, functional beliefs, and social ease.

Participants were told they would receive feedback and results. I never observed the staff do *anything* they promised unless it was negative and harmful to the inmate, but I opted to participate. I recalled that stress was the number one trigger for relapse among alcoholics, so I hoped I might learn something about myself.

Twenty-six inmates participated in this very lengthy test. I was astonished to receive a nicely printed and bound summary of my results. The booklet totaled twenty-five pages and detailed each sector of testing. It explained how the test was structured and the five validity tests incorporated within. Failure to pass any of the validity tests rendered the results void. Centile scores were assigned to each of the fifteen sections,

127

along with an overall centile score. The c*entile score* was explained as the number of people within a group of one hundred that would score lower than the centile number assigned.

Once we received the booklets we were called back and randomly asked to discuss our scores. I looked at mine and hoped I wouldn't be asked to disclose anything. I was listening to inmates give scores such as 12, 23, 18, 31, and 26. Mine was 99. That meant I had max'ed the test; there could be no higher score. Fortunately, I was not called upon; I did not want the attention.

After prison, I sent Dr. Matheny a copy of my printout and asked for his comments and evaluation. He told me the CRIS test had been given over 10,000 times and was designed for professionals and business executives. He said the average centile score was 50, so I doubled the norm. Apparently I had learned a lot about dealing with stress; I certainly had ample opportunity in the recent year.

If I achieved any measure of success or positive skills in the area of dealing with stress, almost all of it came from what I learned in treatment. I learned how to apply each of the recovery concepts to my daily situations and how to change my belief and value system. I learned I could do nothing to change what existed in the outside world; all I could do was change the manner in which I saw and reacted to such things. According to the CRIS results, I learned well.

I asked Wilson if I could work in the education office, teaching other inmates. Many were illiterate and although I only had a high school education I was at the top of the prison pyramid educationally. Unknown to me, the education department was run by a vicious woman named Dewberry. She had made sure it was an all black department and did what she could to maintain it accordingly. The inmates laughingly referred to her as "Miz Quakenbush." I spoke with her about working there and noticed she was extremely cold and distant. She obviously did not want me there and Wilson had other plans anyway. It would not be my last encounter with Dewberry.

Wilson assigned me to clean the halls and lobby in front of the main prison entrance area as part of an inmate crew. I was polishing ashtrays one day when a lawyer came into my work area. He told the guard on duty he wanted to see his client. The guard began looking through paperwork, fumbling, shuffling, and repeatedly searching his material. Finally he said he had no record of the client being there. The lawyer became angry and informed the guard his client was there two days earlier and again demanded to see his client. The guard left for a few moments to consult with his supervisor. He came back and said no one knew where the inmate was but *they thought* he might now be in Tallahassee. I was working, watching, and listening. The attorney was beside himself. He had some words with the guard and left. The federal prison system had lost an inmate and wasn't sure where he was. It was business as usual at Atlanta.

As I was working in the main prison lobby area, several groups of TV crews came in to interview various inmates or staff. I was practically rubbing shoulders with them. One day Warden Jackson walked in as I was mopping a floor. When he saw me, he stopped with a look of complete surprise on his face. He hurried away and I was immediately taken off that job.

I smiled because I knew what happened. I had a high profile status and Wilson put me right in the front of the main prison entrance where I could be seen, photographed, or interviewed by the TV crews coming in. That was the *last thing* Jackson wanted. Fortunately, no one recognized me. I was betting Wilson had his ass chewed by Jackson before the day ended.

I went to work in the food warehouse and it was extremely hard physical work. Three other inmates were also assigned to it. It was huge, perhaps 100,000 square feet or more. Ms. Huffy was a female member of the Bureau of Prisons and was in charge of the operation. She knew how to handle inmates, could be stern when necessary, but I saw nothing mean-spirited about her. A few weeks later another woman took over. Julie Cullen had begun as a secretary and moved up to this much higher paying job. She was thin, with an elongated face, and the inmates referred to her as "horse face." She had apparently gotten the word because she stepped outside one day and someone whinnied. She turned an angry red but was unable to determine who the perpetrator was. She stepped back inside without saying a word.

Julie Cullen was outspoken about her dislike of inmates and was adamant that none should get furloughs or parole. On one of her first mornings in the food warehouse, she called me into the office. She was sitting in front of a calculator and apparently having some problems. "Prouse," she said, "If I wanted to know how many pounds something was and all I knew were ounces, how would I do that?" I was incredulous. I said, "Divide the ounces by sixteen." She said, "You mean, if I had 480 ounces I'd divide that by sixteen?" I said, "Yes." Before she could turn and start punching her calculator I said, "It'll probably come out as thirty or so." She punched the calculator, looked at the answer, and turned to me with an incredulous, wide-eyed look on her face. She thought I was a math genius and couldn't believe I had done the problem in my head. I walked out of the office in dismay.

She was in charge of a vast food warehouse, responsible for hundreds of thousands of dollars, and didn't know how to do a simple third-grade math problem. These were taxpayer dollars hidden behind prison walls. It was beyond mind-boggling.

At the food warehouse, I had repeated run-ins with Ms. Cullen. She was easy to out think, but I needed to be cautious. Somehow, she figured out how to make banners on the computer and was like a small child with a new toy. She made two dozen long banners to hang from the warehouse ceiling denoting what foodstuffs were in each aisle. It was completely unnecessary since we all knew the floor intimately but she insisted. There was a problem. The ceilings were *at least* fifteen feet high, so hanging the signs was going to be difficult.

Since a forklift was used to reach very high storage areas in buildings, she decided that I would stand on a pallet and be lifted up to the ceiling on the forks. Hopefully, the extended forklift and pallet, with my weight forward on it, would not tip the forklift forward, causing me to fall. There was no way I was going to perform this high wire balancing act.

A few days earlier, the OSHA inspectors came by the food warehouse. I watched Julie Cullen and it was obvious she was extremely concerned about them and when they left, she appeared *very* relieved. As she proposed I do the balancing act on the forklift and pallet, I calmly asked what she thought the OSHA folks would say about it. That stopped her in her tracks.

She decided that *she* would get up on the pallet while someone extended the forklift as high as it would go. All of us inmates glanced at each other and stopped working to watch. I wondered if she would take a dive onto the concrete floor, but she managed to get the signs up and in place. I waited until she was all done and back on the floor. She was congratulating herself when I pointed to one of the highest signs that said "Dryed Beans" and I informed her it was misspelled. I saw it when she put it up, but deliberately said nothing until she was down. She didn't believe me but finally managed to find the correct spelling. She made a new sign and did her balancing act a final time. I survived each day by creating lighter moments when I could.

The work was physically very hard. All three of my inmate peers were young and big. Although I was fifty-one, I was in good physical condition. The day consisted of lifting dozens of heavy cases of canned goods and 100-pound bags of rice, sugar, and other items. We had a forklift but it was used sparingly. We also had a huge freezer and refrigerated area for meat and other perishables. We took in truckloads of goods every day, and every Wednesday and Thursday we broke our backs loading and unloading trucks for the main prison and camp deliveries. I refused to be outworked by my younger peers and wondered later about the insanity of that. I wasn't working for a pay raise or promotion. But my parents had instilled a deep work ethic in me and it was instinctive to work hard.

I watched Ms. Huffy split goods between the main prison and the camp, but I had no idea how she did it. I assumed she knew what each facility used based on many years of doing it. I didn't know there was a straight ratio until one day with Julie Cullen.

We were receiving a load of produce and the driver dumped eight bags of carrots on the floor. Julie Cullen was frantically punching a hand calculator as the rest of us stood and watched. As she worked, she casually commented that 25% were to go to the camp and the remainder to the main prison. At that, I reached down and tossed two bags to the side for the camp. She asked what I was doing and I said, "That's 25% of what was delivered, so I put them off to the camp side." With a puzzled look, she said, "Show me how to do that on this calculator." I took the calculator and said, "You can do it two ways. You can divide eight by four since 25% is ¼th of the whole. Or you can multiply eight times point two-five and come up with the same answer."

"Oh!" she exclaimed, "You have to *multiply* by .25!" She was dividing eight by .25 and coming up with thirty-two bags of carrots. Since we only had eight to start with, she was having trouble making the numbers fit. She turned to the other three inmates and said, "Prouse can split all this out without me. He's got a calculator in his head!" and she walked away. Because I had the ability to divide something by four, she thought I was a math prodigy.

The waste was incredible and I often wondered how taxpayers would react if they knew. With both Ms. Huffy and Julie Cullen, their incompetence and inability to adjust what they ordered created massive waste. Several times we threw away huge quantities of food items; we simply threw them in the dumpster. And each time, I secretly wrote down lot numbers, food sources, and tracking numbers. On March 6, 1991, we threw away 5,000 pounds of powdered milk that was so old it mildewed.

On April 5, 1991, we threw out 3,230 pounds of whiting fish fillets with the "Farm Boys" brand showing on one of the pallets. Again, I noted the number of packages destroyed, and recorded the data on the items. The stamp on the packages showed they'd been received on 8-21-90, but this time we were disposing of the goods to make room for incoming shipments. Huffy and Cullen blindly copied one order from another, over-ordering amounts that couldn't be stored. So when space became crowded they just threw food away.

During one episode at Unicor (the prison industry area), one of the inmates said they threw away an estimated $60,000 of materials and items. Guards were seen pulling much of it from the dumpsters and putting it in their cars.

Julie Cullen wanted to control and dominate me but I wouldn't cooperate. She would order me to do ridiculous things to embarrass me in front of the other inmates. I would comply and look directly through her, keeping my face expressionless. As long as I said nothing and didn't look threatening, she could do little. But the tension continued to mount and the contest continued to escalate.

One cold, rainy day she ordered me back to my cubicle after an incident. I said little but it was my attitude she couldn't conquer and it was getting to her. The weather was lousy and I was happy to go lie down in my cubicle and read instead of working outside and possibly getting sick. My relaxation didn't last long, however, as the PA blared, summoning me to Ms. Terri Bischoff's office. She was up the chain of command, so this wasn't a good thing.

As I entered her office, I noted two large male guards, one black and one white, and they both glared at me. I knew Ms. Bischoff and Julie Cullen were good friends because I heard Cullen talk about the two couples going out together. Bischoff said, "Prouse, if you don't want to end up in trouble, you better do exactly as Ms. Cullen says." I had a Columbo routine in prison where I did my best to play dumb and ask questions. I looked at Bischoff and said, "Let me make sure I understand. If I do *exactly* what Ms. Cullen tells me to do, then everything will be okay. Is that right?" Bischoff answered yes. I was then ordered back to the food warehouse. I'm sure Bischoff called Julie Cullen and told her the problems with me were over.

The first thing Cullen did was tell me to take some items back to the far corner of the warehouse and stack them. I did so, but didn't return. After all, she hadn't told me to come *back*; she sent me to the back and I stayed there.

A long while later she found me and was irritated that I was still back there. With a blank face, I said I promised Ms. Bischoff I would do *exactly* as told. I didn't want to get into trouble, so that's what I was doing. Julie Cullen looked at me, shook her head, and walked off. I don't think she thought her problems were over.

At the end of each workday, Julie Cullen would routinely pat us down to make sure we weren't stealing items. I noticed she got dangerously close to my crotch each time and would show just a hint of a smile when she did it. The other inmates also noticed it, and I told them I was going to surprise her some day and squat down so she could get a handful. They were delighted with that idea.

The inmate who drove the forklift was released and I was assigned that job. We rarely used it, but I had to go to the prison motor pool and get a license. There was no checkout, no nothing; they just gave me the license. I never drove a forklift before but got pretty handy with it. Since I could no longer take pride in an ILS instrument approach or nice landing, I made the forklift my surrogate aircraft. I took pride in being able to manipulate the forks and put things where they needed to go with little effort.

I was using it to unload a truck one day and had an accident. The truck had a collapsed spring on one side and was heavily tilted as it approached the loading dock. As I maneuvered the forklift onto the truck, I caught a fork and bent it due to the uneven surface. This unfurled a storm of attention from the prison administration. Several of the prison authorities came over and looked at the forklift, concluding that I must've done it intentionally. So my license was pulled and I was sent to work elsewhere.

Word quickly spread around the camp and by the time I got back that evening I was taking some jabs about it. "Man!" they would say, "You can fly an airplane and you can't drive a forklift?!" I laughed and said, "I need about fifteen rum and cokes and an icy ramp, then I'd do just fine." They loved it.

I tried several times to get out of the food warehouse but Wilson wouldn't allow it. Other prison managers had asked for me, but Wilson was determined to keep me there. Now he needed another plan.

He sent me to work in the kitchen for a guard named Jameson. Racial prejudice abounded heavily throughout the prison and Jameson was the worst of the worst. Black inmates would often stand around, shoot the breeze with Jameson, laugh and smoke. The others would have to work. There was no subtlety about any of it.

Jameson didn't discriminate about *who* he discriminated against. We had Mexicans, Cubans, Puerto Ricans, several Native Americans, an Iranian, and others. If someone wasn't black, then they were all fair game.

Jameson seemed to relish giving me the worst jobs but I shrugged them off. Until I was released it was all just something to do and made no difference unless I allowed it to. One afternoon Jameson told me to clean the underside of the ovens. I lay in a pool of fetid, greasy water as I scrubbed grease and dirt from the bottom of the ovens.

But the power of mind and spirit is without form or boundary, and I remember thinking, "This isn't the most pleasant place I've ever been, but at this very moment I'm not hot and I'm not cold. I'm not in pain. I'm not hungry, and I'm not thirsty. I'm not sick and I'm not dying. This isn't the best place I've ever been, but I'm okay. At this very *moment*, I'm okay."

Fortunately, I only had to work for Jameson a couple of days when Wilson came up with another plan. Sorting mailbags at Unicor was considered the worst job in the prison and that's where he sent me. Most inmates made 12 cents an hour. Unicor made mattresses and repaired endless millions of mailbags for the U.S. Postal Service. Inmates working there made a whole dollar an hour.

A large truck would back up to the long, steep cement chute leading to a basement area and discharge thousands of bags. The sorting area was dusty and dirty, creating a dusty veil for the lights in the room. The bags were individually shaken, sorted, and stacked in one of three piles, small, medium, and large. Every bag shaken contributed to the dusty environment. I learned quickly what the bag size was simply by the weight. It was unending stoop labor but I could detach and transport my mind to far places as I stooped, picked up a bag, shook, and stacked it. The days went by faster than my time in the food warehouse, and I was happier sorting mailbags than anywhere else.

Several days into the job I stood in the noon chow line. I was dusty and dirty from head to foot. Wilson sat at the staff table as I passed by in line. He looked at me and grinned, " How yew like yo' new job, Prouse?" I grinned as big as I could and said, "I like it fine, Mr. Wilson. It's the best job I've had." It was not the response he expected and his face nearly slid to his chest as he tried to regroup.

No one could take my attitude. That belonged to me. I could do whatever I *had* to do, handle *whatever* they threw my way, and I could do it *as long as* I had to.

A short while later I went from the worst job in the camp to the best. Wilson was in hot water because the orderlies (janitors) weren't keeping one of the buildings in decent shape. He wasn't doing me a favor when he assigned me that job; he was covering his butt. He knew I would do a good job and he could relax. He also assigned Grady Mayeaux to the job. Grady and I were cube-mates and it was a break for both of us.

We got up early and finished early. There was lots of cleaning and concrete floor waxing, so I left my mark on the same floors I saw when

I arrived. No one bugged us. We could do our own thing as we worked and that was nice.

I had many moments to reflect back and the severe turn in my life never failed to sadden me. A collage of memories flooded me. Prison life seemed difficult to believe. My days as a young, adventurous cadet, full of promise and a bright life were bittersweet to look back upon.

Saufley Field - Into the Air - 1961

After completing pre-flight training I headed over to Saufley Field for the Primary phase. Since it was located in the same large Pensacola complex, I didn't have far to travel. Many in my preflight class were college graduates and received their commissions upon completion of Preflight. I was now saluting many of those I just shared the previous sixteen weeks with. It was strange to see the Ensign boards on their epaulettes.

Class work was more of the same – aerodynamics, navigation, and most of the subjects we studied previously. We moved away from theory into the more practical applications. There were new subjects such as aircraft operation – engines and systems of the Beech T-34 Mentor we would soon be flying. We learned the principles of operation, the parts of an engine and their functions, along with the electrical, hydraulic, and pneumatic systems. Navigation involved current technology, rather than dead reckoning and celestial concepts. We advanced from the formulas in aerodynamics to what would actually occur once we climbed into the cockpit. Half the day was devoted to class work and the other half to flying. The rapid pace always seemed just ahead of where I was.

I saw cadets wearing a gold bar roughly three inches long. It designated those who had soloed; another plateau that earned respect, separating them from the rest of us, and with it came additional privileges.

The most notable was liberty in civilian clothes while the rest of us had to wear dress whites everywhere we went.

There were four training squadrons. One was an all-Marine unit where I was assigned. Flight 18 was typically Marine-like in that the instructors took great pride in pushing us harder than our other three Navy counterparts. The assignment of instructors to students was a moment of great anticipation. Upon arrival, we got the word as to who was feared, who was a "screamer," and who was a lucky draw. I drew First Lieutenant Cary Watkins and hadn't heard anything about him. He seemed pleasant enough when we were introduced. I learned he was from Ohio and flew helicopters during his previous duty assignment.

I was in awe of anyone wearing gold wings. As we readied ourselves for the first introduction flight I prayed I wouldn't get airsick. I spent many hours sitting in a T-34 cockpit mock up studying and rehearsing flight procedures. I talked myself through as I touched and named switches, moved controls, and simulated starting the engine. On October 31st 1961, I took my first introductory flight with Lt. Watkins. I was nervous as I sat in the front cockpit while his voice filtered through my headset. He started the engine and the moment it roared to life my mind went blank. I could remember nothing from all the hours spent practicing.

Everything Lt. Watkins did was seemingly effortless and I marveled at that. The takeoff was exhilarating as we accelerated and lifted off. He demonstrated how the propeller slipstream wanted to pull us off the runway to the left and how right rudder would keep us aligned down the center of the runway. After demonstrating some basic things such as holding the plane straight and level in flight he told me to take the controls. Immediately the altimeter began to wander up and down as I gained and lost altitude while the airspeed slowed then increased correspondingly. The wings seemed to roll about the fuselage and the nose wandered left and right. I was all over the sky as I briefly took the controls for the first time.

We flew over landmarks I had to memorize and information was coming faster than I could absorb as Lt. Watkins continued demonstrating first one thing then another. I struggled to keep up. Then it was my turn to fly again and I began to wonder what sort of superhuman was required to control a machine like this. I could only concentrate on one thing at a time while two others went awry. Gratefully, I did not get airsick although I had a bag close by.

Our second flight took place the next day, and he commented "Nice hop" in the remarks section of my training form. I believe it was my attitude more than my ability that earned the comment. Due to bad weather it was five more days before we flew again. I saw my first above average marks on that flight. He wrote: "No warm up needed due to above average progression in stage," and "Nice control throughout hop." I struggled and felt completely inept, but he apparently saw something else.

I liked Lt. Watkins. He was not abusive, as some of the instructors were, but he was extremely demanding. Between his perfectionism and my frustration I began to dread each flight, yet once it was completed I had an adrenaline overload. Then I would repeat that cycle all over again for the next flight. Training became a constant paradox.

In Preflight we watched a training film of a T-34 entering a spin, filmed from another aircraft close by. Then the film switched to the interior cameras in the spinning aircraft, presenting a dizzying view. The ground rotated rapidly and violently as the aircraft plunged toward the earth and the spins tightened and accelerated. I found myself dry-mouthed as I anticipated having to perform such a maneuver.

The training syllabus introduced spins on the seventh flight and I was extremely tense. When the moment of truth arrived I executed the procedures exactly as I practiced them on the ground; power off, nose high above the horizon, increasing backpressure to prevent the nose from dropping. The airspeed bled off and the aircraft began to shudder with the approaching stall. Then it kicked violently over into the spin. Suddenly the earth appeared straight down and we were on a corkscrew, twisting dizzily as we hurtled toward the ground. Centrifugal forces increased as the turns tightened and I counted each turn, one...two... three...then I neutralized the controls, checked the throttle in the closed position, applied opposite rudder, and suddenly the spinning ceased. I neutralized the rudder, eased the nose back up keeping the wings level and it was done.

I breathed a sigh of relief and the fear was gone. Once again, the fear of the unknown disappeared. I was even anxious to repeat the maneuver.

Another lesson learned, another experience reinforced, and from that moment I looked forward to performing spin recoveries, often receiving above average grades.

As we progressed, Lt. Watkins' tolerances tightened even more. On December 7, 1961, we landed at an outlying field. He climbed out of the rear cockpit, patted me on the shoulder, and told me it was time for me to solo. It was the moment every student works toward. I was elated *and* apprehensive. With a mixture of confidence and fear I added power, took off...and was in the air all by myself for the first time. In 10.7 hours Lt. Watkins had taken a student who previously had only ridden in an airplane twice and prepared him for a safe and competent solo in an airplane categorized as "high performance" by the FAA.

I flew with a soaring heart. I had complete freedom. There was no instructor to guide or correct me, and it was up to me to get the airplane back on the ground. What a day! Later, I humorously wondered if there had been any significance that Pearl Harbor Day had been the day selected for me to launch alone. When I returned to Saufley Field Lt. Watkins performed the traditional cutting of my necktie, the lower half of which still resides in its place of honor in an old scrapbook along with the solo certificate signed by him. I had earned my solo bar.

He wrote in my training jacket, on January 15, 1962, "This student has the potential of being an excellent aviator," which I took as high praise from a flight instructor who seldom praised but whose interest in me was never in doubt. On January 16, 1962, I completed my final check ride, ending the Primary phase of flight training. Lt. Watkins' final entry before our farewell said: "Marcad Prouse is an excellent potential officer. During my association with him he has always done his best and has always presented a fine military appearance." In spite of my continuous feeling that I was never quite good enough, I ended this phase of training with a 3.05 flight grade and 3.48 cumulative score. This was well above average and more than enough to earn me a slot for the highly sought after jets at Meridian, Mississippi. It was time to leave Saufley and move into the Basic Flight Training phase.

Onward and Upward – Cadet Life

From the beginning, almost all of us aspired to fly jets, aware that the pipeline in the Marine Corps consisted of two main branches – jets and helicopters. With rare exception the top grades got their choice of jets and once those slots were filled the remainder went to helicopters. I did well so my options were open, but could never get past the nagging feeling of inferiority when it came to education. I listened to stories about Harvard, Yale, and all the Ivy league schools, colleges and universities of every size. I heard tales of fraternities, fast cars, girls, and campus life–and sat as a mute listener always hoping no one turned my way and asked an embarrassing question about my own experiences.

I felt I would have a shortened career as a Marine officer due to my lack of education, so I decided that flying helicopters would better prepare me for being ousted into the civilian world. I *wanted* jets and the exciting flying they offered, but I chose the helicopter pipeline instead.

George Perry, my roommate in Primary, sat on the sidewalk as we prepared to leave Saufley. He had tears in his eyes after being denied jets and struggled to understand my decision to turn them down. We packed up and headed twenty-five miles northeast of Pensacola to the small town of Milton, Florida and NAAS (Naval Auxiliary Air Station) Whiting Field. There they flew the much larger T-28's from two adjacent fields, North Whiting and South Whiting. The T-28 was a large propeller aircraft that dwarfed the T-34.

Again, we began with an academic schedule moving into advanced applications with more direct connections to actual flying. There were more classes on aerodynamics, navigation, communications, engineering (the T-28 engine), meteorology, FAA and air traffic control communications and procedures.

I drew a brand new instructor named Herb Hawn, a Navy Lieutenant just assigned to the Basic Training Command. I was to be his very first student. He was from Arkansas, a bachelor with a pleasant southern accent and a mild-mannered, congenial disposition. When I returned from Vietnam as an instructor, I learned that new instructors were always assigned above average students as their initial charges, which was a good news, bad news sort of thing. For the instructor it meant he didn't have a student that required extreme supervision. But for the student it often meant a lost opportunity to excel because the instructor was inclined to grade toward the average column.

Decades later, Herb Hawn apologized for not grading me higher, exclaiming that I was the best student he ever had. He said he simply didn't know it at the time. I never felt cheated because I never thought I was as good as most of my previous grades indicated.

I climbed into the cockpit of the T-28 for the first time and heard the coughing roar of a truly powerful engine. Herb was patient, but he had high standards. He took me through fam stage (familiarization) and in spite of several below averages in headwork for doing dumb things he wrote, "Prouse is eager, knows his procedures cold, and is always thinking." On the next flight he wrote, "Student knows how to use his head," even though I never felt on top of things. Yet my marks for airmanship kept climbing. Training was relentlessly competitive; there was never a let up during the entire eighteen months. Extreme pressure was part of each day and attrition took its toll. From the days of Preflight we steadily lost people.

Watching a friend depart was always awkward. Sometimes there were tears which they tried to hide as they said their goodbyes and watched their dreams end. I would watch them walk away, carrying their sea bag, and fear would grip me. I felt sure I would follow them at some point.

The days passed rapidly as I completed fam stage and moved into basic instruments where I was reassigned to another Navy instructor,

Lt. Terry Farris, an even-tempered, excellent instructor. I began flying "under the hood" for the first time, moving to the rear cockpit. There I would rely solely on cockpit instruments for flight with no outside visual references. This was an important part of any aviator's training. It was also a phase that separated a lot of students from their dreams of flying.

I'd had two flights with Lt. Farris during fam stage, and picked up handfuls of above averages from him, so he was familiar with me. He took me through the 12-lesson syllabus and I successfully passed my basic instrument check. Not all my time was spent studying and flying. I spent the weekends with my buddies as we hit the bars and met girls. There were Navy Waves working at Whiting and I met one who was extremely attractive. Mickey was a shapely, long-legged blonde with blue-gray eyes. She won the Miss Whiting Field beauty title and we became a twosome. She was personable, outgoing, had a great sense of humor, and was fun to be with. During the week I was studying or flying, but when the weekends came I was with Mickey.

The final requirement in Basic was carrier qualification and we learned and practiced carrier-style approaches and landings. We learned about the mirror, the meatball, the Landing Signal Officer (LSO), communications, and flight deck operations. We flew 13 practice flights in preparation, slowing the aircraft to its minimum controllable speed and precisely maneuvering it to a small, targeted landing area. This was a demanding phase of training.

A very large mirror was located to the left of the touchdown area and a small, round orange spotlight, known as "the meatball," was reflected into it at an upward angle providing the proper glide slope to the pilot. A pilot was able to visually acquire the mirror and meatball from a considerable distance on the approach. Extending outward from both sides of the mirror were single rows of green datum lights, located precisely at the middle of the mirror. A proper glide slope angle was indicated when the orange ball was centered between the two rows of green datum lights. Keeping the meatball centered while maintaining a precise airspeed and rate of descent was challenging.

The LSO stood by the mirror and monitored every approach. He was specially trained and qualified after watching thousands of approaches.

He had a radio and talked to each pilot throughout the approach. He held a switch that could turn the datum lights from green to flashing red indicating the pilot should immediately wave off, or abandon the approach. The LSO would grade each segment of the approach using phraseology peculiar to carrier operations and each student would be debriefed in detail upon landing.

Finally, qualification day arrived. Circling high above the USS Antietam, nervous and apprehensive, I watched the small shape in the water with smaller objects buzzing around it. I anxiously awaited the call from the ship announcing our deck time had arrived. It came, and we descended quickly toward the ship. It loomed ahead, an impressive gray shape, as it became very real, with its long white, frothy wake trailing behind and the destroyer escort off to the right side. I became hooked on the adrenaline and excitement.

I came around and made my first approach, watching the mirror and the meatball. As I picked up the meatball, I called "Roger ball" and rolled out in the groove. I fought to keep my eyes on the mirror and the meatball as the landing area of the carrier filled my windscreen. Then suddenly there was a solid thump and I'd made my first carrier landing! I added power and lifted off again, executing one of two touch and go's before the first arrested landing.

It was exhilarating and the word *orgasmic* was just barely a stretch. After my second touch and go I came around for my first arrested landing. I went through the procedures for the hundredth time and this time when I touched down I was slammed forward in my harness as the hook picked up the arresting cable. I stopped and rolled backwards, watching the smooth, ballet-like hand signals and movements of the sailors in various colored shirts, each of which designated their job on the flight deck as they moved me into position for my first deck launch.

Carrier operations are extremely fast-paced and there's little time between aircraft landing and taking off. The entire flight deck is a beehive of activity. I was cleared to takeoff as another aircraft approached close behind and I added power, checked my instruments, and looked at the very short deck in front of me. It did not appear physically possible that an airplane could fly in that distance, yet I knew they did so I released the brakes and began to roll. Incredibly, the plane leapt into

144

the air before I reached the end and the plane flew beautifully. After two touch and go landings, followed by six arrested landings, I was carrier-qualified. I had a good day and the LSO was generous with his grades.

Several times during Basic training I changed my mind about flying helicopters and filled out a new preference card. Then reluctantly I went back and returned to helicopters. I preferred jets, but was trying to force myself to plan ahead for the eventual outcome. But after carrier-quals in the T-28 I was hooked on jets and wanted them regardless of all other considerations.

Back at Whiting, I replaced my single solo bar with a new double bar device indicating successful carrier qualification. I eagerly went to the Student Control Office to make a final change to the jet pipeline but was surprised to discover the deadline had passed.

I accepted the disappointment and prepared for the assignment to helicopters. Shortly after, I was summoned to the Marine Aviation Detachment for a meeting with the Colonel in charge of all Marines. Two other cadets were there and I was called in first. It seemed they needed three places filled in the jet pipeline and since I had the top grades of the three I was being offered the first slot.

I eagerly accepted but asked if I could go home on leave because I had a serious problem in my personal life. I was given seven days leave and three days proceed time, for a total of ten days before reporting to NAS Beeville, Texas. I left the Colonel's office, unable to believe my good fortune.

I turned my attention to my problem. Mickey and I spent a lot of time together in a very torrid relationship. In the movie, "An Officer And A Gentleman," a small town local girl fakes pregnancy in order to marry her cadet and become the wife of an officer and a pilot. It's her ticket to the higher plateaus of life and she grabs at it.

The movie was scripted decades after Mickey and I met. I was fond of Mickey, but had no permanent plans for us. I had been honest about that and now it was time to say goodbye. As far as I knew she wasn't looking for anything lasting, either. I had a long way to go before I got my wings and that was going to take precedence over all else.

As I was finishing up at Whiting, Mickey informed me she was pregnant. I panicked but managed to collect my thoughts enough to suggest we go to a doctor and confirm it. She balked, coming up with a number of excuses, all of which triggered suspicion. I went home on leave with this situation unresolved and although worried, I was also highly doubtful she was actually pregnant. While home in Wichita I wrote Mickey and told her I DOR'd from flight training (Drop On Request) and was going to take a job in a Wichita aircraft plant. I invented a number of reasons resulting in my sudden decision to abandon flight training and remain home.

Within days I received a letter from Mickey telling me she miscarried and was ending our relationship. I was relieved that the dilemma was over. I saved the letter for a long while just in case. I never had an abundance of strong personal self-esteem and the idea that our relationship had been a ploy did nothing to help that.

Jets - 1962

I reported to NAS (Naval Air Station) Chase Field, Beeville, Texas for Advanced Jet Training at noon on Friday, August 10, 1962. For the previous two hours I watched jet fighters crisscrossing the Texas skies as I made my way across the flat Texas landscape. I was nervous about going from a slow propeller airplane to a jet that flew nearly twice as fast. Back came the voices inside; I struggled to rid myself of the self-doubt. This was the last hurdle and I *had* to believe I could handle it.

This final phase of flight training would last about six months. If I made it, I would pin those wings of gold and receive my second lieutenant bars as a commissioned Marine Corps officer. I had come a long way from a condemned house in Arkansas and a chaotic home in a housing project in Wichita with two alcoholic parents. I was so close to finishing...if I could *just* make it.

I checked into the base and reunited with a number of close friends who arrived before me. We spent the afternoon laughing and drinking at the officer's club. As evening fell they suggested we head into town to a local drive-in called "Cain's." It was a hot meeting place for cadets and the good-looking girls of south Texas.

At Cain's my buddies immediately descended upon a car full of laughing girls but I hung back, drinking more beer. Finally, I thought I had enough to drink and nervously rehearsed some glib things to say, so I approached the driver. When she turned to look at me I was smitten.

147

She had the most beautiful brown eyes and suddenly I felt as awkward as a first grader. I forgot what I rehearsed and slurred something about her beautiful brown eyes. I was making no sense and wished I could retrace my steps and disappear. She neither smiled nor spoke. I felt like an ass and was sure she concurred, so I turned and walked away.

A little later, she got out of her car to go inside. I got a good look at her and almost sobered up! She was wearing turquoise shorts, with a nicely contained derriere and shapely legs. I couldn't take my eyes off her. But I was not going to make a fool of myself a second time, so I stayed by my car and drank.

I saw her the next day as my cadet buddy Conrad Hamilton and I were coming back from the small town of Beeville headed for Chase Field. I took care of some routine tasks in town as I prepared for my stay in Beeville. Speeding past, I glanced over at Cain's. There she was, about to walk into the restaurant with a friend! I hit the brakes and swerved into the parking lot. Conrad and I walked in and feigned surprise at seeing them. I was very nervous, but sober and sensible, and I asked if we could buy them coffee. We were invited to join them.

I learned her name was Barbara Burns and she worked at the bank. After some small talk I asked if I might call her sometime. She paused, and said yes. We began to date, and she became the love of my life. She was everything I dreamed about with all the qualities and virtues I ever imagined. She was exceptionally pretty, with a great smile, a lovely laugh, and a cute figure. Beyond that, she had old-fashioned values. She was openly honest, unpretentious, and completely without guile. I loved her soft south Texas accent and lit up whenever I was with her. She was the most wholesome and sweet girl I ever dated.

Her family was not well to do. They worked hard, farmed, and at one time ran a small dairy operation. Her dad had also worked in the oil fields as a roughneck. They lived in a home that would embarrass some, but Barbara never hesitated to ask me in. I immediately hit it off with her mom and dad. Her mother was where her looks came from, while her dad was lean, rawhide tough with a white-haired crew cut, and as unassuming as Barbara was. I liked them a lot. She had a younger brother, Robert, and an older sister, Norma Jean, who possessed Hollywood beauty and was married to a local rancher.

148

I was completely captivated with Barbara. I thought of her constantly but was only able to see her on weekends. The schedule ahead of me was intense and I was so close to completing, but I worried she would meet someone else and I would lose her.

When flight training resumed, I was immediately immersed in more classroom work, the same subjects again but escalating to advanced levels. Once the class work was completed and exams passed, it was time to start flying.

I was assigned to VT-24, one of three training squadrons at Chase Field. My instructor was a tall Marine Captain named George Morris. All students would first fly a very long syllabus in the F9F's, then wrap up their final days of flight training in the single seat F11-F Grumman Tiger, the airplane of the vaunted Blue Angels.

Throughout flight training I was fortunate in the flight instructors I was assigned to, and George Morris perhaps epitomized that the most. He was a gifted pilot, a patient instructor, an excellent officer, and a good man.

I was entering the big leagues as I transitioned into a fast, high performance jet airplane. I climbed one echelon of challenge after another and progressed through the dream of becoming a pilot and Marine officer. The one just ahead was my last bastion to conquer. My first fam flight with Captain Morris came on September 6, 1962.

Again, I spent hours and hours studying and practicing cockpit procedures, closing my eyes and locating switches. Virtually all the other students were moving to the F9 from their previous jet trainer, the T2J, which I'd passed up while headed for helicopters. They were accustomed to fast speeds, high climb rates, and the whisper quiet cockpit sounds of jet engines. I had to double my efforts to overcome this training deficit.

Nothing was familiar as I put a G-suit and a torso harness on for the first time. For the first flight I would mostly be a passenger as Captain Morris started the engine and taxied us out. On the runway I was still trying to absorb the complicated checks required after engine start when suddenly we were hurtling down the runway and were airborne. The silence was eerie. Captain Morris' voice came through my helmet in a manner I never heard before, quiet and clear, with no competing engine noises. I fought off the claustrophobia of my oxygen mask, another unfamiliar item only worn a few times previously.

We climbed higher and flew faster than I ever had before. I felt mentally inadequate and seriously questioned my ability to keep up. All the while, Captain Morris kept talking as he showed me the training area landmarks and demonstrated the airplane's performance. I marveled at his confidence and skill.

Letting down, he demonstrated the field entry procedure from the five-mile initial fix into "the break." The break is a mid-point down the field, aligned with and over the active runway, where an aircraft suddenly banks sharply and makes a 180 degree turn, entering the downwind leg for landing. I was ill prepared as we approached at twice any speed I'd ever seen and Captain Morris smartly snapped the plane into 90 degrees of bank and pulled 4 G's in the turn. My head bounced hard off the canopy and I was glad to be wearing a helmet. In the midst of the high G turn he put speed brakes out, dropped the landing gear, eased the flaps out, and we turned on our final approach. It happened so fast I couldn't keep up and felt totally lost.

Unlike a propeller aircraft with instant engine power response, a jet engine has a considerable time lag to it, and the need to add or reduce power must be anticipated well ahead of the actual time it's needed. After the first landing Captain Morris passed control of the airplane to me and we stayed in the landing pattern while I performed 5 landings. Still in a fog and mentally trying to catch up to the airplane, I was surprised when he debriefed me after landing and noted in my training jacket, "Student seemed to have feel of power and added or took it off in landing pattern as necessary." I picked up two above averages during a flight in which I felt completely incompetent.

The next day I flew with another instructor, set my altimeter 1,000 feet off, and picked up my first below average for headwork in this phase. He commented that it was "a rather nice hop" except for the headwork error. This was a serious mistake that I never made a second time because I realized it could have killed me in instrument conditions.

I was glad to have George Morris back for the rest of my fam flights. His next comment in my jacket was "student is smooth and hardworking." I wondered why he would write such a thing because I started from so far behind and was struggling just to earn average status.

George Morris took a personal interest in me beyond his role as my flight instructor. He was quietly demanding and set such an example of flawless performance that I had no excuse for coming up short. We spent extra time after the flights talking about life in the Marine Corps, what I should hold myself to as an officer and many thoughts and ideas about flying.

He did something I never heard of another instructor doing; he invited Barbara and me to his home for dinner and drinks. George and his wife Dottie instantly liked Barbara. A certain distinct barrier has to exist between instructors and students and I clearly understood that. George took a chance by breaching that barrier and bringing Barbara and me into his home, but I never crossed the line.

I saw Barbara on the weekends and could hardly wait for them to arrive. I lit up when I could be with her but our time together always seemed so brief. Then the weekend was gone and I was back to the intensity of the task ahead. With each passing day I slowly became more competent under George's tutelage. I had good days and bad days, but nothing disappointed me more than to disappoint Captain George Morris.

I progressed through the lengthy syllabus and it was time to go aboard the carrier once more. This time carrier operations involved hydraulic catapult shots off the forward bow of the USS Antietam, another new experience for me. Coming aboard ship in a jet was considerably more demanding than it was in the T-28. As we headed for the U.S.S. Antietam I was anxious but well prepared.

Preparing for my first cat shot, I followed the smooth, ballet-like hand signals of the deck handlers and edged the nose wheel up over the shuttle while they tensioned the aircraft down. I ran the engine to one hundred percent, saluted the catapult officer, and put my head back awaiting the unbelievable acceleration of the hydraulic catapult. I was so nervous that I almost hit the water as I went over the bow. With that exception I had an excellent day at the ship. Once the first cat shot was behind me I was ready to do it again and again. Some say if the thrill of a catapult shot lasted a few seconds longer they would never get married.

VT-24 was my training squadron and I completed that phase on January 16, 1963, moving a few hangars down to my final squadron– VT-26. At the end of the day I finished well in the F9, building my grades to a 3.07. It was a marked contrast from my first flight with Captain Morris and I had learned so much from him. I was not the same cadet from a few months earlier.

Gold Wings and Gold Bars

VT-26 pilots considered themselves the elite of Advanced Jet Training. Fighter pilots all, they were flying the sleek Grumman F11-F Tiger Jet, the fast, high performance airplane the Blue Angels were using to dazzle spectators all over the world. It was a first for us students because the airplane had only one seat, which meant there would never be an instructor with us. Not even for the first fam hop.

It would also be the first time we flew an airplane with an afterburner and the ability to break Mach 1, the speed of sound, which we would do as part of our training. It was an airplane with knife-edge thin wings, designed for high altitude flight and perfect for smooth formation work.

I was now the first student for Navy Lieutenant Ed Holmes. He was a big man, likeable, easy-going, and eager to instruct. Before climbing in the cockpit, I had to complete a rigorous simulator syllabus in an F11 mockup as we covered the normal procedures and all the emergencies.

On January 31, 1963, I flew my first F11-F flight with Lt. Holmes in an accompanying chase plane. I broke Mach 1, flying faster than the speed of sound, and picked up an unprecedented six above averages with no below's. His written entry commented, "Student was exceptionally steady for 1st flight in aircraft." This was fun flying, I was in the home stretch now, and couldn't wait to get in the air each day – the end was in sight.

We moved into Air Combat Maneuvering, or "hassling," as it's called and I loved it. I read everything I could about tactics, hoping to become an adept student of this rapidly moving aerial chess game. There were moves and counter moves for each situation. I was aggressive and enthusiastic to get in the air. I flew my final flight in the training syllabus on February 20, 1963, ending 19 months and 3 weeks of intense effort.

I accomplished it without receiving a "Down," or unsatisfactory flight, something as rare as a golfer's hole in one. In all the years since, I have only known a few who could lay claim to that. However, I considered it more luck than skill.

I asked Barbara to marry me and she said yes. I was happy to find someone I wanted to share my life with but frightened about giving up my freedom. No matter how I approached it, I knew one thing–I did not want to lose her.

On February 25th, 1963, Barbara's twentieth birthday, I graduated from flight training and could hardly believe I had accomplished my life dream. The graduation ceremony began and I glanced at Barbara, so beautiful and so loving as she shared this moment with me. I was touched and flattered when Captain George Morris arrived and presented me with the gold bars he had worn as a second lieutenant. It was a deeply meaningful gesture on his part and I asked if he would pin one on while Barbara pinned the other. Then she placed those coveted, precious gold wings directly over my heart. It was over. I was now a designated Naval Aviator and Marine Corps second lieutenant.

The day seemed surreal and I couldn't believe this part was over. I worked as hard as I possibly could, the daily pressure was extremely intense for over a year and a half, and now it was done. *I could return to my Native community now; I had made it.* I knew that many others along the way wanted their wings as badly as I did and had worked just as hard. But for whatever reason, they fell short. I was enormously grateful for whatever hand Providence played in my completion.

Barbara and I went home to Wichita for a much needed break. The drive north took thirteen hours but they whirled by in our excitement and joy. Barbara stayed with my sister and I stayed with my dad. She was an immediate hit with my family and all my friends, who quickly sensed her open and undisguised wholesomeness.

My relationship with my father was turbulent for a number of years and worsened during this visit. He had been recruited by NASA, had a good paying job, but was living alone in a small, dirty apartment. He and his last wife parted company but neither bothered with a divorce. There were cases of empty liquor bottles stacked in the small kitchen and when I attempted to talk to him about his drinking he became angry and arrogant.

My leave was coming to an end and one morning I picked Barbara up at my sister's and said, "Let's go to Oklahoma and get married right now." It was impulsive, but I was going to California and Barbara was going back to Texas. I had my wings and commission, my emotions were in orbit, and I wanted Barbara as my wife.

Barbara paused for a moment then said okay. I called Coy Blankenship, who was a close friend from high school, and asked if he and his wife Mona would drive to Newkirk, Oklahoma with us. Several hours later we were all standing in front of a Justice of the Peace in Newkirk as Coy and Mona slipped off their wedding rings and loaned them to us for the ceremony.

We returned to Wichita, had a brief two-day honeymoon and it was time for Barbara to go home to Texas. I headed west to the Marine base at El Toro, California. I promised Barbara we would have a regular wedding in Texas, the kind she'd dreamed of with friends and family, a wedding cake, reception, and all the rest. A short while later we cancelled those plans when Barbara told me she was pregnant. I was concerned that her parents might be angry with us, but was relieved to find they were not.

As I headed to California, I glanced down at my wedding ring from time to time, adjusting to the idea that I was now married and moving into a new phase of life. Hollywood could not have scripted my life any better.

Marine Attack Squadron 311

In April 1963, I arrived at Marine Corps Air Station El Toro (MCAS El Toro) accompanied by an old family dog I agreed to take from my father. Base housing was unavailable so I found a tiny place in Silverado Canyon, high in the hills surrounding El Toro. Barbara joined me several weeks later and I introduced her to our small rented kitchenette with one bedroom and barely enough space to turn around in. Nothing dampened her spirits, though, and we happily began our married life. All my dreams had come true. I intended to join a fighter squadron, but was disappointed to learn most of their flying consisted of grinding around on boring GCI flights (ground controlled intercepts). My friends in the A4 Skyhawk squadrons were enthusiastic about the airplane and the mission. Nearly all the flying involved low altitude, high-speed work, with a wide variety of weapons and I quickly decided I wanted to fly the Skyhawk – and I never regretted it. A young Navy pilot who would later seek the U.S. Presidency was also flying the Skyhawk. His name was John McCain.

Barbara joined me and we made new friends at a whirlwind pace, virtually all of them fellow Marines and their wives. Our squadron quickly became our extended family and the other wives immediately welcomed Barbara. Compared to the Air Force a Marine squadron was much smaller and compact. There were twenty-eight pilots – mostly first and second lieutenants, a few captains, one or two majors, and a lieutenant colonel topped the pyramid as commanding officer.

The older wives were wonderful about taking the younger ones under their wings and squadron camaraderie was not the sole province of the pilots. The wives developed very close and lasting relationships.

Squadron happy hours commenced at 4:00 P.M. on Friday afternoons at the Officers Club, restricted to squadron members only. Woe to the unfortunate pilot whose wife violated that rule and walked in. The Happy Hours were loud and raucous as each squadron staked out a long table with their squadron symbol or mascot perched upon it proclaiming it as *their* table. As the evening progressed the squadron symbols became trophies for other squadrons to steal and display in their ready rooms. I always stayed until the O'Club door was closed and locked for the night.

The drive back to Silverado Canyon had hairpin curves, switchbacks, steep climbs and descents and was challenging in good light when sober; but at night it was treacherous. I wrecked our car the first two consecutive Happy Hours as I made my way home late at night. I lied to Barbara the first time since the damage was slight telling her someone hit me in the squadron parking lot while I was flying. The next Friday, I did considerably more damage to the opposite side of the car and she heard me arriving home as the peeled back chrome trim scraped loudly behind me on the concrete. I walked in, told her I hit the mountain, and went to bed.

Although I was embarrassed by the accidents, I shrugged them off. It was part of the pilot persona to fly hard and drink hard. I vowed to drive slower coming home at night, but I never considered easing up on the booze.

I made scant pay as a cadet and at graduation took out a stiff loan, known as a "dead horse," to buy the new officer uniforms I would need upon commissioning. Barb's pregnancy was starting to show but she hadn't bought one single piece of maternity clothing due to our tight finances. Yet she never said a word. I came in one afternoon and she greeted me with her smile and usual hug and a kiss. A few minutes later she stood on her tiptoes to get something from a cabinet. She was wearing a loose, baggy top and as it rode up over her slacks I noticed her swollen tummy with the zipper half unzipped to accommodate her condition. Suddenly I felt ashamed. I had not taken the time to consider her need for maternity clothes. And she'd never complained once. The next day we went to Sears and bought her several outfits with a credit card. She was so happy that I felt even worse at being so inattentive.

Barbara was extremely well liked by everyone and there was no shortage of support as she came closer to delivering our baby. Our lives could not have been scripted better. I was burning up the skies in jet airplanes and married to a beautiful lady who was going to have our first child.

The Douglas A4B Skyhawk was a highly maneuverable, sleek, single seat, single engine jet attack airplane. I climbed into it for the first time on May 1st, 1963. A mere touch on the stick brought instant response and I only had to think the airplane into doing what I wished. The roll rate was the fastest in aviation at that time.

Our first child was born prematurely on August 27, 1963. I was flying and upon landing the SDO (Squadron Duty Officer) informed me my wife was at St Joseph hospital in Santa Ana having our child. I was startled because she wasn't due for several more months. She had fallen and broken her water.

Delivery came thirty hours later, at 4:27 P.M., and I was amazed at the peaceful calm she displayed as labor was induced. Nearby, clearly audible in the maternity ward, someone was screaming as their labor hastened, but Barbara remained calm and serene. Neither Barbara nor I were able to hold our baby after the delivery as he was immediately taken to the intensive care unit. I got a glimpse of him through the glass windows and was unable to absorb the overwhelming miracle of life, struggling to accept that I was a father and we were now a family.

Scott was a big baby, considering the early delivery, and everything went well. Word rapidly reached the squadron and I walked into the Ready Room to a large announcement emblazoned on the blackboard. The A4B had three stations on which to hang ordnance, one under the belly, known as the centerline station, and one on each wing. When we dropped ordnance it was known as "pickling it off," and in large broad chalk strokes on the blackboard was the announcement "PROUSE'S

WIFE PICKLED HER CENTERLINE". We were an irreverent bunch, and the wives often grimaced at our callous humor.

A few days later I brought Barbara home while Scott remained in an incubator for several more weeks. Months earlier we moved out of Silverado Canyon into a small apartment in Santa Ana. Finally, we brought our son home and began our life as parents. Barbara was only twenty, the youngest wife in the squadron. I was twenty-four.

We had dreams and goals and neither of us were sidetracked with the temptations of an easier, softer way that appealed to many. Neither of us had come from a life of ease or privilege and we were dedicated to expending the effort required. Then, suddenly we were parents, responsible for another small life, and at first it seemed unreal.

Barbara was a natural mother; there was none better. She was born for motherhood and I realized how lucky our son was. From the beginning she was a much better mother than I was a father. She did it effortlessly, seemingly with no need for adjustment, while I often came up short. I loved Scott, but was having trouble transitioning from such a free spirit to someone who changed a diaper. Barbara more than made up for my shortcomings and was patient as I slowly adjusted to fatherhood.

My profession was dangerous and I lost several close friends. This way of life was not without peril and I attended a number of memorial services. I heard the sad and somber strain of Taps and watched missing man formations fly overhead. With a young wife and new son I made arrangements for their lives without me. I took out additional insurance and made a will, recalling another young lieutenant who recently died without either, leaving his wife and young child in a disastrous situation.

The pilots in 311 were superb to a man. Being an average aviator in this group would have been sufficient for anyone, but a strong competitive spirit was instilled into each of us. Captains Don Rowe and Speed Shea were openly recognized as being superior aviators among us while we each worked to catch them. Our camaraderie defied description. We flew as a band of brothers as we put our complete trust and confidence in each other whether we were leading the flight or flying wing position. I literally trusted each man with my life.

We were approaching the one-year preparation time for an overseas deployment. We again qualified aboard the Navy's carriers, first the

USS Yorktown, then the USS Hornet. Later, we would qualify on the USS Oriskany, receiving a letter of commendation from the Chief of Naval Operations for the best performance aboard ship by any Marine squadron. I was flying with the best pilots in the Marine Corps.

I made first lieutenant and was offered a chance to attend Naval Justice School. If I accepted I would become the squadron legal officer, an important squadron job which would freeze me in the squadron for another year and guarantee a slot for the upcoming overseas tour. I accepted and went thirty miles south to Camp Pendleton for the seven-week school, knowing it would lock me in for two more years of flying. Typically, new pilots flew their first year in a squadron. Then they were sent to a non-flying billet for a year (or sometimes more) before making their way back into a flying slot. I wanted to maneuver around that and remain actively flying in my squadron.

Naval Justice School was the abbreviated military version of Harvard Law School, and we covered the entire Uniform Code of Military Justice in those seven weeks. I barely had time to eat and sleep between class work and studies and was introduced to the unique manner of thinking that takes place in the courtroom. I returned to the squadron as the new legal officer.

As we prepared to go overseas the squadron went through extensive inspections, testing, and scrutiny by senior Marine Corps officials. We performed well on all fronts. Prior to deploying overseas every pilot had to go through the two-week Marine Corps Escape and Evasion school, known for its brutal conditions and harsh regimen. It took place high in the Sierra Madre Mountains at a Marine facility known as Pickle Meadows and no one looked forward to going there. Base camp was at 6,000 feet and tops could exceed 11,000.

Our final exercise was to avoid capture for a week as each nine-man team made their way across rugged mountains to a safe area. The remote and formidable mountainous area set an ominous tone for this exercise. The sense of realism was extreme. Fatigue and hunger sabotaged caution and I had a foreboding sense of imminent capture. I trailed behind the main body and was able to escape both times my team was ambushed and captured. Once, the aggressors were inches away as I lay underneath some thick and painful thorn bushes trying to still my pounding heart as they searched for me. I was the only one in my team not captured during this final, difficult week.

On the home front other things were happening. Barbara had only gained fifteen pounds in her first pregnancy and was quickly back into snug fitting skirts when she informed me she might be pregnant again. The doctor confirmed it and eight days less than one year from Scott's birth we welcomed another boy, Jay, into our family. Everyone began inquiring if we were Catholic, to which I would normally respond, "No, we're just horny Protestants with very poor birth control."

We began preparations to point our aircraft toward the Far East and in February of 1965, I took a month's leave. While at 13432 Wake Avenue in base housing we had many good times and lived next door to outstanding Marine neighbors. There was a feeling of sadness as we said goodbye to the Marine Corps family we grew so close to during the previous two years. We made the long road trip to Beeville, Texas after bidding farewell to friends.

Barbara would live in a tiny house next to her parents, a source of comfort to me. I knew she would be carefully watched after and our two small sons would be close to loving grandparents. It would be a long time before I saw my wife and children again. And there was always the possibility I would not return. Barbara was tearful and I kept kissing her and my two little sons just one more time, trying to find the appropriate moment to walk away. Finally, I turned and walked to the waiting airplane.

Japan and Vietnam

War is an ugly thing, but not the ugliest of things; the decay and degraded state of moral and patriotic feeling which thinks that nothing is worth war is much worse. A man who has nothing for which he is willing to fight; nothing he cares about more than his own personal safety is a miserable creature who has no chance of being free, unless made and kept so by the exertions of better men than himself. – Sartre

In preparation for the upcoming deployment we received twenty brand new aircraft. Earlier, we became the first west coast squadron to receive the latest model of the A4, designated the A4E. It had more power, more speed, and could carry more payload with quicker engine response time and better fuel efficiency. We were going into war with the best airplane our country could provide us.

In the twelve months preceding our overseas deployment date we spent approximately 165 days away from home, mostly on two-week training deployments to Yuma, Arizona and Fallon, Nevada.

We were to be the first squadron to fly the A4E eight thousand miles across the Pacific, requiring extensive planning and test flying. We would refuel in the air twice before reaching Kaneohe, Hawaii, once more over Midway Island before landing at tiny Wake Island, and again before reaching Atsugi, Japan. From Atsugi it was a short 400-mile flight

163

southwest to our home base at Iwakuni. We would have a day of rest in Hawaii and at Wake Island before completing the Pacific crossing.

We began our squadron movement on March 23, 1965, as we moved twenty airplanes, twenty-eight pilots, and 206 squadron personnel to the Far East. I was to fly in the first flight of ten, split into groups of five; I flew 6.3 hours across the Pacific en route to the Marine base at Kaneohe. Captain Don "Digger" Rowe was my flight leader in the five-plane flight and I always enjoyed flying with him. Our time aloft was over four times the normal flight time for a single sortie. Adding to the difficulty was the thick rubber "poopy suit" we had to wear to protect us from ocean exposure in the event we had to eject over the Pacific. It was skin tight, difficult to get into and out of, and almost impossible to urinate from if the need arose. Upon landing in Hawaii my muscles were so cramped it was difficult to get out of the cockpit without help.

Several of us lieutenants took advantage of our short night at Kaneohe and went to Duke Kahanamoku's where Don Ho was cutting his very first album in front of a live audience. He was a former Air Force pilot, a spectacular performer with a rich baritone voice. He put on a fabulous show. Later, he would become a Hawaiian legend. We ordered drink after drink to his oft-repeated phrase "Suck 'em up!" while he entertained the audience. Barbara later bought the large $33\,^1/_3{}^{rd}$ record album and my piercing whistle can be heard amid the applause at the end of the song, "Pearly Shells".

It took three legs, 17.7 hours, and four air-to-air refuelings to reach Japan from the California coast. Within two weeks we were notified that we would be heading for Vietnam, to a new airstrip being built on the coastal beaches fifty miles south of Danang – at a place called Chu Lai. It would be the first time the Marine Corps employed a combat expeditionary airfield in actual combat. The flying would be extremely challenging.

Although we were only in Japan a brief while we crammed a lot of flying, drinking, and touring into a short period. We were introduced to the "Happy Yen" dice roll at the Friday Happy Hour. It involved rolling dice for a huge amount of Yen contributed by all the squadron members. The first two winners were pilots not known for being wildly outgoing and they picked up their winnings to the disappointed mutterings of their peers. I won the following week and my fellow pilots exploded in wild celebration as I gathered the pile of money and departed. The exchange rate was 360 Yen to one Dollar American and I had more money than I thought I could spend. I had one hour to be off the base and gone or I forfeited my winnings if caught.

I was drunk most of the weekend and found myself in a distant Japanese town with no recollection of how I got there. I was the only American around. I joined a Japanese street parade—and suddenly discovered it was an anti-American demonstration. However, I was drunk and fearless and I exited the demonstration without incident. Eventually I found a train and made my way back to Iwakuni with the help of some polite Japanese. Much of the weekend was lost in a blackout, along with all my money.

On May 29th and 30th we flew our aircraft to Cubi Point, Philippines, for the final staging into Vietnam. I had to fly on the C-130 with the remaining pilots two weeks later. My last night in Japan was spent with my lifelong best friend, Marine First Lieutenant John Dodson, who was flying F8 Crusaders in a photo squadron. We spent the last of my Yen and got smashingly drunk. I was horribly hung over the next morning as I boarded the hot and crowded Marine C-130 for the long trip to Chu Lai. By mid-June all VMA-311 airplanes and personnel were in Chu Lai.

Our combat runway was made from interlocking pieces of aluminum, and was less than half the length we needed to operate from. We used JATO bottles (jet assist take off) for the thrust required to get airborne and we landed into carrier arresting gear. Chu Lai was hot, desolate, and primitive, with no air conditioning. An ice cube or cold drink of water was a rare luxury usually reserved for debriefing after a combat mission. The runway and airfield operations area was a stone's throw from the South China Sea; the short runway paralleled the coastline in a northwest-southeast direction. Marine infantry secured the small Chu Lai perimeter and the area just beyond belonged to the Viet Cong in all directions.

A high mountain range rose to the west and Marine artillery lit it up at night with H & I fire (harass and interdict). Fine powdery sand invaded everything, clinging to our sweating bodies and creeping into

165

every part of our equipment and personal belongings. Our food was cans of C rations eaten cold or heated with blue-flamed Sterno tablets. We built writing desks and makeshift stools out of disassembled ordnance crates. It was a celebration day when we received plywood floors for our tents and could get out of the sand.

As a young Marine I was convinced our cause was just. I never questioned the credibility of my government and accepted the information they disseminated. However, I viewed the rules of engagement as sheer folly manufactured by Washington politicians. Eventually, my opinions about the war changed and after a few decades I looked back with sadness, anger and disgust.

On the second day I flew my first combat mission in the nearby area of Tam Ky led by our Executive Officer, Major Jack Parchen, an outstanding officer and pilot. He had begun his Marine career as an infantry officer in Korea. As we cranked up combat operations with more and more sorties he became the de facto leader of our squadron in spite of being second in command. Sadly, the weak link in our squadron, both in the cockpit and on the ground, was our Commanding Officer.

On August 18th, 1965, the Marines launched the first full scale American ground offensive of the war known as Operation Starlight. A Viet Cong regiment, just eight miles south on the Van Tuong peninsula near Quang Ngai, was gathering for a full-scale assault on our small airbase at Chu Lai. Operation Starlight was a preemptive search and destroy mission to thwart the attack and prevent the loss of Chu Lai. Every component of Marine Corps might was poured into this battle including naval gunfire, infantry, artillery, and air support. The squadrons at Chu Lai were heavily engaged in this seven day operation. I flew five missions during the operation. More than six hundred Viet Cong were killed while fifty Marines died and two hundred-fifty were wounded. The first two Medals of Honor for the Vietnam War were awarded during this battle, later known as "The Battle of Chu Lai." VMA-311 received the Presidential Unit Citation for this engagement.

During our time in Vietnam we flew combat missions almost daily. The arrested landings and JATO takeoffs were the norm, adding another dimension of challenge to the missions.

I applied for a Regular commission in the Marine Corps and was sure I would be passed over. They were very competitive and I was positive no officer with a high school education would be selected. To my surprise I was one of three lieutenants in our squadron to receive one. When I received my wings I was given a Reserve commission but the step up to a Regular commission opened new doors for a career in the Marine Corps.

I received my first Air Medal and gave the ribbon to Sgt. Ed Hill and the medal to Staff Sergeant Tex Butler, the two NCOs in charge of the Airframes and the Hydraulics shops. I wiggled my way out of the legal officer job and was the Officer in Charge of those shops. I had sixteen enlisted Marines under me and they worked heroically under devastating conditions. I felt the two NCOs deserved the medal and ribbon more than I did.

On August 24, 1965, I had an extremely close call. Lieutenant Gus Xavier and I were standing hot pad duty when we were scrambled for a close air support mission. Gus was a close friend who would die in the mountains surrounding the Ashau Valley. I was section leader that day and Gus was my wingman as we launched. We arrived on the scene and learned the Marines were pinned down by heavy weapons fire coming from a tree line.

We pounded the position with bombs and rockets. Shouts of excitement came over our headsets as the Marine controller on the ground told us we'd destroyed the guns. The tree line was now quiet. I asked the FAC (forward air controller) if he wanted more aircraft launched as a precaution and he said yes. I told Gus to climb to a higher altitude and relay the request for another flight. I told him come down and join me if he saw me roll in on another target.

Suddenly the FAC reported enemy soldiers moving up to flank them from the southeast and asked if I could strafe. I replied that I could. I saw uniformed troops moving through a rice paddy where he indicated. We were briefed that a North Vietnamese unit was in the area so I was expecting to see uniformed troops if they were involved.

I pulled around in a tight high-G turn, straining my neck as I looked back through the top of the canopy to keep them in sight. I kept my eyes on the troops as I reached down, charged the guns, and came around to strafe. There were approximately forty troops in the open with nowhere to go as I rolled out and headed for them. I bore down on them and opened fire at point blank range as I walked the rudders back and forth to spray the entire area with twenty millimeter high explosive rounds. I intended to kill as many as possible; there was no way I could miss. *I was incredulous as nothing happened – the guns failed to fire.* I pulled up hard in another high G turn and started to come around a second time. I looked down and saw that I missed the gun-charging switch by an inch. I mistakenly selected the switch next to it and failed to arm the guns. The odds of that happening were almost nil.

I radioed that I was making a second pass and noticed that Gus had dropped back down and was ready to follow me back in. There was a pause, then the controller on the ground said, "Hold it! Hold it! Don't strafe! They're Marines!" I shuddered and felt a cold chill. He had mistakenly targeted our own troops. By the grace of God I barely missed killing or wounding a whole platoon of Marines. And I'd literally missed by an inch. I was at home in the cockpit and the chance of making that mistake was extremely slim. Since then, I have never heard of friendly fire casualties without saying a silent thank you prayer to God for sparing me that day.

There were three other squadrons now flying out of Chu Lai, comprising eighty aircraft, and Chu Lai was a beehive of activity. On the night of October 28th, 1965, as I was falling asleep in my tent, explosions lit up the night sky just over the small ridge to the flight line. Viet Cong had infiltrated and were blowing up and machine-gunning aircraft, managing to destroy three and damage several others. I grabbed my .38 pistol and started over the ridgeline but stopped as I considered the likelihood of being shot by other Marines in the darkness and confusion. I did not want to go home a casualty of friendly fire.

When we left Japan for Vietnam, we took the two scrawny squadron dogs we inherited. One of them had pups shortly after arriving in Chu Lai. I took one of the puppies and named him "Dammit." He was my constant companion when I wasn't flying. I mixed powdered milk from C rations and carefully nurtured him as a tiny pup. Barbara sent me worm medicine and dog food as he got older. I spent many hours training him and although he was only four or five months old he was smart and obedient.

As the gunfire and explosions continued, I settled back with Dammit next to me. He was on full alert due to the noise and activity. Dammit slept next to my cot and some hours later, when things settled down and we were all asleep he began to bark. A grenade exploded approximately fifty yards away; leaving a large crater in the dirt road running through our tent area. Dammit's barking was probably responsible for the Viet Cong avoiding our tent area and saving us from a grenade blast.

The monsoon season arrived in October and we averaged thirty inches of rain per month, the moisture penetrated everything we owned. Low cloud cover and reduced visibility hampered air operations. We resorted to a tactic known as "low and slow," delivering ordnance from much lower altitudes while extending ¼ flaps and slowing our airspeed greatly. Although it allowed us to deliver ordnance under adverse weather conditions it reduced our maneuverability and increased our exposure to ground fire.

During this time the Marine Corps changed its overseas rotation system. They shifted personnel to other squadrons and began the changeover to individual replacements. I was assigned to VMA-223, back in Iwakuni, Japan. I was sad to leave the squadron I flew with since getting my wings; but I also had many good friends in 223 and was happy to go back to Japan. But I was going to miss Dammit.

I loved my little canine pal and was deeply attached to him. In a brutal and violent war, where the countryside was ripped and scarred, where people died every day, he was a quiet refuge. The look in his eyes, the wagging tail and body language, and the smell of his fur when I nestled my head in his neck, gave me a precious peace. I would miss him dearly.

My good friend and squadron mate, Gus Xavier, was to keep him until I returned, which I expected to do very shortly with VMA-223. I intended to take Dammit home to the United States. I sadly said goodbye and left him in Gus' care. Gus would soon lose his life attempting to help the embattled Americans at the battle of the Ashau Valley. He was awarded the Silver Star for his courageous actions. My intentions to return for Dammit died in the twists and turns of war, and I never saw him again.

I barely adjusted to my squadron when the Commanding Officer, Lt. Col. Wilson, called me into his office. Brigadier General Marion Carl, an extraordinary Marine legend from WWII, was losing his current aide and looking for a replacement. General Carl was Assistant Wing Commander of all Marine aviation in Vietnam. Every squadron in the Asian theatre was to nominate one pilot for the job, and then the commanders of the three Marine Air Groups would narrow those nominees down to one each. The general himself would select from the final three. Lt. Col. Wilson wanted me to be the VMA-223 candidate.

Although the request was flattering, there was no way I wanted any part of that. My Commanding Officer talked to me at length about the career advantages the assignment would offer, trying hard to persuade me to say yes. I respectfully refused. It was difficult since I was a first lieutenant talking to a lieutenant colonel. He let me off the hook after I reluctantly said I would think about it. I left his office hoping he would forget about it.

A few days later he called me in again, asking if I reconsidered the opportunity. Again I respectfully declined. I left hoping I would not have to deal with this again. I was wrong. He approached me once more and the pressure was mounting at this point. *Then* it occurred to me that if *every* squadron had to put a candidate forward the law of averages would surely work in my favor. I reluctantly said okay, reasoning that the numerical odds would take care of me.

I knew General Carl's aide from my days at El Toro. Lieutenant Joe Maiden, soon to be Captain Maiden, was a graduate of the U.S. Naval Academy – well educated, handsome, smooth, and polished. He was everything I was not. I was rough around the edges, came from an alcoholic home and Native American community, had trudged through high school, and was an ex-enlisted Marine infantryman. I was hardly the picture of a General's aide. Furthermore, I had no desire to be one, notwithstanding the fact there was a certain career distinction in being selected for such an assignment.

Before I knew it, I was awaiting an interview with the Marine Air Group (MAG) 13 Commanding Officer, Colonel O.E. Howe. Lt. Col. Wilson wrote a glowing endorsement, describing his impressions of me at Chu Lai. He reiterated those as a member of his command. In the waiting area I mixed with a number of other nominees, all excitedly hoping they would be picked for this assignment.

Once in front of Colonel Howe I again stated my desire to remain in my squadron, thinking he would surely select one of the more eager and enthusiastic candidates. My plan seemed to be falling apart when a few days later I became one of the three finalists and would be talking with General Carl very shortly.

A week later two other candidates and I met in a waiting room outside an office where General Carl was preparing for our interviews. Lt. Joe Maiden sat at a desk in the waiting room and I made a last minute appeal, asking him if there was any way to avoid this assignment. Joe said he could tell the general he knew me personally and I was incompetent. This solution was not very palatable, so I declined.

Once inside the general's office I gazed at this Marine legend. He was nearly a quadruple ace, with 18 ½ kills in WWII, and had earned *two* Navy Crosses, second only to the Medal of Honor. Added to those were *five* Distinguished Flying Crosses and many other lesser medals. He was a test pilot of indescribable renown in the days when aviation was transitioning from props to jets; and pilots were dying daily during that difficult and dangerous period. He set dozens of records in aviation and had no peer in the current active world of Marine aviation.

He was known as one of the finest pilots to ever grace the skies and was selected to command the first Marine jet squadron. He also led America's very first jet aerobatic demonstration team. I knew of him by personal reputation only. The General was known to be somewhat controversial. He was feared by many and never did I think I would be standing in front of him.

Standing at attention, I answered his questions until he finally gave me a chance to speak freely. I told him as quietly and politely as I could that I wanted to remain in my squadron and continue flying. I thought

171

he wanted a volunteer and the other two candidates desperately wanted the job, so I assumed I was off the hook.

I returned to the squadron area elated as though a ton had been lifted off my back. I invited every VMA-223 lieutenant I could find to join me at the officers club for drinks on me.

A week later I walked into the squadron Admin Office and was told to pack my bags because I was the new general's aide. It was a crushing moment. I was a Marine, however, and an order was an order, so I packed up and headed for Danang, Vietnam. I had managed to stay in a tactical squadron for nearly three years when most lieutenants were only allowed one, so I had no reason to complain. I thought my flying had finally come to an end.

Life with a Legend – BGen Marion Carl

I did not like the idea of being a general's aide but was determined to do it well. I had three days of on the job training before Joe Maiden departed. Three weeks would have been more appropriate. Everything was foreign to me as I learned the daily routine and who was who in the command staff at Danang. Then there was the complicated phone system along with dozens of other small details to memorize, none of which had anything to do with flying an airplane.

I was in the midst of full bird colonels, a few lieutenant colonels, and an occasional general. I was extremely uncomfortable. Joe Maiden left and I was on my own. My first day was hectic as I met the aides of the other generals when Lieutenant General Victor "The Brute" Krulak arrived for an impromptu visit and inspection. Krulak was short in stature but his name evoked fear. He was legendary throughout the Marine Corps. General Carl and I were there when his entourage arrived and the activity was frenetic as people rushed everywhere in preparation. I found General Carl, and said, "Sir, everyone is telling me what to do and I'm confused. Since I'm *your* aide I thought I better come ask what *you* want me to do." There was a hint of a smile as he told me to take the jeep and go back to Group Headquarters and make sure they knew General Krulak was on the way. As I headed for the jeep I ran straight into General Krulak and while he may have been short I had no problem seeing the three stars on his collars.

I snapped a salute saying, "Good morning, Sir," hoping he would continue on his way. Instead, he returned my salute and stopped directly in front of me. I stood at attention as he looked up at me and said, "Who do you work for, son?" I heard stories of people who looked down at him, which seemed the normal thing to do, but I knew that was an invitation to absolute disaster. With my eyes straight ahead as I looked over the top of his head, I replied, "Sir, I'm General Carl's new aide, Sir." He paused and said, "He's a good man. Take care of him," and turned to leave. I saluted, exhaled, found our jeep and drove away.

Anytime I had a question of *any* sort, I went directly to General Carl. It was the beginning of a lifetime relationship between this legend of a man and myself, although I had no idea at the time.

The aides for the other generals felt sorry for me. General Carl was a quiet man with a no-nonsense reputation; people were uneasy and fearful around him. He was tall and slim but sinew strong. It was easy to imagine him growing up on an Oregon farm. I liked him almost immediately. I was on the job a couple of days when he called me into his office. He said, "This is probably the only time in your career you'll be working directly for a general. I see this as a fifty-fifty thing; fifty percent involves what you can do for me and fifty percent involves what I can do for you because I'll be writing your fitness report." I nodded quietly, but I was blown away. What an extraordinary attitude for a general to display toward his aide. I thought my job was simply a one-sided proposition and I was there to do whatever he wished.

Before Joe Maiden left I asked if the general ever did any flying. Joe's eyebrows shot up and he said, "Oh yeah! He flies fifty to sixty hours a month." That was a *lot* of flying so I asked, "Do you ever go with him?" Joe replied, "No, he does all the flying; you won't get to fly at all."

General Carl flew everything the Marine Corps had, but he did most of his flying in the UH-1E "Huey" helicopter. It served his purpose best by allowing him to get directly into the battlefield areas and observe first-hand what was going on. The first time he told me to call for a Huey I asked if I could go and he said yes. A lieutenant from the helicopter base at Marble Mountain, located five miles away to the east, landed at our helicopter pad and we walked out. I rode in the back with the gunner while we spent most of the day in the field. I didn't enjoy riding rear seat in the Huey, but it was the only way I could get in the air.

One morning when the general was gone I noticed a Huey NATOPS manual on his desk and I hurriedly began scanning it. The thick NATOPS manual contained everything to be known about the aircraft, its operating limitations and procedures, along with all the emergency procedures. After scanning it I placed it back on the general's desk before he returned. A day or so later he asked me to get a helicopter for him and as we walked to the helo pad I began to ask him questions about things I read in the manual. We got in the helicopter, I took my place in the back, and we lifted off. This time we unexpectedly returned to Marble Mountain and he told the lieutenant in the copilot position to get out, then turned to me and told me to get in the seat. From then on I became the copilot and did much of the flying when we weren't in the middle of a lot of shooting. I logged eighty hours of stick time in the Huey and became comfortably proficient.

I never failed to go with him and we spent many long days flying together, occasionally returning late at night after the mess hall was closed. Someone would let us in and we'd eat a quiet meal together. He talked very little and I grew comfortable with his silence.

Most of our flying was unauthorized and we were doing it anonymously since we never used a call sign. When high-ranking officers flew they always had an accompanying aircraft in the event of an emergency but we always traveled alone. We were hit twice and each time it was kept quiet. On one occasion we took a hit through the main rotor blade. Upon landing the general met with the squadron CO and I was surrounded by lieutenants. As they looked at the rotor blade, one of them asked me, "Does he *order* you to fly with him?!" I replied no and he retorted, "That's the only goddamned way *I'd* go with him!"

Christmas, 1965, in Vietnam was hot and rainy. I thought about Barbara, Scott, and Jay back home in Texas and was glad they were safe. I wrote a "last letter home" in the form of a poem but hoped it would never be sent. Rarely did I go a day without writing a letter to

Barbara or she to me. At times I would go days without mail and then finally receive several of her letters at once.

Tom Eldridge received his regular commission with me a few months earlier. He was sent to VMA-211 when I went to 223. He died on December 29th, 1965, after being severely wounded through the legs by machine gun fire as he made a run on an enemy position. He almost made it back, but crashed twelve miles south of Chu Lai. The area was so hotly contested it took nearly two years to recover his body. Tom, or "Taz" as he was known, had been a good friend; we had some great times together. We were all shocked at his death. It was a huge loss to the squadron and those of us who knew him best agonized over his death.

Ted Lamparter was a close friend who was in my preflight class in Pensacola and again later at Whiting Field. He and his wife Candy were a handsome couple and I spent many evenings with them and their little daughter. Ted dropped out of flight training at Whiting Field and I lost track of them. Somehow they received word that I was killed in Vietnam and wrote Barbara a heartfelt letter expressing their condolences. Barbara was extremely shaken when she read it, rushing to get my latest letter to check the date on it. She and her mom decided they would have received the dreaded knock on the door by two Marine officers if I had been killed. Still, Barbara was very anxious and distraught for the next few days, until she received another letter from me. She wrote to Ted and Candy, who were mortified by their mistake, but Barbara graciously thanked them for their concern and for taking the time to track her down.

The base at Danang offered creature comforts I never had at Chu Lai. I was eating at the General's Mess and the food was excellent. Liquor and ice were both available, and I was now living in a hooch versus a tent.

There were some Red Cross girls in downtown Danang, another place off limits for us. They lived in an old French home and were known for their parties. One night I was drunk and a number of my buddies suggested we drive into Danang and party with the Red Cross girls. I was the only one with access to a jeep, the general's, and I agreed to drive—without getting permission from the general. We stuffed a record number of lieutenants and a couple of captains in the jeep and off we went. I remember very little about the party except we weren't welcome. The girls grudgingly gave us some drinks as a buyoff for our departure.

On the way back someone noticed we were missing part of our original crew and had picked up some strangers in their place. It was too late to turn back so we pressed on. Approaching the base I realized we were spectacularly overloaded, everyone was solidly drunk, and we were going to have a difficult time with the Air Police manning the gate. I put the gas pedal to the floor and ran the gate. After an exciting chase they finally caught us when we turned into a dead end street. For unknown reasons they did not write us up, which would have been catastrophic when the general got the paperwork. I think they were so amazed at the audacity of our group they were willing to grin and shrug it off.

A short while later someone actually stole the jeep. The Chief of Staff, Colonel Bronlueewe, was irate and I heard him tell the general that he recently heard the jeep driving in late and he knew something was going on. The theft of government property was a serious matter and an investigation was ordered. I took a deep breath when I noted the officer assigned to the investigation was a captain who was on the trip with us. He and I both decided this was a delicate matter and should not be over-investigated. The jeep was eventually found twenty miles away at a Naval field medical center.

On February 14, 1966, I was airborne with the general and Operation Double Eagle was in progress. Helicopters were everywhere as Marines engaged the enemy on the ground. The general and I were orbiting and saw several helicopters target a wooded area firing rockets into the midst of the trees. Without using a call sign, the general told them to cease fire while we assessed the situation. Passing over a hot area at a low altitude was dangerous, but we made a pass and observed two enemy who appeared dead. When we came around a second time, one was gone. Without warning the general landed in a rice paddy next to the wooded area and asked if I wanted to go in and get him.

Every fiber in my body was screaming, "Hell no, I don't want to go in there!" but when my mouth opened all I heard was, "Yes sir." I grabbed an M-16 rifle and walked to the edge of the wooded area, the sound of the chopper's blades cutting the air behind me. The cover was thick and I had to make several attempts before I found an opening. The thick brush was drowning out the sound of the Huey engines still running in the distance. It was dark and foreboding inside the heavy cover.

I moved slowly and quietly, glancing all around. I had the feeling of being watched. It occurred to me if I were the wounded man in this situation I would take someone with me. I was not supposed to die on the ground like this; I was supposed to die in a cockpit — and I was only two months from going home. I wondered if this man had a wife and family as I did, and I wondered if he also hoped to survive long enough to return to them. Suddenly, I did not want to find him. I was scared and knew I would shoot at any movement. Guilt coursed through me. I was a Marine, dedicated to killing the enemy, and I did not want to kill this man.

I picked my way slowly, scanning every part of the brushy area and the shadows. I glanced down and was startled to see an AK-47 with blood on it. The front hand guard was shattered, probably due to the rockets from the other aircraft. I knew it belonged to the man I was looking for – and I knew he had to be close by. I heard the gunner calling me from the edge of the woods so I took the AK-47 and made my way out, glad it was over.

I came out of the woods into the rice paddy and saw that another helicopter had landed. I walked over to the general. The other pilot saw me walking with the rifle and radioed a request to the general asking if he could have the rifle. The general was not supposed to be doing this kind of flying and didn't want any evidence of it, so he told me to go give the AK-47 to the other helo pilot. I was angry about giving it up and as I handed it to the other helicopter pilot, I said, "Next time you want one of these you can go in and get it yourself!" I stormed back to my own Huey.

We lifted off and again circled the area. Suddenly a figure burst from cover and ran down the side of a creek. The gunner in the back opened fire and the general yelled at him to cease firing. We chased the man down and hovered, the rotor wash was beating the tall grass down and exposing the man. He was to the left side of the Huey near the General's window. General Carl motioned for him to come out as I watched. With adrenaline coursing through my body I shouted over the intercom, "If you'll set this f-----g thing down I'll go get him!" In the excitement I forgot that I was talking to a General, but he ignored me and landed as the man came out. Prior to coming out the prisoner bent down and dropped something in the creek but it was too deep to retrieve anything. I brought the man back, but another helicopter landed and took him back to Quang Ngai where he would be interrogated. Both the general and I hoped no one recognized us.

A month later, on March 20th, I would repeat this exercise but it would be in a more open area, in the midst of a firefight and withdrawal of Marine troops during another operation. This time there was two VC and they split up. We caught one and turned him over to another helicopter.

When I joined General Carl I thought I had seen the last of my days in the air. In reality I got to see a whole different sort of air war with him. I saw and experienced a lot and got a first hand, up-close look at the brutality of war – the dead and dying, and the struggle to stay alive.

In his quiet way, the General made sure I gained an education during the four months I was with him. Even though I fought the assignment as his aide, I developed a real fondness and respect for this legendary officer. I was with him daily for four months and shared some remarkable experiences with him. He was the most humble man I've ever met, completely unimpressed with himself and his many legendary accomplishments. He was honest and genuine, completely unpretentious, and he was his own man.

I left the General on April 6, 1966, and returned home to the United States. He was slated to return three days later. As I left him I said, "General, I did everything I could to avoid being your aide but I would have missed so very much if I had been successful. I'm truly glad it worked out the way it did." Our paths never crossed again until two decades later.

The next day about two hundred of us were packed like sardines in the Marine C-130 with no room to move in any direction, but I didn't care – I was headed home. As we took off, I looked back and saw the coastline of Vietnam disappearing behind us. All my experiences of the past year and a month seemed surreal.

Vietnam disappeared behind me and I inhaled deeply. It was over. The war marked me in ways I didn't realize at the time. As an A4 pilot I knew I was responsible for the deaths of people on the ground and wondered how many might have been innocents caught in the war. I was glad I never saw the people I bombed, rocketed, or strafed. As I came in fast, there might be a fleeting glimpse of movement or activity, but I never had to deal with close-up encounters. Fighting from the cockpit sanitized that part of the war. But my time with General Carl put me on the ground and I observed the destruction up close. I saw bodies alleged to be Viet Cong carried away from a battlefield over poles, much like a hunter might bring out a deer – limp, bloody, mangled, and impersonal. But I knew each of them had loved ones who felt about them as Barbara and my family felt about me. It was difficult to shrug that off and hide behind my shield as a tough Marine.

I saw a wounded American on the hospital ship Repose with his intestines resting on his stomach inside a fluid bag to keep them moist. But I saw nothing compared to the daily horrific scenes the Marines on the ground were exposed to. I did not regret my part in the fighting; I knew I answered the call of my country, but the war changed me.

Years later, I regretted the sacrifices of my comrades. Tom and Gus were forever frozen in my mind as young twenty-five year olds. They would never know the joy of children and grandchildren.

Barbara left our two small sons with her mother in Texas and met me at MCAS El Toro. I was in for another treat once we headed home. I saw my wife for the first time in thirteen months and she was beautiful! It was wonderful to kiss and hug her for the first time in over a year. She lost weight during my absence; her arms and legs were thinner. She had also started smoking; I asked her to stop and she did.

We decided to go to Las Vegas for several days before going home to Texas. I wanted to go via Greyhound bus so I could just sit and soak up the American landscape, free of rice paddies, bomb craters, and the sights of war. I was in uniform and when we boarded the bus we couldn't find two seats together. I asked a woman if she would mind switching to the row ahead, telling her I hadn't seen my wife in thirteen months. To my surprise she refused. Before I could react a gentleman sitting a row back said, "Here, Lieutenant, you can have my seat and I'll sit next to this bitch!"

Barbara was jubilant and happy. She was gushing with news of the boys, describing how they'd changed as she showed me all the latest pictures. We were two people euphorically happy at being together again.

I was anxious to get home and see my sons, so a few days later we boarded a plane and headed for San Antonio. Barb's mom met us with the two boys. They had grown so much since I'd left. When I left for Vietnam Jay was a non-distinct looking six month old and he had turned into a cute nineteen month old little boy with his mother's brown eyes. Scott was taller and heavier, now two and a half, and talking, which surprised me. When he called me "Daddy," it was a sound I wanted to hear over and over. I coaxed him to say it again and again. Both boys immediately came to me with no hesitation and my heart was bursting with love and gratitude. I had so much to be thankful for, a beautiful, sweet, loving wife and two wonderful little boys. I was alive and away from the killing.

FPC Atlanta – Prison 1990-91

For the most part, I was somewhat laid back in prison, or at least as much as one can be in that place. Fear is a state of mind and I opted to accept whatever took place. I got along well with most inmates although I didn't go out of my way to be friendly. I had much more difficulty with the guards.

I sat in the mess hall at the end of my second week. I made no deliberate effort to learn names, but as I looked down the chow line I knew almost everyone's name. Most of the inmates were not first-timers, they were in trouble most of their lives. Most were not accustomed to decent treatment and lived by the rules of the jungles they survived in. Prison is meant to de-personalize. Inmates were called by their last name only, or it was prefaced with "Inmate".

Anytime I met someone I used their first name and the result was surprising. To simply acknowledge their humanity by using a first name evoked an unexpected reaction. I patronized no one, but was generally treated with respect in return. A few even called me Captain as they nodded and spoke, surprising me. Most smiled when they spoke, also surprising me.

In prison, everything is a quid pro quo and everything has a price. There's an underground economy and I paid an inmate fifty cents to iron my best set of khakis for visiting day. They were only worn for visits and I could usually get a couple of weeks out of a set, since we kept the visits short. I didn't want Barbara to spend an entire day in a prison visiting room. It was too much for me as well.

One can buy most anything in prison. Booze and drugs were available for a price. A large guard was known to help ease their way in. I disregarded the quid pro quo rule and often wrote letters home for inmates who couldn't write. If I could help someone, I did; I wasn't going anywhere so it was no big deal. I wrote a successful appeal for a young African-American inmate and I thought he was going to hug me when he learned he would be transferred to Miami. His wife and six kids were too poor to visit him in Atlanta. It felt good that I was able to help.

I received little favors also. One of the kitchen inmates whispered to me one day, "Go look under your pillow." I discovered a delicious bacon and egg sandwich. Prison food was atrocious, so this was a delightful treat. I stuck it under my shirt and made my way to a bathroom stall where I could close the door and eat it without being snitched out by someone.

One visiting day early in my confinement, Barbara came in and handed me an envelope. She had a large, clear plastic purse that allowed the guards to quickly inspect it, but their mood determined what she could bring in from week to week. The envelope contained another check from Charlie Young, again for $10,000. I was stunned. I told her to hold onto it and let me think before she cashed it. For a solid month I struggled with whether we should accept it or not. My mentor and many friends thought we should. Still, I wasn't so sure. We would need the money when I got out, but I didn't think that made it okay. I had an insurance policy that provided a small amount of income but it seemed to exempt alcoholism. Denny Olden, a Northwest Captain in charge of our pilot insurance program, made a trip to the insurance company. He pushed our policy through so Barb was getting a small amount to survive on day to day. In light of that I didn't think it was right to take Charlie's check.

I thought about the Lord's Prayer and the phrase that says, "Give us *this day* our daily bread." It didn't mention anything about next week's. We were getting by, day to day, so I told Barbara to send it back to Charlie. Giving $10,000 back was a hard decision when I was making twelve cents an hour, but I thought it was the right thing to do. I wrote

Charlie another long letter, thanking him and explaining why I was returning the check. I told him the gesture itself contained more value than the amount of the check. Charlie then enrolled us in a monthly food plan from Harry and David's. Barbara began receiving a gourmet meat and dessert of the month. I could not have afforded the gold stamped packages the food came in, much less the food itself.

There were five or six other pilots in prison, all of them drug smugglers. One was a former Northwest pilot, whom I liked, and another was a former Delta pilot who was a snitch. The others came from varying backgrounds. Dewey, a former Air Force pilot, ran the laundry and was an aging, long-term convict. He had flown for a drug cartel in South America before being caught. One pilot had been a superbly credentialed defense attorney in the Pittsburgh area, exceedingly well known and highly successful. He told me that a million dollars in cash stacked on a table in front of him was an irresistibly powerful sight. I had no desire to associate with this group, so I kept my distance. I was the only pilot there who had not been flying drugs for hire. I received some interesting job offers that would not require an FAA certificate.

One day I saw the prison SWAT team run by. A couple of years after I left prison, this SWAT team goon squad would go through the buildings where I once lived. They would brutalize the inmates and send seventeen of them to local area hospitals, including one who was blind and defenseless. Prison officials split up the wounded, sending them to various hospitals to cover up the scale of the beatings. The Atlanta Journal-Constitution reported the story but it quickly died a smothered death, as do most prison stories involving misconduct by prison staff.

One of the regular prison guards was Parker. Every time he was on duty he came in with three or four times the normal required urine kits. He was fascinated with watching inmates urinate and would stoop down so he was inches away from their penis. I would soon encounter him.

Emory University supplied teachers to instruct five college courses per semester at the prison. Since I had no college background, I intended to take the courses. The Atlanta prison staff harassed the teachers, making them wait for prolonged periods of time, losing their paperwork, and giving them a hard time in general. Still, they persevered.

185

Pell Grants allowed me to take the courses. I began with a course in remedial math even though Julie Cullen thought I had a calculator in my head. I refreshed my algebra skills and made a 4.0 in the course. Next, I took English 101, from Dr. Jim Bryant. After I got out of prison, I learned he was also an ordained minister and I honored his request to speak at his church one Sunday morning.

As I began my English course, Dr. Bryant asked for a writing sample. We were to write several pages about ourselves since that required no research. I turned my paper in with the others. The next week he handed all the papers back with the exception of mine and said he wanted to see me after the class. I immediately thought I failed the first assignment. Instead, he took me aside and encouraged me to write a book, saying he had never been so impressed with a first draft of anything. Although I was surprised and flattered, I looked around and thought the prison bell curve was so low that almost anyone who could write a complete sentence would score high. So I shrugged off the compliment and forgot about it.

I made a 4.0 in that class as well as English 102, which Dr. Bryant also taught. I was dumbfounded when again he pushed me to write, saying, "I think you have several books inside you." Next, came a marketing class and I pulled a 4.0 there also. We only had five classes to pick from and one or two were Biblical courses. I didn't care what the subject matter was; I wanted to learn and make the time serve me instead of me serving the time.

I was in a work camp and we worked all day. Classes came at night, after the workday was over, so one needed to be motivated to pursue class work. After I got out of prison, the powers that be killed the Pell Grants for inmates☐a brainless error that will cost society in the long term.

The prison had a nice visiting room. It had new facilities, an all-glass view of the outdoors, vending machines (owned by guards), and shiny floors. It was their showplace and they hoped everyone thought the back end was as attractive as the visiting room. It wasn't. Each inmate was allowed fifteen visitors on a list approved through the NCIC, the National Crime Information Computer. A normal person could process a request in thirty minutes. In prison, it took three to six months.

The total of fifteen visitors was all inclusive and included lawyers, family members, and friends. I fed in application after application, timing and staggering them to not draw attention. When I got one back, I would send it to Barbara and tell her to make a copy to be sent to the potential visitor. She would tell the person to be sure to bring it with them because it was likely the original never made it to my folder. I learned early that prison staff couldn't get a piece of paper from one side of the room to the other without losing it. Several times, a visitor came in from out of town to see me and was told there was no approval form in my file. They would present the copy and the guard in the visiting room would react as though he just witnessed magic. The guard could *never* understand how a visitor could have a prison approval form in *their* possession. Without having it, several would have come long distances only to be turned away.

One weekend, Scott, Barbara, and Dawn came for a visit. The guard at the desk was trying to match their forms to their individual driver's licenses, which were on his desk. Scott stood, watched, and remained silent as the guard shuffled three driver's licenses among the forms, unable to get them matched up. Finally, the guard gave up in exasperation and waved them in. Scott was astonished at the guard; I was not. I informed Scott that the guards picked for the visiting room were the crème de la crème, so he could only imagine what was in the back of the prison.

Another weekend, the guard who handled the visitor applications motioned me over. He was one of the minority of white guards and said to me, "Prouse, don' put no mo' applications in fer visitors," and I simply said okay without any additional response. He continued, "I wuz goin' through yo' file and yew got fohty-three in there." I kept a straight face and said nothing. I knew they were too lazy and too incompetent to count so I took advantage of it. It was one of the rare times in prison when their stupidity worked in my favor.

Barbara was allowed to hug and kiss me when I entered and departed the visiting room, but we could have no contact during the visit. I was searched before I entered and as I departed. Still, there were ways to get things in. We had virtually no medical help so I got some band-aids and aspirin in. I had a paper-thin khaki jacket and the Atlanta winters were cold and wet. As a Marine, I learned the worst thing that could happen to a POW was to get sick, and I did *not* want to get sick in prison. A family member wore my old Marine field jacket in to visit me one day. I ditched the paper-thin khaki jacket in the bathroom and wore the field jacket back into the prison. It helped immensely. There were all sorts of contraband visible in the prison, but the unspoken rule seemed to be, "If you can get it in, you can keep it."

I had tiny back and forth moments about ever flying again. In view of all that had occurred, a return to the cockpit seemed impossible. Sanctions were put in place to make sure of that. But as the days went by I continued to apply what I learned in treatment and had fleeting moments where I could dream the impossible. One of my daily meditation readings said, "Before any dream can come true, there must first *be* a dream." For me, the challenge was how to dream while keeping it balanced with harsh reality.

I found peace in pleasant memories of Barbara and me when we were young and just starting out. We had been so happy and much adventure lay ahead.

The Dream of Flying Again

I was stripped of everything and the FAA demanded two years of "demonstrated sobriety" before I could approach them about getting my medical certificate back. Since booze and drugs were plentiful in prison, I was concerned the FAA would force me to begin from my release date. My regular FAA doctor made numerous attempts to contact the prison to establish random drug tests for me but gave up after the prison refused to respond. A doctor I was in treatment with offered to come out and do the random drug screens. It was a surreptitious and risky maneuver because I would go to the hole if caught. We slipped into two stalls in the men's room and Bob would pass the specimen container to me. I would provide the sample and pass it back under the stall. Bob even paid the monthly cost, about $35, another appreciated kindness since I was only making $19.20 per month.

I didn't know if the FAA would accept what we were doing, but it was the best I could do. It turned out not to be a problem.

Two weeks into prison, Barbara came to visit and gave me some startling news. Nine of my fellow pilots had begun making our monthly house payments. Two were people I knew by name only. I was repeatedly struck in the heart by things people did for us, and this was another of those moments. Once I was out of prison, I made four strong attempts to get them to stop but Ed Landers told me each time, "We meet every six months and when we get ready to stop we'll let you know." They never stopped during our time of struggle.

These acts of kindness stood in sharp contrast to what I daily witnessed in prison. One day I walked into the prison office area and behind a plate glass window I saw three guards handcuffing a large African-American inmate, tears streaming down his cheeks. The inmate was young, perhaps twenty-three, over six feet, and three hundred pounds or more. The guards told the inmate his father died and they were taking him to the hole to prevent him from trying to get to the funeral.

We had three inmate counts each day. The first was at 4:00 P.M. and was a standing silent count in the individual cubicles. The next was at 9:00 P.M. and everyone froze where they were as the guards came through and counted. The third took place at night as we slept.

The housing areas were laid out in a large U shape, with cubicles going completely around the U. One guard would walk in one side of the U and make his count going all the way around. Then the second guard came in the other side and did likewise. They both disappeared outside to compare numbers and no inmate could move until they announced the count was clear. Rarely did they get it right the first time. The record occurred one night as they made nine different count attempts before both of their numbers matched. My prison journal notes a number of nights I was late for my college class because the guards began their counts at 4:00 P.M. and were still trying to get them right when my class started.

I met Howard Shapiro a day or so after entering prison. He knew I was the alcoholic pilot who had just come in and he introduced himself. I wasn't particularly interested in talking with him but I was polite. Then he told me he was a compulsive gambler and belonged to a recovery group. He was in prison as a direct result of his gambling, having embezzled funds to engage in his addiction. Once I knew that, I became more interested in speaking with him.

Howard was five feet ten and weighed two hundred and seventy four pounds. He had sad, baggy eyes and a strong Boston accent; we had absolutely nothing in common. He was a well-educated CPA from a wealthy family in Boston. He lived a life of privilege in his Jewish community, but became the disgrace of his family. He received no mail and had no visitors.

If I was challenged to pick one inmate among the five hundred who would end up as close to me as a brother, Howard would have been in the last ten inmates remaining.

He was a charter member of the recovery group I started and was there every week. We talked about recovery constantly. I began to learn more about compulsive gambling. We logged countless laps around the walking track in the evenings and during the weekends. It was not uncommon for us to walk thirty miles on a weekend as we talked. When I left prison, he told me he had recorded our walks and we'd logged one thousand miles together. We could have walked from Atlanta to one hundred miles shy of Amarillo, Texas.

Howard was my only close friend among the inmates and we looked forward to spending time together once we were both free of prison. I listened to Howard talk about his gambling and it occurred to me how similar it was, in many ways, to my alcoholism. As he related situations, he would say, "and then I'd place a bet." If I simply substituted the words, "and then I'd take a drink," the two addictions became interchangeable.

There were differences, however. Howard pointed out that he could go to the horse track, place a bet, then attend a recovery meeting and no one would know. He said, "You can't drink a beer and go to a meeting because they'll smell it and know you drank."

He adored Barbara because she would send him a card once a week. And she sent him a daily meditation book that he cherished. Since he received no mail and no visits, these things were special for him. It was against the rules for her to correspond with another inmate so she put a Happy Face at the bottom as her signature. Howard could hardly wait to show me each card.

With one exception, Howard was the only inmate with an advanced degree. Dewberry grudgingly allowed him to work in the education department, but before it was over he would have some harrowing experiences with her. Howard loved helping the other inmates and was a dedicated teacher, spending many off duty hours working with them.

Everyone in the education department was black except Howard. Dewberry brought another African American inmate in, Ron Westmoreland, whom she liked. Ron hadn't even completed high school and Howard watched as he struggled to understand basic fractions,

191

unable to find the common denominator. He was inept as a teacher but Dewberry gave him fives on his work report while giving Howard threes. This kind of treatment was pure, blatant racial discrimination but it was simply the norm at the Atlanta Federal Prison.

Mysteriously, Dewberry appeared to wield heavy influence in the camp and prison area. I concluded she must have something on the higher-ups because she got away with extraordinary things. It was widely rumored that she was a heavy cocaine user. Paranoia is a strong by product of heavy cocaine use and hers rivaled Captain Queeg's; the only thing missing were the ball bearings.

Few people attempted to help inmates but Ms. Levi was one who did. She was an enthusiastic worker who somehow managed to get into the education department after Howard's arrival. She was well thought of by the inmates, but Dewberry disliked her intensely. A federal mandate required that every inmate should leave with a minimum eighth-grade education and Dewberry was unable to meet even that minimal requirement.

A short while later, Ms. Levi and Dewberry had an explosive blow up. Dewberry could be heard yelling in the compound as she screamed at Ms. Levi "You've invaded a black department!" A week later, Ms. Levi was gone, and so was any chance she brought to the inmates for educational help.

Prior to prison, I enrolled in a financial planning correspondence course. A requirement for the course was a small, hand-held Hewlett-Packard financial calculator. Dewberry took an instant dislike to me and refused to allow it in, saying it could be made into a bomb.

I wrote to Ms. Ginger Current, the registrar for the college, and informed her of the situation. I minced no words as I described the situation in the prison. I strongly emphasized that all correspondence between us *must* remain confidential, or I would be in a position of serious jeopardy if she disclosed anything.

Ginger Current wrote Dewberry a letter saying the calculator was vital to completion of the course and that it should be obvious to anyone. Dewberry called me in and angrily demanded a copy of my letter to the college. I had no access to a copier and I informed her no copy was available. She demanded I write the college and have them send her a copy. I informed her that the prison was able to read all my incoming or outgoing mail but there was no provision whereby I had to *retrieve* letters so they could read them. Dewberry said she would write the college and get a copy. I told Barbara to call Ginger Current to make sure that didn't happen or I would end up in the hole.

Ginger Current informed Dewberry the prison would have to subpoena any correspondence they wanted and then called Barbara to inform her. Dewberry called me in and said she received a copy of my letter from the college, which I knew to be a lie. It was clear Dewberry was going to do everything in her power to thwart the calculator coming in and prevent me from taking the course. An inmate seldom challenges the prison system since it is nearly always a losing proposition. I went to Mike Michaels, an inmate who had been locked up a long time, and sought his advice. Mike was a bright guy and knew more about the intricacies of prison life than I did.

He informed me I could file a Form BP-9 against Dewberry, but cautioned that I should be prepared to go to war if I did because she would come after me with everything she had. He told me I would need to steamroll her because I would get buried if I lost my resolve. He emphasized I should not make this decision lightly. I told Mike I just wanted to do my time and be left alone. Mike said it didn't work that way. Either the prison staff would pick me to pieces if I chose to be passive or I would have to stand and fight.

Many things happen to inmates in prison. If an inmate causes trouble, guards can (and do) plant drugs or other contraband in his locker and send him to the hole. "Diesel therapy" is a means whereby inmates can disappear for weeks and months, then surface at some prison thousands of miles away. In the meantime, the stress can be immeasurable to family members until the inmate surfaces. There were some specially configured prison busses for this procedure.

Without warning, an inmate is handcuffed, led away, and put on one of the busses. The busses are driven ten to twelve hours a day for several weeks. At the end of each day the bus arrives at an en route prison where the inmates are locked up for the night. Early the next morning the routine begins again. One or two daily restroom stops are made and the rest of the day is spent handcuffed to special bars in front of each seat. If it's

193

winter, the heat is kept off while the driver and guards wear their jackets and the inmates freeze. No personal effects are allowed so clean clothes and toiletries are a problem. No mail comes or goes for the duration of the trip; then it takes months for mail to catch up. After a week or two on the road, most inmates have had enough and are pacified.

I filed the BP-9 against Dewberry and the struggle began. As expected, it was refused at the local level and sent back to me. I followed Mike's guidance and filed a BP-10. Dewberry submitted a written rebuttal, lying through her teeth. Having been a Marine Corps legal officer, I kept documented notes with dates, times, and quotes. I noted every single detail, every letter written, and every letter received, along with dates for those also.

I buried her with facts. The BP-10 came back denied again, this time from a higher echelon in the prison system, but Dewberry was becoming worried. I filed a BP-11, this time going well beyond the Atlanta regime, outside her area of influence; I threatened legal action in addition to the request for the calculator. I won.

Wilson called me in and said "things had been worked out." I went to Mike Michaels because I wanted to pursue the BP-11 and make Dewberry eat crow. Mike gave me some sage advice. He said, "Remember what you wanted when you started this. You've got it. You won. I suggest you take your winnings and leave the table." He was right. But even though I won the battle I lost the war, because the struggle ate up so much time I was unable to take the course. I knew I made a mortal enemy in Dewberry and had to watch my back. There were many ways for them to get to me if they wished, and I could do nothing about it. I never had problems with the inmates but the guards and staff were impossible. Nearly everything that occurs in prison is a result of intimidation. Nearly always, the prison system does the intimidating, but once in a while an inmate wins. I was hoping that Dewberry would back off now that she knew I would fight.

My release time came and Howard still had a year to go. As we walked our final laps around the prison track the night before my departure, he broke down and wept. We had shared so much together. Howard had dropped seventy pounds and was down to a svelte two hundred and four pounds when I left.

He was finally released and went back to Boston where he began the downhill slide back into his addiction. I saw the signs developing and cautioned him repeatedly. He was soon gambling again. He severed contact with me and I didn't hear from him for nearly fifteen years.

Prison was a nonstop world of Catch-22 insanity. Cretins ran the prison. I thought that confinement and separation from the free world would be my punishment. Living in that insanity day after day, power-less to do anything but accept it, *that* was the punishment. It was also, in some ways, like being the only person alive in a cemetery. It is a system *so bad* that those who have never experienced it cannot believe it and, thus, in the most ironic way, the system protects itself.

Prison is a different thing to different people. I saw inmates come back to prison like it was a homecoming, almost happy to be back. They were back in familiar haunts with three hots, a cot, and a weight pile (outside workout area where the weights were kept). It was not that for me; down deep my Comanche roots longed to be free, to feel the breeze of freedom on my face, smell the rain in free air, to be able to hug and kiss Barbara, and be rid of the sickness of prison.

I had countless more experiences in prison. Learning to cope with them and the insanity of the prison system challenged me. I found myself grateful for all I learned in treatment. Recovery concepts became my means of retaining my sanity. Many inmates approached me over time and asked how I did it, how I could appear to remain unaffected. I did it one day at a time, shorter when necessary.

I left federal prison on August 8, 1991, after serving eight months and three days. Even as I left, the guards played their games. I gathered my few belongings in a cardboard box and headed for R & D. I passed Wilson and he said, "I'll keep a job open fo' yew, Prouse." I responded, "Just make sure it's not one you need to fill right away," and walked past. Knowing he had a life sentence there and would probably die in that madhouse gave me great satisfaction.

Inside R & D, Ms. Ndebe had my papers on a desk where I could see them. Instead of processing me out, she busied herself with sorting mail. She kept glancing my way to see how I was reacting. I knew it was the same stuff I had dealt with for eight months. She was the one who made me come back every night for a week as she teased and taunted me about bringing a recovery book in. I refused to let them get to me the entire time I was there and I wasn't going to surrender now. I laid my head back against the wall and dozed off. Ndebe awoke me, shaking my arm and telling me I needed to sign my release papers.

I received $125.60 from the prison. I had $100.60 in my commissary account and the prison gave me $25 to assist me in the free world.

I was slated for six more months in the federal prison halfway house at Tenth and West Peachtree Street in Atlanta. Eight months and three days may not sound like much to some, but it was an eternity to me. As a convict, locked up and confined, the rain smelled and felt different. So did the breeze. I missed the smell of the earth and the leaves in the fall. I looked at the moon and wondered what it would look like from the outside.

Years later, after I spoke somewhere, a man said to me, "Fourteen months in the prison system? Man, that's nothin'! I spent eighteen years there!" I looked at him, smiled, and said, "Hey, good for you. You win!" It was a long time for me.

I walked out of prison and Barbara was waiting in the parking lot. She waved and smiled as I approached. "I love you!" she yelled and ran to me. I laughed, hugged and kissed her, free of any guard stopping me. We survived this part of the ordeal but much more lay ahead. She was truly the wind beneath my wings and I felt we could survive anything together. In her own way, she went through as much as I did. Even though we stood there in the shadow of the prison, we were both free for the moment.

She told me six pilots came in from various places and were waiting just outside the prison area in a church parking lot. Glenn Eggert and Bill Rataczak flew in from Minnesota the night before. Colie Smith and Dayle Yates came down from Gainesville, Georgia, and Mike Phillips drove down from Cumming, Georgia. Vic Manussier made the trip from Alabama. I shook hands and hugged each one of them. Normally, the standard time allowed for the trip to the halfway house was two hours, but Ndebe ate up most of my time as she played her games. I was released at 9:24 A.M. and was down to a thirty-six minute deadline for reporting to the halfway house in downtown Atlanta. I had to cut the reunion short and head for the Dismas House.

Regardless of what I saw and experienced in prison I accept responsibility for allowing myself to be put there. My job, for the rest of my life, will be to continue to move past any anger and resentment and prevent it from intruding on my peace and serenity. Hatred destroys the hater, and resentments are like taking poison and then waiting for the other person to die. I'm still working on those things.

Prison put me in situations that I probably would never experience elsewhere. I lived in circumstances I never imagined with people I could never have pictured. Prison tested my character, my will, and my spiritual cornerstone. As I walked away, I was at ease with what I learned and felt I had acquitted myself well. I knew I did not possess the power to do it all alone. I thanked God for the strength, the grace, and the dignity He granted me in a dark and horrible setting.

Halfway House

I was called into the prison administration office one Friday afternoon and informed that Congressman Ben Jones would be in the following day to visit me. I was surprised and had no idea why he was coming. I had been in prison for quite some time at this point. Later, I would discover that Juanita Marsh, the founder of Anchor Hospital where I went through treatment, set up a meeting with him. She invited a number of pilots from Birds of a Feather that were also there. All of them discussed my situation and Ben agreed to visit me.

Juanita Marsh was a state judge. She was a beautiful and stately woman, and I guessed her to be in her mid-sixties. I often remarked to Barbara that she must have been breathtakingly beautiful in her younger days. She had a soft, aristocratic, Southern accent; everything about her exuded class. Her family had been the victim of alcohol and drugs, which led her to establish Anchor Hospital. She became one of my strongest supporters my first week at Anchor.

Congressman Ben Jones was an actor prior to going to Washington. He was well known for his role as "Cooter" on the hit TV show, "Dukes of Hazard." Ben also knew a lot about alcoholism and recovery. Since I lived in his congressional district, he was interested in my situation.

Juanita Marsh and Ben Jones arrived to visit me on June 8, 1991. Barbara was also there. The visiting room was buzzing as the inmates recognized Ben. Most did not recognize him as a congressman but they were excited about seeing "Cooter." Juanita asked the visiting room guard if we could use one of the small, closed off rooms reserved for lawyers and their clients. The guard refused because Juanita was a judge. When Ben Jones heard this, he went over to the guard and informed him a judge had to be a lawyer *before* they became a judge. We then got the use of the room. Ben was laughing and shaking his head at the blatant ignorance; I informed him it was the norm.

Ben's visit rattled the prison administration. Ben told me he saw me on TV and was impressed with the way I handled things. He went to see the camp administrator and then paid Ms. Bischoff, Julie Cullen's supervisor, a visit. He was pushing to get me the maximum amount of halfway house that could be awarded – six months.

This was exciting news to me and I was also in awe that a congressman would come see me. Shortly after Ben's visit I noticed a deafening silence in much of the harassment I got from the guards. As the months passed, Hurlman, the guard who was there when I was first admitted, made several attempts to intimidate me in front of other inmates. Early in my incarceration, he intercepted and read a letter in which I specifically cited the prison administration's blundering incompetence and he threatened me with serious consequences. Once, he called me into his office where three black inmates were present. They were laughing and visiting with him, and one was propped back in a chair with his feet on Hurlman's desk. Hurlman used me for show and tell as he attempted to intimidate me in front of the others. I said nothing, but simply stood and stared at him. Once he was done, I was permitted to leave and Hurlman continued his visit with the other inmates. He confronted me repeatedly but was unable to intimidate me.

Hurlman approached me one morning after Ben's visit and was clearly nervous. He awkwardly attempted to smile and be pleasant to me. I remained quiet and kept a straight face but smiled inwardly, enjoying every minute of it as he uncomfortably shifted back and forth. Finally, he managed some words and hurriedly moved on. It was clear he was worried now that I had a congressman backing me. He wasn't the only one in prison administration who was concerned.

The prison was notorious for missing release dates. I never saw *anyone* released on time. Sometimes the prison delayed the release a week, sometimes a month, but it *never* occurred on the actual release date. One inmate succeeded in getting his lawyer involved and the prison was going to be fined $1,000 for every day they delayed his release. He was immediately released. Another inmate was anxiously packed and ready to go when the prison informed him he would have to spend *another year* there. He became suicidal and I spent some time with him and tried to talk him through things. He got out the following day after he managed to reach his lawyer. My release date for halfway house was set for November 1, 1991. But I mentally prepared myself to be there until Christmas. I refused to set myself up as virtually every inmate did.

Now that a congressman was involved, I began to think they just *might* pay some attention and let me out when my date arrived. Finally, they called me in and informed me I would be getting six months in the halfway house. That was almost unheard of; three months had been the previous record.

Adding to the prison's legendary incompetence was their blundering consistency in assigning probation locales. When I first arrived in prison an inmate left the administration office and walked by me shaking his head. He was operating a drug boat out of Texas when he was arrested and the boat seized. As a Texas resident he hoped to return home upon release. But thus far, the prison assigned him to a probation office first in Kentucky, then many months later to Tennessee. Finally, more than a year later, he was being sent to North Carolina. He said it might be easier to move his family to North Carolina than get the paperwork corrected for his Texas home. A year or more could easily be eaten up by errors and reprocessing.

True to their modus operandi, when my paperwork came in just days before I was to be released, they assigned me to a probation office *in Boston, Massachusetts*. With mere days before my release, I could see the writing on the wall with another month or two in prison. I informed them Congressman Ben Jones was coming to the prison to pick me up on my release date. I made that up, but they got the paperwork straightened out in record time. I left the prison on August 8, 1991 and headed for the Dismas House in downtown Atlanta, located at Tenth and West Peachtree. I reported in and began to settle into my new surroundings.

Dismas House was staffed and operated very much like the prison. Racial prejudice permeated the halfway house, so nothing changed. Dismas House was in a decrepit building with torn and mismatched carpet, scarred furniture, and rusted bars over the windows. At the lecture for the fire drills, we were told it would burn to the ground in four minutes, and I didn't doubt it.

Ms. Gladys Scott, a ponderously obese lady, was the director. Ms. Doris Lawrence was assistant director and she was a vindictive, mean spirited scripture-quoting woman. I sized up the situation pretty quickly.

I was assigned to Dorm seven, bed twelve. Danny Jordan, a fellow inmate from the prison, preceded me and finagled me into the only dorm with windows. What a difference windows made over time.

There were sixteen beds in the room. Mine had a mattress approximately two inches thick, with heavy folds and creases from the baggy, fire-retardant mattress cover. It sagged like a hammock and again I hoped my back would be okay. I had a small locker in which all my personal belongings had to fit.

I was given some free time that day and went home with Barbara. Being with her again was dreamlike, nearly surreal. We felt like newlyweds again. Later, I lay on our couch and relaxed. I dozed off for a few minutes and Barbara said she just kept looking over at me, thinking how wonderful it was to see me there once more. I made several tours of my home, experiencing the wonder of being in a place I once took for granted. I walked into the bathroom and just stood there. It was silent and I was the only one in it. It was a far cry from the madness of the prison facilities.

We went to Southlake Mall and I bought a Sony Walkman. In prison, I used one to escape from my surroundings. Before I left I gave it to an inmate who was poor and wanted one. After the mall we drove to Anchor Hospital, where I had been a patient.

The halfway house required an inmate to obtain employment within ten working days or return to prison. I wrote Anchor from prison and asked if they had anything available. I emphasized that I didn't want them to create a job for me; I would be willing to take anything available. I offered to work on the room cleaning crew, in the business office, or any other place they could use me. To my surprise they wanted me to work in the counseling department.

I was apprehensive and didn't feel qualified. They assured me I was and they wanted me working with other alcoholics and addicts. The following day, August 9th, Barbara picked me up at the halfway house and drove me to Anchor. As I saw the sign for Anchor Hospital, I remembered my fear and disgrace on the night we first drove down the hill. Now, it was warm and welcoming. I instantly felt at home as I walked through the main entrance. I had such good and grateful memories of the place that saved my life and taught me so much. The staff was warm and gracious and I could feel their love and support. It was so different from the prison setting I'd just come from.

I had to be back at the halfway house by 3:00 P.M. so Barbara and I hurried back and I checked back in at 2:53. I turned in all the documentation I needed for automobile privileges, but those would be a while. Since I was already starting a new job the next day, I was told I would have eight hours of free time on Sunday. I was elated. The following day, Saturday, August 10th, I signed out of the halfway house and Barbara picked me up. She took me to Anchor where I spent eight hours in an orientation period by Karen, another employee there.

For the next few weeks Barbara would get up at 4:30 each morning, drive all the way from Conyers to downtown Atlanta, pick me up at 6:15, and take me to work at Anchor. Then she would drive back to Conyers, work all day at her job in an office supplies store, drive back to Anchor in the late afternoon, pick me up, and take me to the halfway house. She would get home around 6:30 P.M., eat, go to bed, and start all over the following morning. She never complained and tirelessly did this until I obtained driving privileges.

I made $6.75 per hour working as a CA (clinical assistant), while Barbara made $6.50 in her job. The halfway house took twenty-five percent of my gross for the privilege of living there. After taxes and FICA, I was left with very little. In a forty hour week I grossed $270, with $67.50 going to the Dismas House. State and federal taxes, along with FICA, took an estimated twenty-five percent more, leaving me with $151.87. Then I had to save ten percent of that, leaving me with a week's net of $136.68 – or a net hourly pay of $3.42 per hour.

But attitude is everything. When asked how I could possibly survive on what was left, I reframed the situation. I would smile and say,

"In prison, I made twelve cents an hour and I'm now grossing $6.75. That means I've just received a pay raise that is 56.25 times my previous pay. If I can do that *just one more time* I'll be making $379.69 an hour!"

The halfway house was an improvement over the prison in some ways, but it was more confining during the time I had to physically be there, which was most of the time. There was a common area in which males and females came and went; there was a men's floor and a women's floor. When I was physically in the halfway house there was no place to go except my floor. I wasn't allowed outside unless I was going to or from my job. In prison, I could at least go outside and move around. Later, when I gained home privileges, I could sign out and go home for a day or so.

The staff at the Dismas House was cut from the same cloth as the prison guards. When those qualities are combined with power and control, it becomes a twisted and aberrant environment. Most inmates wanted to return to the prison once they got a taste of the halfway house and staff. I would counsel them to hang on and get a job. Once they could get free of the halfway house and go to work, it would be worthwhile. Going to Anchor each day and being around real human beings in a clean and sane setting was ample reward and reason enough to appreciate my new semi-freedom. I could deal with the rest.

Dismas House was an offshoot venture of the Catholic Church. Yet it was *not* a non-profit entity so they took twenty-five percent of my gross wages. They spent nothing to maintain the building or its fixtures. The food situation was nasty beyond words and there was an exorbitant charge for it. Food was furnished by the lowest bidder and wheeled in each morning on platforms stacked high with trays. Each meal was in a cheap, flimsy clear plastic container and the trays were put into a refrigerated cooler. I ate two meals during my first week and never touched another. Things that should have been brown were green, and things that should have been green were brown. The most troubling items were unrecognizable and multi-colored.

My decision to stay away from the food was a good one because there were several serious epidemics of food poisoning. During one such period, a resident named Dewitt became violently ill and asked to go to Grady Hospital. Ms. Lawrence refused permission as she taunted him saying, "If you're such a religious man, why don't you just pray about it?"

My time during the day at Anchor was wonderful. I began this new experience worried about my ability to work with alcoholics and addicts. Working in a field such as recovery was unlike anything I'd ever done, but I discovered I was good at it. Not because I possessed innate talent and intuitiveness, but because I cared deeply about the people. The patients knew I was still an inmate in the halfway house. They knew of the hardships I was still undergoing, and they watched me try to set an example as I went through the days of my own struggle. I had to walk the walk, not merely talk the talk.

I made myself vulnerable to the patients, sharing things I never would before. In turn, they opened themselves up to me and we did a lot of good work together. In my sixth month at Anchor I was awarded Employee of the Month and it came from my peers. I always pooh-poohed Employee of the Month awards, but I valued this one.

I continued to deal with the staff at the halfway house. As part of the harassment, they would sometimes order me to assume "the foul weather" position. I had to get down on all fours and put my head on the floor between my arms. It had the appearance of a Muslim with his head down in the praying position. It also had the appearance of a very subservient bow before the staff member. When ordered to do so, I would look them in the eye, get down, and face the *opposite* direction, with my derriere aimed their way.

Staff members would come in at 3:00 A.M., turn the lights on, and roust me or someone else out for this purpose. On one occasion, one came in at 4:00 A.M., turned the lights on, and began wiping the blinds. It was crazy.

I joined a Vietnam Vet recovery group that was a stone's throw from the halfway house. Eddie was the counselor. I liked him a lot. He was a former Marine machine gunner in Vietnam and a transplant from New York City; a good guy and effective counselor. Months later I opted out of the group. I was an alcoholic, period, and treatment and recovery stressed that I was not unique or different. Most of the guys thought they were unique due to their service in Vietnam. Anyone who did not serve in Vietnam combat was viewed with disdain, and I objected to that. So I told them, "I'm going to drop out of this group. I'm a Vietnam vet who saw combat, but I'm not special or unique. What works to get others sober works for me regardless of who I am or where I've been." I wished them well and said goodbye.

A few dedicated people came to the Dismas House from one of the local recovery groups and conducted meetings with us. I rarely missed one unless I was working or unable to attend. I was grateful for the sacrifices they made to spend time with us.

The clock and a resident time card controlled all my daily movements. I clocked in and out when I went anywhere. If I left a place I had to call and get permission to go to the next and the staff member noted the time and place on my card. Once I left *that* place, I had to repeat the process. Thus, they always had a location and phone number where I was. If the place had no phone I was not allowed to go. Periodically, I could get released for two hours to get a haircut or go to a movie, but not often.

If the halfway house called a number and the resident wasn't there, the resident went on report and lost privileges. If two hours elapsed and they still hadn't found him (or her), they issued an escape report and the person was returned to prison when found. I lost privileges several times because the staff member pulled the wrong resident card or failed to make the proper note on mine. Twice, they wrote down the wrong time and were off by an hour, causing me to lose home-visiting privileges and receive extra duty. I bought a small Radio Shack recording device and a mini tape recorder. The microphone stuck to the phone with a suction cup and picked conversations up clearly. I'd call, ask who I was speaking with, ask if I could go to a certain place, get permission, and then verify the time. That stopped the problem for the most part and I was able to void a couple of DR's (Delinquency Reports) because I had it on tape. If I was dealing with Lawrence she paid no attention to what was on the tape, so I lost privileges and got extra duty.

One halfway house monitor was a gent I liked named Felker. He had bright eyes and obvious intelligence, with a good sense of humor. I wondered *what* he was doing there.

We all had to be clocked in by the 9:00 P.M. curfew. The resident cards were in a file box, supposedly filed alphabetically, and a monitor pulled the cards as the resident stepped up to clock in. If the monitor couldn't find a resident's card, which was not uncommon, everything stopped until it was found. If that made ten people late who were waiting in line early to clock in, so be it – privileges were taken. I had to stand in line a number of times while they searched for my card because they filed it under every letter in the alphabet except P.

One Saturday night, I was attempting to clock in and they couldn't find my card. There was a long line behind me and the time was approaching 9:00 P.M. I thought I saw my card and reached over the counter to check. Ms. Wanda White was on duty and she was a woman who rivaled Ms. Lawrence for sheer malice. She verbally assaulted me for reaching over and I angrily said, "Lady, I'm just trying to find my card!" Ms. White yelled, "Mah name's Miz White and ah ain' no lady!" I looked at her and said, "You're absolutely right, and I'll never make *that* mistake again!" All the surrounding residents exploded in laughter while Ms. White stood with a puzzled look on her face.

Felker was on duty Monday morning as I clocked out to go to Anchor. His eyes were twinkling as he bent over and whispered, "Understand you and Ms. White had some words." I grinned, looked up and asked if he'd heard what was said. He laughed, winked, and said he had; I grinned and winked back. Felker was a good guy but there were precious few in the corrections system I could say that about.

Ms. Lawrence delighted in writing me up for a number of DR's over the weeks. She invented things to write me up for, usually citing a fictitious rule. I knew the rules because I read them, and *her rules* were not in anything I was given. So, I would politely ask her to show me the rule and she could not; the DR stuck and I lost privileges.

I was certainly trying *not* to cause trouble because I wanted to go home and see Barbara. That was far more important to me than confronting Lawrence or Ms. Scott. I went to my "counselor" about all the nonsense. Mr. Yeatter was timid, subordinate in the chain of command, and he was also white, in the minority, and impotent to do anything. He advised me not to question or challenge Lawrence. I was in the habit of documenting things in writing and Yeatter told me not to because "it creates paperwork." In prison or halfway house speak that translated to "more work," which they all tried to avoid. More than that, it also added to their inability to arbitrarily deny things that were a matter of written record. Again, as in prison, it was insanity run amuck. I ignored him and continued to document situations.

Eventually, I earned automobile privileges and was allowed home visits. Finally, I was able to spend Friday night home, then finally, Friday and Saturday nights. I always had to report back to the halfway house by 9:00 P.M. on Sunday evening. While home, I could go nowhere without phoning in and being released from place to place, but I was so happy to be home that nothing else mattered. The halfway house assigned me a secret number each time I left on the weekend. They would call me in the middle of the night and I'd give the number. It never occurred to the staff that if I wanted to spend a night away all I had to do was to tell another person my number and have them repeat it when they called.

Finally I arrived at my release date of January 31, 1992. I walked out for the last time, leaving my resident card behind. I spent 424 days in the prison system. I did them all one day at a time, shorter when necessary. Walking away with the ability to go where I wanted, when I wished, knowing I would never again have to deal with the idiots running the insane asylum was incredible.

Free at Last - 1992

Nothing is as cherished as something taken for granted and then lost. It was strange to move around without being chained to a telephone and living under a twenty or thirty minute deadline to get somewhere. I had to adjust to the idea that I could go get a haircut, see a movie, or visit a friend – without getting permission. I put my tape recorder away.

I reported to my probation officer, Mr. Jack Briscoe. I knew things were looking up when I saw his college diploma and heard him speak in complete sentences. He lectured me on what my obligations would be during the three years of my supervised release. He painted examples of dire consequences from some of his recent experiences with inmates; it was obvious to me that I was just another convict in his view. It made no difference if I robbed a bank, raped someone, dealt drugs, molested children or flew an airplane drunk – a felon was a felon, period. I left our first meeting with a clear understanding I could not depend on him to come to my aid for anything, nor would I totally trust him. As part of the initial procedure he inspected our home. I had nothing to hide and was completely unconcerned.

A probation officer has the earthly authority of God Almighty and can arbitrarily make a probationer's life miserable if he so chooses. Briscoe could have decreed that I report to him daily, if he wished, or any of a dozen other things that would handcuff a released inmate while he's free. He did none of those.

As time went on and he came to know me, I believe his picture of me changed. He learned I was serious about my recovery and was a strong participant as I traveled and shared my recovery story with others. I needed written permission from him each time I left the local area. My travel area was specified by county boundaries and I carried that document with me.

There were times when I called him spontaneously for permission to go somewhere due to a change in our plans; perhaps I needed to cross a particular county. Later, he told me no one ever did that; they just went. But I took no chances. I dotted the i's and crossed the t's. I had come too far, and paid too high a price, to return to prison for stupidly ignoring the conditions of probation. Jack Briscoe rarely bothered me or had me report in. He stopped by the house two or three times the entire three years I was on probation. Another probation officer laughingly said, "He doesn't have time for you; he's too busy chasing all the violators!" Briscoe was a good and decent guy and the law of averages finally kicked in when I was assigned to him.

One requirement of probation was to report any contact with police or people with criminal backgrounds. Two days after my release from prison, Barbara and I headed for our beloved north Georgia Mountains. I hungered to go back for so long. In prison I longingly looked at photos we took there and I recalled the cherished moments we spent together in that setting. Part of our normal route to the mountains took us across a county that was now out of bounds for me, so we altered the routing. I was never on that particular stretch of road and thought it was a four-lane highway with normal speeds. It wasn't and I was pulled over for speeding.

As the cop wrote the ticket, I knew he would be running my driver's license and tag number. I knew he'd get a hit saying I was a felon, so I told him I had just gotten out of prison before he even began checking. I watched in my rear view mirror and when he got out of his car I did the same. He said he was going to lower the speed so I wouldn't lose any points on my license, gave me the ticket, smiled, and bade me good day. I was surprised at this unexpected break.

I swore out loud as we got under way, because I now had to call Briscoe and I'd only been out of prison two days. Barbara put things in perspective with her soft and comforting voice. She said, "Why don't we just go on up to the mountains and have a good day. After all, it wasn't a DUI." She was right – it *wasn't* a DUI. We started our day all over, something I learned how to do in treatment. We had a magnificent day in the place I longed to return to for so long.

It was a beautiful and soulful homecoming as we entered our peaceful refuge. We found our favorite spot, eased our way across the huge boulders in the rushing water, and ate KFC fried chicken as we sat. We held hands and walked the mountains as the peace and the beauty settled about us. As we left, I stopped and pointed out the calm, placid pool we talked about just before I headed for prison. We weren't there yet but much of the turbulence was behind us and we were moving closer.

I was working at Anchor Hospital and getting better at working with alcoholics and addicts. I could not be a counselor because of the requirement for four thousand hours of work in the field, plus the exams and boards required for a CAC certification. So I co-facilitated groups, worked in admissions, did one-on-ones, and was immersed in the treatment process. By the time I left Anchor I had accumulated 3,200 hours in the field. None of this had been mandated by the court; it was something I wanted to do.

I worked with many brilliant doctors and counselors but the best counselor I ever worked with was Bernard Carter. He was a short, dynamic man, always dressed to the nines. He exuded a strong spiritual aura that seemed to envelope him. He was clever and gentle, yet he could immediately cut to the chase and clear the air of BS. I did groups with Bernard on Wednesdays and Fridays. I awoke on those mornings excited about the upcoming day.

He was masterful and kind. He would debrief me after each group and never failed to find some kind and generous things to say about my participation. I genuinely loved the man. He died a few years later of prostate cancer, a blow to us all. He truly touched the lives of thousands of people. He gave husbands back to wives, wives back to husbands, and moms and dads back to their children. I had little doubt that he had a special place in heaven.

Juanita Marsh founded Anchor Hospital and it was her child. She was chairman of the board of directors and came through the hospital at least once a week, taking time to talk with every patient. She knew I was hurting financially and after I was there a year she offered me a higher paying position in the marketing department, where my pay would take a considerable jump. She also told me I would always have a place at Anchor.

I was deeply grateful to this wonderful lady but told her I thought my place was with the patients. Although I was only making $6.75 an hour, I was receiving so much more in terms of serious emotional satisfaction. I felt I was giving back just a little of what was so freely given to me. I would have felt guilty leaving the patients I loved to advance my own financial position. Juanita's assurance that I would always have a place at Anchor provided a psychological safety net and much needed comfort. I felt secure for the first time in a long while.

I began thinking more about flying again. Most I knew considered that a closed issue. In addition to the loss of all licenses and my medical certificate, Judge Rosenbaum put sanctions on me that closed the door. I checked with the Air Line Association Attorney, Pat Brennaman, and he told me the FAA would not make it easy for me to get in a cockpit again. I hadn't expected they would.

I was told the FAA required me to start from the ground up, and that my beginning point would be a private license. I never had one because I came out of the Marine Corps, took a test, and was given a commercial license with an instrument rating. My hope was to go back and re-take the tests for the airline transport pilot (ATP) rating. In itself, that presented a formidable challenge. The ATP is the airline equivalent of the Ph.D.; there is no higher certificate. I thought they would surely waive the lower licenses if I could perform to the highest standard in the industry. The FAA's firm stance meant I would have to start at the very bottom and work my way up.

No pilot I knew believed it was doable. When I received the news I was crushed. I sat down and all I could do was breathe in and out. I tried to be still, to calm the disturbance within me, and quiet the voice of impossibility.

The next day at Anchor I was at the copy machine when Pat, the head of medical records, approached. She only had a couple of items so I told her to go ahead. She placed copies on the machine, set the controls, and asked how I was. I replied that I wasn't doing well. Without looking at me, she continued making copies and asked what was wrong. I told her, "I just heard from the FAA yesterday and they said if I want to fly again I must begin at the very bottom."

She was immersed in making her copies and without looking up responded, "Isn't that grand!" Astonished, I wanted to say, *Are you nuts? Didn't you hear what I just said?* Instead, I asked, "What do you mean?" As she lifted her copies from the machine she said, "Isn't it grand that you're going to be able to start working on the thing you want to do most?" Then she turned and walked away.

I stood there dumbfounded. Pat knew exactly what to say and gave me a lesson in attitude that really hit home. I thought about her comment the rest of the afternoon. I drove home after work and told Barbara, "If I think this is impossible, it *becomes* impossible. If I change my attitude, it's doable. If I do this like I do sobriety, one day at a time, I can do it. If I look at it as a time to go back, relive, review, and refresh the things I learned as a cadet in 1961, then the whole picture changes." It was about my attitude; it had *always* been about my attitude.

I could not begin the process because of the sanctions the judge placed on me. I contacted Peter Wold and asked whether he thought there was any chance they could be lifted. Frankly, I didn't think so. Peter caught Judge Rosenbaum one day at the courthouse and asked if he could speak with him in chambers. As they talked, I finally learned what the judge's intentions were the morning of sentencing. He told Peter he intended to sentence me to four years. He thought briefly before telling Peter he wanted to hear from me before considering whether he would lift the sanctions.

I spent several days writing an eleven-page letter. While lengthy, it didn't begin to touch on many issues I thought important. I sent the letter to Peter and asked him to edit it down to no more than two or three pages. A couple of days later, Peter called and told me to leave it as it was. He said it was one of the most remarkable letters he ever read and assured me the judge would never put it down once he began. I still didn't want to send it, but I'd learned to trust – so I mailed it.

Near the end of the letter I stated, "Even if you choose to help me, I still have a monumental struggle ahead because I must go back and re-earn each of the four licenses I need. Most of my fellow pilots say they could not possibly do it, and many of my closest friends have doubts it can be done. I *know* that somehow, some way I can do it. I must quit flying commercially when I'm 60, so time is running out."

Peter had to take a motion to the judge to have the sanctions lifted and I wanted to pay him. He refused, saying, "I believe in you, and I'm staying to the end, wherever that is." Once again, his kindness left me speechless. Peter did a number of things for me over the course of several years, always refusing payment, and always because he simply believed in me. I had little I could give him, but I would gladly have agreed to whatever he asked and paid him over time.

I thought we had an almost nil chance of success, but Peter called me a week later and excitedly told me the judge had lifted the sanctions. What lay ahead still had the heavy mantle of impossibility, but the removal of the sanctions made an attempt possible. Later, when interviewed about me, I saw this tough judge say on television, "That letter may have been the single-most moving document I have ever read. I sat at my desk and wept." His statement stunned me. I had no idea it had impacted him in such a way. I knew I did not possess that sort of power or writing ability. I knew there *had to be* some divine guidance helping me craft that letter!

I was now free to go after the licenses, despite starting from a deep bottom. I had come to believe life is not about falling down, but is about getting back up. We *all* fall down at some point in life. We all suffer defeats, experience moments of ignobility, and have moments of regret and shame. None of us have lives of unblemished perfection and completely stalwart behavior. For those who think otherwise, I am convinced they've set their standards too low.

My heroes have always been people I've admired for their courage, their tenacity, and their unwillingness to quit in the face of adversity. I've watched individuals face horrific diseases and courageously deal with them. I've seen people severely injured and disabled, yet refuse to be seduced by self-pity and defeat. I've watched people rise from lives of unspeakable horror and abuse and then shower the rest of us with the beauty of their spirit. I came to believe that "adversity truly introduces us to ourselves," as I read in a daily meditation book. My job was to keep putting one foot in front of the other, no matter what.

After Congressman Ben Jones visited me in prison, several recovering congressmen began corresponding with me. I knew nothing about any of them prior to that. Congressman Jim Ramstad from Minnesota asked if I could meet with them and on March 25, 1992, I flew to Washington, D.C. for that purpose.

Upon landing I made my way to Capitol Hill. I had two hours before the meeting so I walked the halls of the Cannon and Sam Rayburn buildings and looked at the many familiar names on the doors. I went outside, where the expansive lawn was freshly cut, and inhaled the delicious smell of the grass. I was in a suit and tie, wondering how I had come so far. Six weeks earlier, I was wearing prison khakis.

Every Wednesday at noon these six congressmen met for a brief recovery meeting. Two were extremely guarded about their anonymity, but the other four were open and comfortable with their recovery status. They were all humble, openly honest men. They welcomed me and made me feel comfortable. I met Rod Chandler, from Washington, who would become a lifelong friend, and Bill Emerson from Missouri, who has passed on now. The four who were quite open about their sobriety were anxious to help me, and I was surprised by their willingness and enthusiasm. My morale skyrocketed as I returned home the next day more enthusiastic than ever.

Strange as it may seem, even the power of four congressmen was not enough to assist my return to flying. As time passed, they made several strong attempts to help me, but politics blunted each one. The real value of their support was the heartening effect it had on me personally, and I drew on it during dark times.

Before attacking the licenses, I had to have an FAA medical certificate. Not quite a week later, on March 30th, I flew to El Paso, Texas to begin that process. A Northwest Captain and Vietnam squadron mate, Bob Polhamus, paid my $437 airfare. Once more, I was the beneficiary of the kindness of others which allowed me to push ahead when otherwise I would not have been able.

A recovering pilot has a number of obstacles to clear before regaining his or her medical certificate. One of those was a meeting with a specially designated FAA psychiatrist. The FAA rigorously looks for mental, emotional, and neurological problems in returning alcoholic pilots. I was to meet and speak with Dr. Larry Wharton in El Paso, Texas. I immediately liked him and we spent ninety minutes as he examined me. Typically, the interview lasted an hour, but Dr. Wharton was fascinated by my situation, all the media coverage, and my prison experience, so he spent extra time with me. Then I was sent across town to Dr. Mike Fitts, Ph.D., a psychologist who worked with Dr. Wharton. I spent five hours taking a series of eight neurological exams to determine if alcohol had impaired me in any way. Many of the exams were timed with a stopwatch and involved performance requirements. I was exhausted by the time the tests were completed.

I called Barbara from my motel and told her I could not be more tired if I had worked seventy-two hours nonstop in a coal mine. Everything hinged on my El Paso trip. If I failed here, then every door slammed shut on any hope of ever flying again. The pressure and stress were beyond measure.

When the reports came back I could hardly believe they were mine. I suffered no damage and the report gave my IQ as 141, classifying me "in the top 1% of men my age for IQ and ability." I worked with people in the treatment center who were organically damaged by alcohol. I could only wonder, "Why them and not me?" as I slipped into deep gratitude for my good fortune. A few days later, as I sat in a hospital group with two people who were not so fortunate, I could only conclude I survived purely through God's grace and nothing else. I drank as hard as they had and could have been every bit as damaged.

On April 30th, 1992 I went to see Dr. Dick Harper for my FAA physical examination. Slowly, things were coming together, but I still had to get past an approval from the FAA and there were many squares yet to fill.

The next day, I received a phone call from Patrice O'Toole in Washington, D.C. She was calling from Congressman Ben Jones' office and wanted me to come to Washington to testify at some hearings involving alcohol and drugs, offering to fly me up there. Another congressional aide, Cathy Taylor also called, this time from Jim Ramstad's office. Ben Jones was working with Jim Ramstad. I went to Washington on May 13th for several days of hearings being conducted by former Senator Harold Hughes. He was openly and publicly known as a recovering alcoholic, having been elected as Iowa's governor after getting sober, and later to the U.S. Senate. Senator Hughes devoted his life to the treatment of alcoholism and addiction. The hearings were looking at alcohol and drugs and they wanted my input as to my experiences in prison, and any programs I saw or took part in.

The next morning I was taken to the huge room where the hearings were being held. It was exactly what I had seen on C-Span, with cameras, green covered tables, and a huge crowd. I was immediately nervous, wondering why I agreed to do this. I was briefed that the day's hearings would involve panels of three people each and each panel would be allotted fifteen minutes. That meant I would only have to talk for five minutes and I decided to maneuver and sit between the other two panel members. Shortly before my panel was called, an aide came to me and said the other two had been rescheduled and I would appear alone. It was a frightening development.

I had faced fear before, so I did what I always did. I said the Serenity Prayer, asked God to still my fears, and to allow me to speak from my heart. When it was my time, I walked to the table, sat down, and looked up at the nine members of the board. Harold Hughes had a craggy look and a deep theatrical voice. He had a conspicuous sense of presence as he looked down and addressed me as "Captain Prouse."

I have little recall of what I said, other than God granted my wish and let me speak freely from the heart. Throughout the previous panels I was aware of considerable noise in the room as people came and went and I had become accustomed to the buzz of that activity. I spoke for only a few minutes when I suddenly became aware of silence in the room – it startled me.

I concluded my remarks and Harold Hughes looked at me for a dramatic moment. He paused, then said in that powerful voice, "Captain Prouse, I am going to recite Winston Churchill's shortest speech. 'Never give up. Never, *never* give up. Never, never, *never* give up!" and he declared a fifteen-minute recess. He and other members of the board then came down and spoke with me privately. Once again I conquered my fear and walked through one more amazing experience.

I asked Ben Jones if he thought he might be able to get me an appointment with Dr. Bart Pakull, chief psychiatrist for the FAA. Dr. Pakull decided which recovering pilots would get their medical certificates. I enjoyed success whenever I could meet people face to face and talk with them, but I wasn't sure if Dr. Pakull would be willing to meet with me. Ben was gone when I returned from the hearings, but left me a note telling me I had a noon appointment with Dr. Pakull. I went to Dr. Pakull's FAA office on Independence Avenue. He had heard much about me due to the media coverage.

Dr. Pakull asked if I would like to have lunch and I said yes. It was a beautiful day and we sat in a sidewalk cafe as he bought me a sandwich and some coffee. I liked Dr. Pakull and was open and honest as I answered his questions. Shortly after that meeting I received a Special Issuance FAA medical certificate. The FAA could have buried my request for years and I knew that. Dr. Pakull apparently felt okay with my recovery and, to my amazement, the certificate was in my hands a short while later.

Nineteen ninety-two was nearly halfway gone and I was banking on my congressional support to get my licenses reinstated. The FAA hinted they would look favorably upon that in light of all I had done in recovery. Still, weeks passed and nothing was being done. I began to get the feeling they were stonewalling and I notified the two congressmen who had gone to the FAA. There was little they could do but make another inquiry – and receive the same answer again.

Nothing was being done. I told Barbara I needed to get busy. From the very first I had learned that recovery is an action program and I reminded myself of that. "Faith may move mountains," I was told, "but you better bring a shovel."

I told the congressmen I thought the FAA officials were waiting for the new Clinton administration to take over on January 20th and would then deny our requests as they slammed the door and said goodbye. That's precisely what happened. But I was studying and by the time we got the anticipated bad news, I had already passed two of the four exams. Although disappointed, I was glad I'd moved forward anticipating the FAAs inaction, and was well ahead of the process.

Some months after President Clinton came into office, I passed another exam. There was one written exam remaining but I could not take it until I acquired a commercial license. Thus far, it had taken ten and a half months from start to finish and I worked over 2,000 questions, problems, and exercises. My average score on the exams was 94. I was *never* content to just get by; I *had* to do my best.

In the meantime I was still working at Anchor Hospital, where I spent a total of twenty months. Every day was packed with heavy emotional effort on my part and I was drained when leaving the hospital each night. I had dozens of intensely personal experiences as I worked with patients from every walk of life. I will never be able to count the hugs, the tears, the break-through moments, and the life-changing events I was privileged to be part of. Each of those helped cement my own recovery.

On Friday afternoons we said goodbye to patients who completed treatment. Family members were invited and I stood at the back of the assembly room and watched. I saw families coming back together and the look of hope on children's faces. I saw people leaving who changed radically in the time they spent with us, and I knew no paycheck could ever equal what I felt in those moments. In spite of the $14,040 I earned annually at Anchor Hospital, it was unlike anything I had ever done before. It was one of the richest times in my life.

Coming Home From
Vietnam - Flight Instructor

The spring of 1966 was in full bloom and Vietnam was behind us. I had orders to the Advanced Jet Training Command as a flight instructor. We would be stationed at the Naval Air Station at Kingsville, Texas, 80 miles from Beeville. We were home.

We bought our first home for $19,500 and settled in. I took a month's leave and still had two weeks remaining. We were repainting the house and working on the inside. My best friend, John Dodson, also back from Vietnam, lived three blocks from us. Barbara and I were outside painting when John stopped by with several other pilots. They were going to the Officers club for drinks. I cleaned up and followed them in my car. I had never been aboard NAS (Naval Air Station) Kingsville so I picked up a visitor's tag at the gate and followed them to the Officers Club. We drank as we always did, fast and hard as we laughed and talked for several hours.

Inside, they were making preparations for a large Monte Carlo party that night, complete with gaming tables, music, and food. Finally we left, planning to return later that night. I departed first and took a wrong turn, no doubt a result of all the drinking. I glanced in the mirror and saw my friends going the other way so I sped up to intercept them when I came around from the other direction. The speed limit was 25 MPH aboard the base. I was going sixty when I noticed an official black Navy car approaching head on and blinking its lights to slow me down. I maintained my speed and as he got closer he blinked the lights more rapidly. I shot him a one-fingered salute as he passed and as I glanced in my rear view mirror I saw the car screech to a halt and turn around.

I had a bad feeling and sped up even more, hoping to beat him to the gate and get off the base before he caught me. I slowed as he rapidly closed the distance before I could reach the gate. He pulled around me and the sentry snapped to attention. I got out of my car and noticed he was an older man in a white navy issue T-shirt with no uniform shirt on, so I could see no indication of rank.

He and the sentry were talking and the man who'd chased me inquired who I was. I replied, "Lieutenant Prouse. *Marine* Lieutenant Prouse," I added, since the Navy also has a lieutenant rank. He said something to the guard and departed. I turned in my visitor's tag and headed home, thinking I may have gotten lucky since nothing had happened.

I stopped at John's where he and the others were winding up with a few more drinks. I had another and described what had just occurred. John said it sounded like I'd been stopped by Captain Yeagle, the base commanding officer. A Navy Captain is equivalent to a Marine full bird colonel so that didn't bode well.

Barbara and I showered, got dressed, and headed back to the Officers Club for the gala party. I stopped at the gate to pick up a visitor tag and was informed by the sentry I was not allowed to drive aboard the base. Instantly my temper flared and I returned to John's house and got his second car, which had a blue officer's sticker on it. Sitting high so as not to be easily visible, I approached the sentry once more, expecting to be saluted through the gate. The sentry stopped me, leaned down, and said, "Lieutenant Prouse, I cannot allow you to drive aboard the base, Sir." Not to be deterred I said, "Okay, I'll have my wife drive." As the confused sentry stood aside, Barbara drove onto the base.

The club was packed as people played slot machines, rolled dice, and spun roulette wheels. I saw John and some friends so we joined them at their table. John pointed out a gentleman in the crowd wearing a civilian suit and asked if he was the man who stopped me. I said it was and John confirmed it was Captain Yeagle.

I was dancing with Barbara when I felt a tap on my shoulder. I turned around and saw the base commanding officer. He said, "Young man, I'd like to have a word with you," so I stepped off to the side. He asked if I knew who he was to which I responded in the negative, figuring the better course of action was to plead ignorance. He stated his rank and name and said he was the base commanding officer. I came to attention and said I had no way of knowing that since he was wearing a T-shirt during our encounter. Embarrassed, he acknowledged he was out of uniform, but went on to say he checked on me and knew who I was. He was soft-spoken and gentlemanly as he said, "You're going to be here three years and it can either be enjoyable or not. I'd like to see you enjoy it." I quickly apologized to him and we were off to a great start.

However, he put sanctions in place barring me from the base and forgot to lift them as I began checking in. Finally, I asked someone to please call Captain Yeagle's office and get the sanctions lifted, which they did. I achieved the distinction of being the only pilot kicked off his base before he had a chance to check in.

I checked into my training squadron, VT-21, and went through more ground school re-familiarizing myself with the Grumman F9F Cougar, and then into the instructor syllabus for the flying portion. I began my IUT training (Instructor Under Training) in the venerable old F9 on May 25, 1966 and, having completed the initial phases of my own training, picked up my first student, John Schedel, on July 18th. He was a Marine second lieutenant, married, and a good student. I knew he would be above average recalling my own flight training days and the number of times I'd been assigned as an instructor's first student.

Navy training command squadrons were about twice the size of a normal Marine squadron and had only a handful of Marine instructors. I served as a flight instructor for two and a half years, flying three times per day most of the time and working twelve hour days. Vietnam was heating up rapidly and we needed pilots so we worked six days on duty with one day off.

Since I never tired of flying I didn't mind that part of the assignment. However, the training command Navy was sadly lacking in military attributes and that wore on me. I was involved in a number of incidents involving Navy personnel and refused to succumb to the unmilitary modus operandi. The Navy instructor pilots were sharp and competent, with a few exceptions, and our small group of Marines hung together and supported each other on the field and off.

I was a no-nonsense flight instructor and told all my students to never show up unprepared. Nearly all the other instructors shared that philosophy. Vietnam was pushing us so hard that a few marginal students slipped through who otherwise would not have made the cut.

I had some difficulty with one of my Navy students due to his attitude. He complained to the Student Control Officer that I was too demanding, so I was told I would only be assigned Marine students. Had I known earlier that was a possibility I might have made the request myself. Days off were precious, but sometimes I gave them up to fly with one of my struggling students because I remembered my own apprehension about flying with an unfamiliar instructor. I cared about each student and was willing to go the extra mile if he was giving it all he had. And most were.

I made Captain in September of 1966. It was nice to pin the railroad tracks on as I recalled my days as a private.

It was wartime and we were pushing everything hard – the enlisted men, the planes, and the pilots. We were losing planes and pilots faster in Kingsville than we had in Vietnam. A loud siren would sound aboard the base when an accident took place, and Barbara could hear it from our house. Although she never said anything to me at the time, she would worry until I came home.

At one point I told Barbara I simply couldn't go to any more memorial services, for a while at least. I couldn't bear to hear *Taps* played or watch a missing man formation pass overhead. I was also getting word of more friends dying in Vietnam. I was in a hazardous profession, but it was the shared risk that bound all of us together so tightly.

I tried not to short my family during my time off. Barbara was an outstanding mom and I tried to be a good father to my two little sons. I loved being with them and was always laughing at something they did. I took the boys with me everywhere during my free time. We made frequent trips to Beeville to see Barb's family and spent lots of time with other Marines. We were still making up for lost time overseas.

I began to re-think my military career. It was the only thing I'd ever done and I loved it deeply, but there were problems. I would have to spend four to six years away from Barbara and the boys if I finished out my career. Marines were the only branch of service that had no overseas tours with dependents. I promised Barbara our family would never be like the one I grew up in, that we would be safe and secure. I wanted her to be a stay-at-home mom regardless of our financial situation. And there was no way I could put my career ahead of my family.

A second consideration was I did not expect to go beyond Major since I was not a college graduate. I wasn't even close, having come directly from high school. I had some strong pluses – a good combat record, a good reputation in the Marine Corps, and a good fitness report from a General. I was a good aviator and that was also a strong factor in my favor.

I waited until the eleventh hour before sitting down to write my letter of resignation in June of 1967. It was a painful and anguished decision. Because I had a Regular commission it would require a year for my resignation to become effective. I saw a boyhood dream come true and flew the best airplanes in the world. I flew with the greatest comrades I could have picked. We were truly a Band of Brothers and never again would I be in the midst of such men.

The Airlines - 1968

All I wanted to do was be a Marine and fly jet airplanes. Many of my friends were already established with major airlines and I began to look in that direction.

I sent out over thirty letters and received three responses requesting an interview. Most airlines wanted a college degree. My military experience and combat record were not enough to get hired. Based purely on where I might live geographically, I selected Northwest Airlines. I received my honorable discharge on July 15, 1968, and started at Northwest three weeks later on August 5th. My best friend, John Dodson, joined me in the same class.

I spent eleven and a half years in the Marine Corps, going in as a barely eighteen year-old private. I excelled all the way through and was exiting as a decorated twenty-nine year-old Captain, aviator, and Vietnam combat veteran. I had done well.

Barb, the kids, and I packed our belongings and headed north to begin a new phase of life. Our one-year-old German shepherd also accompanied us.

Initial training at Northwest required more ground school, this time on the Boeing 727, learning all the systems and airline procedures. We concluded with a Flight Engineer written exam and I put one more license in my pocket to go with the Commercial and Instrument rating certificates.

I disliked the boredom of being a second officer and running the flight engineer panel. I talked about going back in the Marine Corps. Barbara said she would support whatever I wished to do. During our first year at Northwest new hires were on probation and could be fired for any reason whatsoever. We made $550 per month, barely enough to get by when our rent alone was $175. After taxes and utility bills there was little left for essentials.

We were cautioned to walk the straight and narrow, keep our heads low, our mouths shut, and told to be as invisible as possible as we got through the probationary first year. I did pretty well until I flew with one particular captain. He was an Air Force flight-training drop out, highly opinionated, and very irritating. I tried to remember what I was told, but with each trip I was like a sponge reaching the saturation point. Finally, during the fourth and final week, I took strong issue with his comments and persistent arrogance. The copilot was Doug Jones, a decorated Marine ground officer in Vietnam. A short while later, he cornered me and with great concern in his voice said, "Lyle! You can't talk to a Captain that way!"

Every Captain completed a write up at the end of the month on probation pilots. The write-ups played a very large role in whether one got past the probationary year or not. This captain gave me a negative write-up although there was nothing he could point to in terms of my professional performance. Instead, he injected a number of vague and ambiguous comments about me personally, designed to deep-six me later.

Captain Don Nelson was the assistant chief pilot and would later rise to VP of Flight Operations. He was a former Air Force B-52 pilot, philosophically known to be right of Attila the Hun. He called me in for my probationary review and leafed through the write-ups. I knew when he got to the write up because his facial expression changed. He spent some time looking at it then asked what it was all about. I asked if I was supposed to comment and he said yes. So I did, quoting the captain on a number of issues, along with my responses, all the while watching Nelson's face become more and more livid. He began writing across the report and passed it to me. It said, "I have discussed this matter with Mr. Prouse and do not feel he should be faulted for his actions." Two in our class failed to make the probationary cut.

I got off probation, watched my pay double, and replaced the tires on our car along with a few other needed things. A few months later, The Brotherhood of Railway and Airline Clerks (BRAC) struck the airline. The strike lasted six months and I was out of work another four and a half months. I worked a myriad of jobs, usually two to three at a time, to feed the family and make ends meet.

Barbara and I talked of adopting a child even while we were dating. Both of us wanted children and we also felt we should give a child a home who otherwise would not have one. Originally, I wanted to adopt a small Indian boy, but since we had two sons we now turned our attention to a daughter. We chose the Children's Home Society in Minneapolis, and were immediately pushed to adopt a mixed black-white child. We steadfastly insisted upon adopting a small Indian girl and discovered there were two main categories for adoption. The first involved garden-variety infant Anglo children and the second category consisted of older children, those of mixed-race, and those with physical or mental defects. We were put into category two.

For the next fourteen months we pursued this process in the face of repeated frustration and continued attempts to change our adoption criteria. I ran out of patience finally and had some words with our caseworker, telling her that we were not going to adopt any child other than the one we originally came for. Weeks and months came and went. After more than a dozen trips to the Children's Home Society, it began to look like a waste of time. Finally, I had enough and told Barbara we would attend one last meeting before abandoning our adoption attempts. At that meeting we were unexpectedly told we were next in line for an Indian girl. That was exciting news.

A few months later we received a call from our caseworker, Mrs. Doty, who told us our daughter was waiting to be picked up. I asked what her Native blood quantum was and she said, "One third," to which I replied, "That's impossible – unless she has three parents." Our little girl was seventeen days old and Ms. Doty told us she had a club foot, but that did not deter us. We walked in and saw our daughter for the first time. She was adorable. One tiny foot was slightly twisted at birth and was in a cast. We bundled her up and brought her home on October 7, 1970. I was out of work at the airline due to the BRAC strike and the adoption supervisor was reluctant to let us have her. Ms. Doty told the supervisor there was no doubt our daughter would be well cared for in view of the effort we exerted to get her.

Our daughter Dawn came home to live with us. Barbara had her daughter and was on cloud nine. It didn't take long to learn what daughters do to their dads. Her brothers loved and protected her, and their relationship with her was instant and natural. She couldn't crawl or walk past without me picking her up and hugging her as I said, "Thank you for being my daughter." As she learned to talk, she would reply, "Thanks for being my dad," and my heart would melt. One year later, we went to court and finalized her place in our family. Now it was official, with a new birth certificate, and no more fear that someone might take her from us.

We were always open about the adoption and Dawn grew up very secure and comfortable. Barbara always explained that her birth mom loved her so much she was willing to give her up so she might have a better life. *Never* did we want Dawn thinking she was unwanted or abandoned. When she was in the second or third grade, she came home and asked Barbara if she had grown in her tummy. Barbara paused, and then said, "No, sweetheart, you grew in my heart." When I came home from a trip and Barbara related that, all I could do was stand and look at her with tears in my eyes.

During our first ten years at Northwest we endured six strikes and twenty months of unemployment. It was a strife-ridden airline run by a man determined to break the airline's unions at any cost. After a number of strikes and many years of unrest, the board of directors ousted him and we began to slowly morph into a smoother airline.

I made copilot after twelve years and could finally fly again. All flying was split between the Captain and the copilots, so I was able to fly every other leg. Once back flying my morale improved considerably.

After eight years in Minnesota, we decided to move to Georgia. My best friend, John Dodson, triggered that decision by moving to Tampa, Florida. We were splitting up for the first time since 1961, but our friendship would continue as strong as ever for more than forty-two years until John died from cancer. He was closer to me than any brother I could have. I loved him dearly.

Barbara and I made a three-day whirlwind trip to Georgia over our anniversary, March 9, 1976, buying a brand new home in a new subdivision called Honey Creek in Conyers. It was the first time in our thirteen year marriage we ever lived in an affluent neighborhood, the first time we ever had more than one bathroom, and the first time the kids had their own individual bedrooms.

We bought a new camper and were able to put it to use in Georgia due to the good weather and great camping areas. Camping was a family affair; we did as much as we could to build great childhood memories for the kids. As they got older they brought their friends with them and it was a good time for all. We were devoted parents and active with our kids as they participated in T ball, youth football, YMCA Indian Guides, Cub Scouts, and every other activity they were interested in. Barbara was always a room mother and PTA mom.

As I reflected back later, trying to assess the role alcohol played at this time, I could see my drinking escalating. But I still had a comfortable margin of denial that said, "I have friends who drink *far more* than I do and far more often." Alcohol was still in second place behind my family. I also saw how much better the camping trips and the Indian Guide trips could have been, had I not been drinking. Alcohol never added anything to my family; it took away. I never saw that until much later.

Return to Flying – The Impossible Dream

It was 1993 and I was still working at Anchor Hospital. Rick Anderton was a former Marine pilot and former Eastern Airlines Captain now flying MD-80's for Private Jet Expeditions. He called to say they were interested in hiring me. That news surprised me and I called PJE and got an appointment to interview with Greer Parramore, the vice president. I met with Greer on March 12, 1993. Greer was a likeable guy and I had an immediate rapport with him. He was empathetic to my situation and told me he tried to get word to me in prison that I had a flying job waiting when I got out.

I could only imagine what a cushion this possibility would have been had I known. But, as one of the staff members at Anchor said, *not knowing* meant I had to work the recovery program even harder.

After I spoke with Greer, virtually everyone in management came in to talk with me, from the president on down. All were friendly and enthusiastic about me coming to work for them. A short while later, I began work with Private Jet and my pay skyrocketed by forty-two percent to $20,000 a year.

Private Jet wanted me to fly their MD-80s, but for the time being they wanted me working in flight dispatch. That meant I had to take the FAA Dispatch exam, which was essentially the same as the Airline

Transport Pilot test. I took it again on April 5th, one day before starting work for PJE. I scored a 98. By this time I was getting pretty good at FAA exams.

Passing the FAA written exams was only the mid-point of obtaining actual flight certificates. A specified flight program had to be performed and passed for each of the certificates. I looked in several flying magazines to get an idea of the cost and it appeared to be anywhere from $10,000 to $20,000. That closed the door. We were just barely getting by as it was. Barbara said, "I don't know if you'll ever fly again commercially, but I think it's important you regain the licenses. We still have our furniture; why don't we sell it so you can try." I could only look at her. She was offering to empty the house of all we had left so I might get my licenses back. What had I *ever done* to deserve her?

Then, one more miracle came my way. Within a day of Barbara's suggestion, I received both a letter and phone call from Captain Terry Marsh, a close Northwest friend and a man I admired immensely. He had a flight school located in Buffalo, Minnesota, about forty miles northwest of the Twin Cities. Terry wanted Barbara and me to come to Minnesota. We were to live with him while I went through his flight school, *free of charge*, and I would regain my licenses. I had already experienced a number of miracles, but this one was *huge* - out of nowhere the impossible suddenly became possible.

Barbara had to stay and earn a living. She was making $6.50 an hour and would be our only breadwinner while I was gone. My PO, Jack Briscoe, willingly gave me permission to go. I was still under thirteen conditions of probation so I had to coordinate between the Georgia and Minnesota Departments of Correction upon arrival.

Greer Parramore gave me a leave of absence from Private Jet, and I departed for Minnesota on Sunday, May 23, 1993. I moved in with Terry and his wife Susan and began flying on Tuesday, May 25th. I never flew small planes before so this would be an all new experience. In the Marine Corps, some forty-two years earlier, I began with a Beech T-34, which was classified in general aviation as a "high performance" airplane. The world of small civilian airplanes was foreign to me and there was a lot to learn.

In the ensuing days I would sometimes fly as many as three times a day. Terry and his son, Matt, shared the instructional chores. Both were superb pilots and instructors. I always considered Terry one of the finest pilots I ever flew with. We flew together when I was a second officer and also a copilot. I also flew with Kirk Leabo, a young man trying to build time for employment with the majors. As he and I walked over the tarmac for our first flight, Kirk, who looked at my resume and saw my total flight time of 15,000 hours, said, "I'm really looking forward to this. I'm going to learn a lot!" I stopped, turned to him and said, "Kirk, let's get one thing straight. *You're* the instructor and I'm the student. I know nothing about these planes and I expect you to teach me!" And he did. He was a fine, knowledgeable, and patient instructor.

Then the two Marsh's enlisted the help of Bill Mavencamp, who was the locally designated FAA examiner and known to be tough on check rides. They ambushed him by not telling him who I was at first. I met Bill, spent time with him, and enjoyed his company. Bill had strong sentiments about the Northwest pilots who had flown drunk and never would have agreed to be the check airman. But as Bill told me later, "By the time I found out who you were, it was too late. I already liked you." He was a rigorously thorough examiner, but fair in every sense. I enjoyed all my flights with him. The FAA had found out where I was going and they contacted him. Bill said he was told, "Don't make it easy for this guy." When I heard that I smiled and said, "I've heard that since my first day in prison."

On June 28th, Bill Mavencamp worked me over in a twin-engine Piper Seneca. I had a good day flying as I passed my multi-engine Private license exam. Upon landing, he looked at Terry's single engine Cessna Cardinal and said, "You've been flying that plane. I know, because I've heard you on the radio. If you want to go for it, I'll give you two check rides for the price of one." I said, "I don't know, Bill. I haven't been doing any of the practice stuff in it since we switched to the twin engine airplane." Bill said, "It's up to you." I walked inside where Terry was and asked what he thought. Terry grinned and threw me the keys to the Cardinal. Bill and I took off again and I performed well, receiving a single engine Private license. It was only 11:15 A.M. I earned two licenses on the same day, before noon; I'm not sure anyone has ever done that before.

On July 2nd, I experienced a serious down moment. I was taking my instrument check ride with Bill and was on a difficult approach. Bill failed several instruments and I was extremely busy when he also failed an engine. Inexplicably, I nearly feathered the wrong engine, which would have meant both engines were lost. The moment I touched the wrong engine I knew it, but it was too late. I instantly failed the check ride. Bill felt bad but I told him not to, that fair was fair and I screwed up. As a pilot who always took extreme pride in my ability, it was a crippling and humbling blow. Kirk Leabo was riding in the back seat and he was speechless. I dreaded returning to the airport and telling Terry. But Terry was simply Terry - kind, supporting, and empathetic.

I was to have dinner that night with a recovering friend but I wanted to cancel and be alone. I knew that was the wrong thing to do, so I went. As we ate, I told Tres about the day's events. Calling up all I learned, I said it was probably something I needed to experience in the area of humility and would take it as such. I felt like a boxer who had been pummeled and beaten, but it was time to get off the floor and go at it again.

The next day I smiled and said it was time to get back to work. I have always learned more from my defeats than my victories, so I tried to convert this experience into another positive event. The airplane we were using had to go in for its 100-hour check so Terry managed to find another twin-engine airplane, a Beech Duchess. I needed to complete the check ride within the next few days, but I had never *seen* a Beech Duchess before. Except for having two engines it was completely different from the Seneca.

I went to Maple Lake airport where the plane was located and flew two and a half hours with a new instructor, Andy Moses. He signed me off, shrugged, and said, "You won't have any trouble on the check ride." We did all the routine maneuvers, but I only had *one* landing and absolutely *no* engine cuts, failures, or single-engine landings. Andy was convinced I would have no trouble and while I appreciated his confidence, I wasn't so sure. I asked if he could possibly come out the following morning, which was July 4th, and fly with me if we did it early. He agreed to do that.

The next morning was stormy, with thunderstorms and heavy rain, and it was impossible to get the flight in. If nothing else, I was going to sit in the cockpit for several hours and become intimately familiar with the switches and instruments, most of which were completely different from the Piper Seminole. I was in the cockpit when Andy suddenly came out and said the radar showed a small hole around the airport and he thought we might get in a little flying. We started the engines and launched. I asked for engine failures and engine out landings, and got more than I bargained for. We did four of them, all with a gusting 25-knot crosswind. Most *two-engine* landings are difficult with that much crosswind. I had my hands full; however it was a great confidence builder. I was positive Bill Mavencamp would *never* require anything like what I just accomplished.

Although I only had two flights and about three and a half hours in the Duchess, I performed well on the next instrument check ride a few days later. I even laughed when Bill failed an engine and I said, "I'll take an extra second to *make sure* I get the right one this time!" Bill laughed and I breezed through the check ride.

To celebrate, Peter Wold surprised me with a party at his home. Many of my friends from Northwest were there as well as others. A few minutes into the party, Peter asked me to go to his garage and get something, and I walked out to find Barbara. Peter wanted to surprise me and had flown her up at his expense. He thought it would be a fitting way to end this part of the journey. Once again, I was surprised and touched beyond words.

I completed all the check rides. It seemed strange that I could take a breath and relax from the books and the studies. I asked Terry if I might take his Cardinal on one last flight, early the next morning, and just fly to have fun. Of course, he said yes.

On Tuesday, July 6, 1993, I launched from the Buffalo airport just as the sun was coming up. It was a beautiful Minnesota summer day, barely awakening, yet so full of promise and beauty. I flew nearly a hundred miles west, to Montevideo, and watched the rural Minnesota landscape slowly come alive. I dropped down low over the farmland, wanting to be close to the earth as farmers came out to feed cattle and do their chores. I was very low and I could see them clearly. Several times farmers would look up and I rocked my wings in a "good morning" gesture. They waved back and I flew on. I turned north, toward Alexandria, then back to the east as I headed for Little Falls. The myriad of Minnesota lakes shimmered in the early morning light and I delighted in being alive. I was flying just for fun, with no tasks to perform. I felt like the young cadet who soloed so many years earlier. I flew for two hours and thirty-seven minutes before landing and taxiing in at Buffalo. My entire spirit was refreshed, and I gave Terry his keys for the last time.

Terry and Susan Marsh had a cookout at the airport that night and I was to leave the next day. Again, I saw many friends from Northwest, all of whom came to wish me well and support me. Over the weeks, a number of Northwest pilots stopped by the Buffalo airport and gave Terry money to help with my training. No one asked them, they just did it.

For forty-four days Terry and Susan opened both their home and their hearts to me. I was in the debt of so many and struggling to adjust to so much goodness after everything we went through.

I attacked this entire endeavor with relentless study and hard work. It was worth it. I was beginning a new life and I embraced it with joy and gratitude. I was coming out of the darkness from all the shame and moving into the brightness of a new existence.

I went home on July 7, 1993. It was a long struggle and there was more to come. But I regained four licenses, two private licenses, a commercial, and an instrument rating. The only thing left was my Airline Transport Pilot (ATP) license, and the requirements for that would be met later on.

The Return to Northwest
Airlines - 1993

U pon my return from Minnesota, I needed to study for and take the FAA ATP (Airline Transport Pilot) exam. I scored in the nineties on the exam but still had the flight requirements to complete. Those would come later. I also needed to regain my passport, which had been surrendered before prison, and I did that. Each of those events was a significant and meaningful accomplishment on the path back. I spent the thirteen days following my return to Atlanta involved in those pursuits. Piece by piece, I was putting it back together. I returned to work at Private Jet on July 20, 1993.

Captain O.C. Miller was head of the Air Line Pilot Association at Northwest. I met O.C. years earlier in Narita, Japan, when a number of us had breakfast together. That was the extent of my relationship with him. O.C. became heavily involved in my situation and an ardent supporter. He was a gifted individual, extremely intelligent, exceptionally charismatic, clear visioned, and with an ability to view problems from everyone's perspective. But years of management-labor confrontation created a deep chasm of distrust and dislike between the pilots and Northwest management.

O.C. Miller was able to bridge that chasm with the president and CEO of Northwest, John Dasburg. Dasburg held O.C. in high regard, and over time the two of them developed a close and unique relationship based on mutual respect and trust. No other pilot in the Northwest organization ever earned or enjoyed a position to the degree O.C. had.

O.C. kept in contact with me during the years I was gone. I knew he was dedicated to bringing me back to Northwest, but I also knew it was a Herculean task. I doubted it could be done. Yet I was aware that O.C. and Dasburg discussed it on a number of occasions. There were times when O.C. expressed guarded optimism and other times when things looked very bleak. I tried to stay grounded in the reality that no airline would take back a pilot who had so horribly embarrassed them. Added to that was my convicted felon status, and the fact that I was an openly diagnosed alcoholic who captured the public's attention. My chance of winning the lottery seemed more realistic.

On September 20, 1993, my FAA licenses arrived in the mail. I just came in from a 10-hour workday at PJE and was tired as I opened the mail to find them. Moments later, at 6:00 P.M. the phone rang. It was O.C. Miller. He asked me to sit down and began to tell me that, when he took the helm of ALPA two years earlier, he had certain aspirations. He talked of his disappointment at being unable to affect most of the changes he sought, and how disillusioned he became. I knew he was about to tell me my situation was one more such event and how sorry he was.

A voice began to rise inside me, saying, "This is the end and you *must* accept it." I continued to hear O.C.'s words on the phone, but they were fading as the voice inside me grew louder and louder, repeating itself each time and demanding acceptance. Suddenly in the distance I heard him say, "But every now and then something happens that makes all the rest worthwhile. And this is one of them. This is the best phone call I've ever made because three hours ago you became a Northwest pilot again. John Dasburg has personally reinstated you to full flight status."

Incredulous, I had to ask O.C. to stop for a moment. I paused and tried to put the brakes on an emotional train going the other direction. I asked him to repeat what he just said, and as he did so I broke down and wept. Tears streamed down my cheeks and I struggled to speak. It was a moment that never fails to bring tears each time I recall it. As I went through this whole experience, I experienced a depth of negative emotions I never knew existed; I struggled to climb out of places beyond my imagination. In the face of all perceived impossibility, learning of my return to pilot status at Northwest was an emotional high I never before experienced.

I concluded my conversation with O.C. and walked inside where Barbara was sitting. She knew I was speaking with him and when she saw the tears streaming down my face she assumed the worst. I walked to her and she stood. I put my arms around her, drew her close, with my face and my tears against her neck. Unable to speak, all I could do was chokingly say,"We're going back...we're going back."

The following day I looked for Greer Parramore when I arrived for work. When Greer hired me I told him, as an aside, "I have a dream that I might someday return to Northwest and I need to tell you that. I consider it a near impossibility and most likely a fantasy, but I still need to be honest and let you know." Greer looked at me and said, "If that opportunity came and you didn't take it, I wouldn't want you flying as a Captain for me. Your judgment would be faulty."

I walked into Greer's office and sat down. I looked at Greer and said, "It's nearly impossible for me to believe, but last night I was called and told that Northwest wanted me back." Greer beamed, leaned across the desk, shook hands with me, and offered his heartfelt congratulations.

Northwest offered to provide an airline ticket so we might return to sign our back to work agreement, but I declined. I wanted to make the long drive again, retracing the same exact path we took for the trial. I wanted to stay at the same cheap places, but this time I wanted to see how it felt going back to celebrate our return. And that's what we did. Every mile brought us closer to a victory I could never have dreamed, when once it was our blackest disaster looming in the miles ahead. I would look over at Barbara, who rode through all this with me, and was so glad she was beside me now.

Approaching Chattanooga, I picked a random exit and turned off of I-75. I found a phone booth and looked up "Holder's Family Restaurant." George Holder was an elderly inmate in his seventies who had been sent to prison, along with his minister, because they were involved in a church bingo game. Neither had thought it was a crime to play bingo and raise money for the church, but it was gambling so they were sent to prison. It was one more example of how overzealous prosecutors can select whom they will incarcerate. George Holder was a kind, gentle soul anyone would want as a grandfather.

Amazingly, I looked up from the phone book and saw Holder's Family Restaurant across the street, directly in front of me, so Barbara and I drove in and parked. I hoped to see George but his son told me he no longer came to the restaurant. He said prison destroyed him and he was simply waiting to die, with no will to live and nothing to look forward to. Barbara and I always saw George's wife in the visiting room as she faithfully visited him each weekend, and we liked them very much. The son gave us a complimentary lunch; I gave him my name and address, and asked that he pass my best wishes on to George. It was one more prison story ending in tragedy. I never heard from George.

We stopped at an Econolodge and a Knight's Inn on the way to Minneapolis. Our spirits were so high that they seemed like five-star motels. Barbara was radiant as we made our way north. She pointed out beautiful horse farms and meadows as we made our way through the Kentucky landscape into Indiana. Years seemed to have fallen away from us and we both recognized how fortunate we were to have come through this experience intact. The brief visit at Holder's Family Restaurant added stark emphasis to that fact.

We arrived in Minneapolis at 3:30 P.M. on Thursday, October 28, 1993. We checked into room 105 at the Holiday Inn Express, and the following day I reported to the Airport Medical Clinic for my return to work physical. The evening we arrived, we drove out to the Northwest Training Center and I just sat and looked. I never expected to see it again.

My return would normally have been an administrative matter, handled by correspondence. O.C. said this event was of such magnitude that they wanted to have an official gathering at the ALPA office and I should notify any friends. I did, and there was a large gathering on Monday morning, November 1st, as I officially signed my back to work agreement and returned to Northwest Airlines as a pilot. The morning was rich with emotion as so many who supported us were there to share in my return. There was a time when it took courage for someone to say they were my friend in the face of my shame and disgrace. Now, they gathered with us to celebrate an occasion once considered impossible.

I was to work in the training department for a year, in the 727 simulator program, and then transition back to line flying as a 747 copilot. My boss would be 727 Fleet Captain Ken Redeske who warmly and kindly welcomed me back. I couldn't have had a better boss. According to the agreement, I would never be a Captain again, but I was fine with that. I had been a Captain and had no unanswered questions. I was so overwhelmed with gratitude that I didn't care. I was restored, given back my worth as a human being, and I was going to fly again. I was going to receive the retirement I lost, which was one of the knives in my heart, knowing my misconduct brought Barbara to a dead end. I would have less than five years remaining before retiring at the mandatory pilot retirement age of sixty.

Northwest intended to remain silent about bringing me back and said so as we signed the agreement. I knew that would be a grave error as the media seemed to pick up the slightest whisper in the wind. But Northwest was bringing me back to fly airplanes, *not* run their PR department, and I did whatever they asked. After the back to work ceremony concluded, they must have brainstormed that decision all day, because they called me late at night and woke me up.

They asked how I felt about reporters. I replied that I disliked them but did not fear them. They asked if I would meet with two reporters the next morning and I agreed to. Barbara and I arrived at Peter Wold's office the next morning to find Jon Austin waiting for us. Jon was the official Northwest spokesman. We never met him before. Also waiting was Laura Baenen, from the Associated Press, and another reporter, David Carr, standing by for a second interview.

I sensed an adversarial interview immediately as Laura began. I remained calm, however, as I responded politely to her questions. As we moved through the interview I watched a shift in her attitude. An hour and a half later she seemed to almost be on my side, and her demeanor had changed. As the interview drew to an end she turned to Jon Austin, "Was there any opposition to Lyle's return?" she asked. Jon replied confidently, "Mr. Dasburg manages through an Executive Management Team comprised of senior vice presidents. The consensus was that this was the right thing to do. After sitting and listening, *I can assure you* it was the right thing to do."

Barbara told me later that she sensed a coldness from Jon when we first met him; I did not. However, I was focused on the reporters and failed to pay much attention to him. Nonetheless, Jon and I became good friends on that day and remained so until my retirement.

We then did the second interview and it was a touch of deja vu since David Carr was the only Minnesota journalist I spoke with after my trial three years earlier. At that point the future could not have been bleaker. Sitting with him this time, we were celebrating a moment no one could have contemplated.

Northwest anticipated a large negative media reaction to my reinstatement, but it never came. In my view, their willingness to take me back, in light of what they anticipated, only added to the level of courage required. People from all over the country sent me editorials and other pieces addressing my return. If there were any negative reactions I never saw them. The sole exception was Jay Leno. I boosted his career for a long while as he never seemed to run out of material on me for his monologue.

A few years later, I reacted to a Sunday newspaper piece where he allegedly said a joke needed to be demeaning to be funny, which he later denied as a misquote. Reacting to the piece, I wrote him a three-page letter detailing the effect his humor had on me as I was in the deepest valley of my life. It was a calm and measured letter, devoid of anger, merely describing how I was affected. I expected no answer from him; in fact, I never expected him to see it. I simply wrote it for closure on my part and forgot it once mailed.

Two weeks later, in June 1996, he phoned and apologized to me. I thanked him and accepted his apology.

I went to work at NATCO (the Northwest training center) and I could not have been happier. I was overwhelmed with gratitude. Most of the instructors were assigned sixteen simulator events a month but I was to work twenty-two and happily accepted them. I flew simulator support, in either cockpit seat, for Boeing 727 trainees. I hadn't flown in a long while but I quickly became more proficient than ever since I was often spending eight hours a day flying. Emergencies became easy and routine; I felt as though I could fly with one hand as I performed the required procedures. It was a wonderful way to transition back into the actual flying that would come later.

We were coming from ground zero financially and I was going to be spending a lot of days in Minnesota. Captain Jim Hystad and his wife, Joyce, offered me the use of their beautiful home, located thirty minutes away in Wisconsin. They were wintering in Florida. They gave me the keys and insisted I stay there free. I balked so they reluctantly let me pay a small amount for utilities.

I thought about John Dasburg's courage. There were simply no words to describe it. If I failed, if I drank again, or if I had another flying incident, John Dasburg's reputation as a CEO would have been destroyed. The media would have massacred him. He had 50,000 employees working for him worldwide, yet he took the time to care about *one*. He took an unbelievable chance. He had nothing to gain by bringing me back and virtually everything to lose. It was unbelievable.

I knew that O.C. Miller was the lynchpin in my return; I was *certain* no other pilot could have persuaded John Dasburg to take such a chance. He risked his reputation by believing in me, and that strongly influenced John Dasburg, because *he* believed in O.C. Miller.

In the years remaining, I dedicated myself to vindicating both of them and everyone else who stayed the course with Barbara and me. I owed so much to so many, and I knew I could never repay them.

Although I received overwhelming support, I knew there was a faction who opposed my return. My friends told me it was small but I had no idea if it was two, five, or ten percent of the pilots. During my first week back, Clay Foushee, Vice President of Flight Operations, asked if I would address the entire flight-training department at NATCO. I agreed to do so. On a Thursday afternoon I walked into the large conference room to find standing room only, with pilots, instructors, and staff lining the walls around the entire room. There were probably three hundred or more people in the room and I found it daunting.

Chris Clouser, a senior VP and the right-hand man to John Dasburg, approached me and pinned a small microphone on my lapel. He informed me my talk would be videotaped and shown to the board of directors.

I never tried to script what I was going to say. It came spontaneously and from the heart. I knew there were opponents to my return in the room. I acknowledged that and said I accepted it, adding I would probably feel the same way if I had not found myself in such a position.

I spoke of my experiences candidly, asked for no sympathy, and I said I respected everyone's feelings and opinions about my return. Over the course of the next two weeks, many came up to me and said they had changed their mind and were glad I was back. Each time was a surprise; I did not expect anything after I spoke that day.

My year in the training department came and went. Northwest asked for an extension on my return to line flying and I granted it. I spent five more months in the training department, and then I began my recurrent training period in April of 1995 for re-qualification as a 747 first officer.

As the date neared for me to move back into the cockpit Chris Clouser called a meeting. A large number of high-ranking company officials gathered in their boardroom and I sat in their midst. Chris read a document stating that I was to return to the cockpit and begin flying again. He ended his statement saying, "You will conclude your service at Northwest Airlines as a First Officer." I signed the back to work agreement knowing I would never be a captain again and I was okay with that.

The following day I ran into Sarge Martin, Director of Flying, and the man who had to fire me several years earlier. Sarge became a strong supporter and said to me, "I didn't like the part about your concluding your career as a First Officer." I smiled and replied, "I've *been* a captain, Sarge. I have no unanswered questions. While I would love to end my career back in the left seat I'm okay with things as they are. One thing I've learned is that *no one really knows how this will end.*" I continued, "Any time I wonder about the future or what it holds, I simply turn around, look at all that's behind me, the miracles I've experienced, and I have no fear of what's ahead." He smiled and said, "I wish I had your attitude."

Touching the Sky Once Again

I flew my first 747 copilot trip on May 27, 1995, taking Northwest Flight 44 to London, England, and Barbara went with me. We laid over in Brighton and had a magnificent time with the crew. The flight attendants all fell in love with Barbara and made sure she rode in first class both ways. Laughingly, they told me I was not allowed to fly unless I brought her on every trip.

I offered to buy a new three-stripe copilot uniform, but Captain Sarge Martin told me to keep my four-stripes. He felt I earned the four stripes and was entitled to wear them. I just didn't wear a Captain's hat.

Twice I flew with captains who had strong negative feelings about my return. I sensed their feelings immediately, but I remained pleasant, did my job professionally, and granted them the right to feel however they felt without ever saying a word to them about it. Both times they called my hotel room midway through the trip and asked if I would have breakfast with them. Both times they apologized and said they were glad we had flown together. Because I had learned to accept things, even if I didn't like them, I could conduct myself in a way that drew them to me instead of away from me. It was one more thing I owed my sobriety and the lessons learned in treatment.

Each year John Dasburg would spontaneously summon me to his office. I never had any idea when it would be or what we would discuss. I lived a life free of fear, so there was nothing he could ask that I was reluctant to talk about. I enjoyed each of our visits and we communicated easily and openly. I felt a genuine fondness for him and looked forward to the visits.

Eventually, I found myself dreaming about being a Captain again and felt guilty about it. I had been given back so much, so I tried not to want more. Still, I thought, it would be the final vindication. I thought of the circle, so sacred to Native people with all its significant meanings, and I thought a return to the left seat would complete the circle. But I vowed to remain silent. I just needed to be grateful for what I had.

In early 1997, I received another annual summons to John Dasburg's office. Chris Clouser was present, as he always was, and I walked into the office. With barely a word of greeting, John Dasburg looked at me and said, "What can we do for you, Lyle?" I was momentarily startled but my instant thought was *I'd like to be a captain again*. Instead, I responded, "Nothing. You've already done it," and I smiled.

Almost immediately, I regretted it. I thought, *Dammit, they were asking to see if you wanted to be a captain. Now they think you're content to stay where you are, that you don't want to face another captain checkout.* A few minutes later, Chris Clouser said something indicating he thought I was flying as a 747-400 first officer. The 400 was a two-man 747, and since I never flew that position before a move to that slot would have frozen me there for the two years remaining in my career. So I deliberately passed it up.

I corrected Chris and said, "I'm flying the generic 747. A move to the 400 would have frozen me and eliminated any chance I might someday be a captain." Then I immediately changed the subject and segued into something else. I thought, *Good. Now they know what I'm thinking and I didn't have to put them on the spot by asking.*

As we finished our meeting, I walked to the door with John Dasburg. He again asked, "Lyle, what can we do for you?" I replied, "I guess if I wanted something it would be to make it easier for the guys behind me," meaning the returning alcoholic pilots now in recovery. John Dasburg put his hand on my shoulder and smiled, "You've already done that," he said, as we shook hands. I began to walk out the door. Dasburg stopped me and looked directly into my face. "We love you," he said in a soft manner. I paused, smiled, and said, "I love you, too." And I walked away. I came to know the president and CEO of a huge, worldwide airline in a way no other pilot before me. I was completely humbled by that thought.

During the years I was free, I spoke all over the country at the invitation of various groups, some recovering and some not. There was never a charge for the speaking engagements. Occasionally, an honorarium would be offered by a non-recovering entity. Every penny was sent to an Indian treatment center, first in Wichita, then later to one in Shell Lake, Wisconsin. I have participated in many workshops around the country, spoken at virtually all the major airlines, and am willing to go anywhere to help those recovering.

I agreed to speak at the United Airlines three-day alcohol and drug seminar for their flight operations department on April 29, 1997. They flew Barbara in with me. Approximately 125 United employees attended from all over the country. Their entire Employee Assistance Program (EAP) department was there as well as all their chief pilots and many leading professionals in the field.

I was the keynote speaker as the workshop got under way. Concluding my talk, I said, "I'll never be a captain again, but that's okay. I've been given so much back that it doesn't matter, and I'm completely saturated with gratitude for the life I have today." They responded warmly, as they always had before.

Barbara and I were asleep in our room late that night when the phone rang. It was O.C. Miller. He was no longer head of the pilot union but he remained a close friend and confidante of John Dasburg. I was surprised by his call and even more surprised when I heard O.C. say, "John Dasburg just told me he thought you ought to be a 747 captain when you return." Stunned by the news, I relayed it to Barbara who was awake and listening to my conversation.

I lay awake in the dark for a long time afterwards, unable to sleep. I had experienced so many miracles and many times thought to myself, *This is the ultimate; nothing can eclipse this.* And each time I was wrong. In the darkness I had the strangest feeling that God was looking down and grinning as He said, "See, every time you think I've used up my miracles I can always show you one more."

The next morning Barbara and I attended breakfast with all the United personnel. I sought out Poss Horton, the chief pilot from Dulles airport and the person in charge of the workshop. I told him about the phone call the previous night. Poss grinned as he excitedly asked, "Would you announce that at breakfast this morning?" A short while later he called the group to order. I stood and told them about the phone call and the crowd erupted with a thunderous reaction. Barbara was not in the banquet room with me, but she knew I made the announcement because the noise in the hallway was deafening.

I returned to Northwest and put my card in for a captain position. When a slot became available a few weeks later I began the checkout and concluded it on August 28, 1997, receiving my final type rating as a captain in the Boeing 747. Captain Terry Marsh, Fleet Captain of the 747 program, gave me the check ride. Two outstanding pilots asked to fly with me on that day, and Captain Ken Waldrip served as my copilot while former Captain Gene Schmidt handled the second officer duties. Terry worked me over thoroughly, laughing as he threw one thing after another at me and I scrambled to keep up. But I was sober and my mind was quick and clear; I was well prepared, and relished the challenges with good humor and competency.

We taxied in and I shut the engines down. Terry grinned, reached over, shook my hand, and said, "Congratulations, Captain!" Ken and Gene followed suit. I had completed my journey home and was taken by the power of the moment. I returned to the left seat as the sacred circle closed for the final time in my career.

A short while later, I was scheduled to deadhead home as a passenger from Narita, Japan. An FAA inspector was on board and he quietly came to me and said he was supposed to give me a final look-see on behalf of the FAA. I smiled and said I would be happy to do the flying. I put my flight bag in the cockpit. As I stepped back to get something, he said he wanted to speak with me. I stopped to listen as he continued, "Lyle, I'm not here as an adversary. I have the highest regard for you and what you've done. I want you to know that." I smiled and thanked him; what he just said and did was very un-FAA-like and I appreciated it.

He wrote a glowing report on my performance and it made its way up to Chris Clouser, John Dasburg, and back to O.C. Miller, who sent me a copy.

I spent the last full year of my flying career as a 747 captain for Northwest Airlines. John Dasburg entrusted me with a mega-million dollar airplane, a crew of eighteen, and allowed me to fly all around the world. I was a recovering alcoholic, a convicted felon, and he placed these precious things in my hands. What more can be said. I am satisfied that I acquitted myself well and vindicated the faith that O.C. Miller and John Dasburg placed in me. I think I may have changed the minds of some of the nay-sayers and doubters. I wanted to be the best employee on the property; I worked at it every moment.

From the time I first returned to Northwest until my final flight, I experienced the goodness of people. I never flew a twelve or thirteen day trip without six to ten people coming up to me in hallways, restaurants, airports, or hotels, to introduce themselves and say they were glad I was back. The small group of opponents never approached me so all my experiences were positive.

I was in my final year on March 6, 1998, and we were slated to fly from Los Angeles to Osaka, Japan. I was aware of the date, since it was within one day of my sobriety date and two days from my arrest in 1990. Due to the length of the flight it would be an augmented crew, with two captains, two second officers, and one first officer. I was the senior captain and it was my practice to offer the choice of flight periods to the junior captain. The other captain opted to go first, which I expected, since the last half of the trip was the most fatiguing.

The captain I was with had never been particularly well liked, but I'd never flown with him before so I approached this trip with an open mind. Two hours over the Pacific, I was seated in the business cabin and heard the lead flight attendant page for a doctor on board. I asked what the problem was and she said a passenger was having chest pains. Strangely, there were no doctors, nurses, or other medical personnel on board – unusual for a 747 flight.

A passenger came up and said he was once a Red Cross volunteer, but it had been years ago. He was uneasy but said he would help if no one else was available. He and I went back and spoke with the distressed passenger. The passenger was a portly Caucasian male who appeared to be in his late fifties or early sixties. He stated there was no family history of heart disease, he was not on any type of medication, and had no pain

251

in his left arm. In addition to his chest pains, his face was flushed and his breathing somewhat erratic. He was obviously very frightened. The Red Cross volunteer and I walked back to the front of the plane. He said he was unsure, but thought the man was probably experiencing a heart attack. I took his name and thanked him for helping.

I went to the cockpit and informed the other captain that we had a problem and should probably consider a diversion to the nearest airport. He was reluctant. We all knew a diversion would throw the flight into disarray, causing connection problems for passengers. Additionally, it would add hours to an already long day of flying once we got airborne again. He said he wanted to go back and speak with the passenger, which surprised me. If I was flying and the other captain said he thought we should consider a diversion, I would accept his judgment. I climbed into the vacant captain seat while he went back to the cabin.

I asked the other crewmembers what their thoughts were about the situation, starting with the junior man, the second officer. Both he and the copilot thought we could have a serious potential problem on our hands. I summarized my own thoughts and said, "As I see it, the *best* scenario we can hope for is that the passenger doesn't die in the eleven hours of flight time remaining. But once he's in Osaka he will still require medical help and he'll be in a foreign land where he doesn't speak the language or have financial resources. If he dies *before* we get there and we knew about the situation two hours out, it's indefensibly poor and unacceptable judgment to have continued." Both of them agreed. I concluded by saying, "I think the best course of action is to head for an airport and not gamble with this man's life." They both concurred.

I had been downstairs in the cabin for two hours, so I asked the copilot what airport we were closest to and he indicated San Francisco. I told him to get us a clearance and declare a medical emergency. He did so and I was in the process of turning east for the airport when the other captain re-entered the cockpit. Nonchalantly, he said, "I talked with the man and he's willing to continue." We had three hundred and three passengers on board and I felt sure he had discussed all the lost or missed connections and pressured the man into continuing. I said, "He's no longer part of the equation." I almost said, "and neither are you" My counterpart noticed we were turning and said, "What are we doing?" I said, "We're heading for San Francisco."

Somewhat irritated, he asked, "Well, are you taking over?" I responded, "Yes, pass my flight bag up to me, please." Part of the recovery wisdom integrated into my life was separating the problem from the solution. At that moment, the other captain was part of the problem and I needed to deal with the solution.

I made an extensive PA announcement to the passengers and explained what we were doing and why. I asked the passengers to think of this man as their husband, father, or family member and consider what they would want us to do in that case. I acknowledged the connection difficulties and said we would deal with them once we were on the ground. The lead flight attendant came up and said the passengers reacted well and were not complaining at all. That made it much easier on the flight attendants.

I asked the second officer to calculate how much fuel we needed to dump to arrive at our maximum landing weight. After a quick calculation he replied we had to reduce our weight by one hundred thousand pounds. I told him to start dumping fuel and a moment later he informed me one of the two dump valves wouldn't open. That meant we would most likely be unable to get our weight below the allowable maximum landing weight. The weather at San Francisco was rainy, with winds out of the east. There were no approaches from the west due to the high terrain, so we were now faced with a wet runway and a tailwind landing at high gross weight. Minutes later, the second officer managed to get the other dump valve open ensuring we would be able to get down to the maximum landing weight.

The other conditions still meant a dicey landing. I asked air traffic control for a lower altitude to increase our fuel burn. I pushed the power levers forward to a high power setting, and raised the speed brakes to give us more drag while still maintaining good forward speed. We would now burn fuel faster as we continued to dump.

I shot the approach and the landing was smooth as we decelerated nicely on the runway. I taxied into the gate area and was informed over the radio that ambulance personnel would be boarding the airplane to take the distressed passenger off. I made a PA asking for all passengers to remain seated until this was accomplished. I immediately went down to the cabin and was standing there when the medical personnel brought the passenger past me in an aisle chair. The flight attendants had put him on oxygen, but he pulled the mask off as he approached. He looked up and said; "Thank you." I will never forget the look of relief and gratitude in his eyes. I told him he was welcome and wished him well. He was clearly glad to be back on U.S. soil where he could receive the care he needed.

We refueled, re-catered, and taxied back out. The flight attendants could have shut the flight down due to flight time duty limitations but they unanimously opted to continue the flight. I wrote each of them a glowing letter of commendation once the trip was over.

As I taxied out, we received a call over the company radio. The medics verified that our passenger was indeed having a heart attack and was on the way to a hospital. The other captain was listening on his headset and he looked at me. "It was a good call," he said. I knew it was.

In the hours afterward, as we made our way across the Pacific, I gazed at the calm Pacific from the left seat. I sat quietly and reflected.

I was within one day of my sobriety anniversary eight years previous, and two days from the day I risked the lives of fifty-eight passengers. And now, eight years later, God gave me an opportunity to do something good. Perhaps He let me save a life as a result of my sobriety and the miracles that brought me to this moment. I said nothing to anyone as I sat in quiet, prayer-like, humble gratitude.

When I returned home I wrote a letter to John Dasburg. I thanked him for making me a captain, thus allowing me to be the one who made the decision on this flight. Had I been a copilot, I would have been unable to direct a course of action. Quite possibly, the outcome might have been tragically different.

I retired on my birthday, September 29, 1998, at the mandatory retirement age of sixty years. In a way, I left as I began because we suffered the first pilot strike in twenty years, stranding me in Bangkok, Thailand on my final trip. Three days later I made my way home to Atlanta. I would not have my final, celebratory retirement trip with Barbara accompanying me, but it was okay.

As I closed my career, I had regained all I lost except for the material goods. We were financially destroyed in the aftermath of my arrest and imprisonment. I would not have traded all those losses for my sobriety and the beauty of life that I've come to know. It was a difficult journey, and yet also one of miracles and beauty. In exchange for money and material losses, I was given dignity, self-worth, honor, humility, and a purpose for living. My children would escape the horror I witnessed as I watched my parents die from alcoholism. Instead, they had two laughing and healthy parents who loved them, and would to the end of their days. I learned to be grateful for everything that happened *to* me. Without those things I could never have experienced all the things that later happened *for* me.

I remembered that reading from a daily meditation book in the early days which said, "Adversity truly introduces us to ourselves." I remembered the fear inside because I didn't know who was there. Nothing I accomplished was mine alone. I am neither unique nor special. I simply followed suggestions, tried to live according to the principles embodied in a program of recovery, and targeted the next right thing day in and day out. I stayed sober one day at a time, as I remained acutely aware of and grateful for my sobriety. I said "Thank You" a lot to a God of my understanding. I had a wife who steadfastly stayed the course with me and offered encouragement each time my spirits sagged. Finally, Barbara and I were blessed beyond words with friends who came from everywhere. Without them we could not have survived. Today, we measure our wealth in friends and are wealthy beyond dreams.

Two weeks before my retirement, Barbara and I appeared on an ABC Nightline Special with Ted Koppel. Also appearing was John Dasburg and Judge Rosenbaum. The program was entitled "To Fly Again" and was three years in the making because I did not trust media people. In those three years I got to know and trust the producer, Laura Palmer. She produced a powerful program. It triggered a second movie offer, which we declined.

As part of the filming, I accompanied the Nightline film crew to the federal prison, where they wanted to speak to some of the prison staff. At first, I declined to go. Then, knowing the patent disregard that prison officials had for the truth, I decided I should be there. I refused, however, to talk to or shake hands with any of the prison personnel. Several staff members recognized me, including "Throw-The-Book" Cook. Mostly ignoring them, I sat inside my car and watched the Nightline crew put cameras and sound equipment out on the sidewalk directly in front of the main prison entrance. While I looked at the long steps going into the institution, Julie Cullen came out the door. She was wearing her blue guard's uniform and talking with another guard, when she noticed me sitting in my car.

There were many people moving about on the sidewalk but I just sat and watched her. She looked at me again as she walked past. I met her eyes but neither spoke nor acknowledged her. Watching my side rear mirror, I saw her stop, then turn around. She walked back to the car and asked, "Weren't you one of my inmates?"

I looked at her and replied calmly, "No. I was here once, but I was never one of *your* inmates." Not sure of what to say next, she looked at the film crew and the equipment, and asked, "What are you doing these days?" It was a question I hoped she would ask. I said, "I'm a 747 captain for Northwest Airlines." She looked surprised, nodded, murmured something, and walked away.

As I closed the chapter to my Northwest career, another miracle was born. I received a phone call from my former attorney, now my good friend, Peter Wold. He told me Judge Rosenbaum had called. The judge told Peter he'd never supported a petition for pardon in his sixteen years on the bench, but would support mine if I chose to make the attempt. I had never considered such a thing. The odds of obtaining a presidential pardon were almost unfathomable, but I faced long odds many times before. I requested the necessary paperwork from the Pardons Office in Washington, D.C. They sent me a stack of forms and documents I would need to prepare the petition.

Retirement and Pardon

I began the process for pardon in January 1999, and spent two years in that endeavor. Nothing ever came quickly or easily and I was accustomed to that. Judge Rosenbaum wrote a powerful three page affidavit that fills my eyes with tears each time I read it.

In his affidavit, Judge Rosenbaum says in part, "Mr. Prouse was, and is, unlike any defendant who has ever appeared before me."

Judge Rosenbaum continued, "After pronouncing Mr. Prouse's sixteen month sentence and one year sentence on his codefendants, I told them they could delay reporting until their appeals were exhausted. Mr. Prouse's co-defendants opted to defer reporting. Mr. Prouse chose a different path; he told me he had been convicted, sentenced, and should go to jail. In over fourteen years on the bench he was, and remains, the only defendant who has ever said he'd been convicted and sentenced and it was time to go. And he went."

"Mr. Prouse was sent to a prison that did not have a recovery program. He was forbidden to organize one while in custody. In this single regard he was less than a model prisoner – he set one up and dedicated himself to reclaiming his sobriety and his life. Mr. Prouse completed his time and dedicated himself to helping other alcoholic pilots. I am aware of the countless hours he has spent on this program and I am also aware of the help he has rendered to his fellows in the process. Mr. Prouse has

257

materially improved the safety of the passengers who will fly with these pilots."

He then addressed the request from Peter Wold to lift the sanctions he had imposed that would prevent my return to flying.

"I knew keeping a pilot from flying was the greatest punishment I could inflict upon him. I told his counsel that I wanted to hear from Mr. Prouse and asked him to tell his client to write me a letter. I received an eleven page letter about three days later. Before discussing the letter, it is fair to say I had been a federal judge for about eight or nine years when I received it. After that long on the bench, a judge has heard and read about every sob story and claim of personal redemption that can be told.

"Even with this background, Mr. Prouse's letter was one of the most impressive and moving statements I have ever read. It was obvious that he was a gifted writer, but more than that, he had undertaken an amazing personal odyssey.

"Sir, I swear as your affiant, that I have seldom, if ever in my life, encountered a man more richly deserving of a pardon. Lyle Prouse encountered a fall, almost literally, from the heavens in which he had flown so many times. His crime was public, and treated as a comic moment hundreds of times on national television. His reformation and personal triumph in confronting his illness, and ultimately, in confronting himself, deserves the pardon he is seeking.

"I have never met Lyle Prouse out of the courtroom or off the record. But if ever I have a chance to do so, I will tell him, as I now tell you, that this is a man and a citizen of whom this country should be proud. He has served his country well, and when he wronged it, he uncomplainingly paid the price. This is a man who deserves the full rights accorded to an American citizen. I urge your favorable consideration of his efforts to have them reinstated."

It was difficult for me to believe anyone could deserve the redemption I had experienced. I remembered the bitter shame and the thought that I would never rise above it for the remainder of my life, yet the words from my trial judge told me different. He and so many others dared to believe in me and I humbly watched it all in amazement.

Another powerful document came from Rod C, one of the congressmen I had come to know. He was no longer in congress but I valued his wonderful letter on my behalf. Added to that was a warm and supportive letter from Dr. Audie Davis, head of the FAA's Medical Certification branch for 34 years. Dr. Davis personally signed my FAA medical certificate, giving me permission to fly again as a recovering alcoholic. My minister and our county sheriff also spoke up on my behalf.

On October 19, 1999,   I made a trip to downtown Atlanta to Senator Paul Coverdell's office. I finally completed the extensive paperwork in the pardons packet and wanted to see if I could get any support that might draw some attention to my case. Initially, I was ushered into the Senator's office and treated courteously, *until* I mentioned why I was there. Then, as had happened many times before, I saw an invisible curtain descend. While the tone remained polite, I knew the meeting was over. It was a situation I'd experienced many times before and I recognized it immediately.

No politician wanted to be involved in *anything* regarding a convicted felon. The memory of the Willie Horton case and how it torpedoed the presidential bid of Michael Dukakis was still fresh. I was an anathema. Before leaving, however, I pulled the Nightline tape out and asked if someone might *please* give me seventeen minutes of their time and look at the tape. I told them the story was contained in that small amount of time. I said if they watched it and still chose not to help me I would gladly accept it and not bother them again.

I left not knowing if they would watch it or not, but a week later I received a phone call saying they would be willing to help. Senator Coverdell attached a cover letter to my pardon packet that was carefully worded and very non-committal. Still, simply having a letter with his name on it would be helpful. Then he and President Clinton clashed over an issue that made national news, and I was fearful I might become a target of political retribution. I decided to approach Senator Max Cleland. He was a democrat and if willing to sign on I would have the support of a republican and a democrat. Max Cleland and I shared the Vietnam experience and a military background, and I thought he might be supportive. I couldn't have been more wrong.

Senator Cleland was speaking at a church in nearby Lithonia, Georgia, so Barbara and I attended. He had lost both legs and an arm in Vietnam and we listened to his talk. Afterwards, he would be in the church basement signing copies of his book, *Strong at the Broken Places*. Barb and I queued up in the line with a book in our hands. It was an awkward place to approach him and I had only seconds to make my case. Senator Cleland's face gave me the answer before he even spoke, but he looked up at me and said, "The last time I did something like that it cost me six million dollars." I was taken aback but I thanked him and walked away.

I went home demoralized. I had not expected that reaction, but I wrote to his Washington, D.C. office anyway. I gave a brief narrative of my journey thus far. I was calm and measured in my comments. I thanked him for his time, said I understood his position, and that I would continue on alone. I was stunned to receive a letter from his chief of staff two weeks later, saying Senator Cleland would join Senator Coverdell and sign the cover letter.

I sent in my packet hoping someone would look at it. I felt there was a strong argument for pardon based on merit alone, but I feared my paperwork would get sidetracked in a box on some dusty shelf somewhere.

As President Clinton prepared to leave office, two lists of pardons were published weeks apart. My name was nowhere to be found. Television announced the pardon of former congressman Dan Rostenkowski and I immediately sensed the pardon process was more about political payback than a genuine exercise in humanity, so I concluded I would not qualify.

Disillusioned and frustrated, I told Barbara I thought we could forget about a pardon. A day or so later, having collected my thoughts, my entire attitude changed. I said to Barbara, "Look at all we've been given back. Look at all the miracles. And here I stand angry and frustrated because I don't get one more. I'm letting it go; I don't need it. I have so much more than I ever deserved or could have hoped for, and I simply don't need this one."

A few days later, on January 20, 2001, Barbara and I came home and saw eight messages flashing on our answering machine. The first was a message from Laura Palmer, the producer at ABC Nightline. She was so excited she never even identified herself but I recognized her voice as she said, "You just received a presidential pardon! Everyone here is so excited for you! We're all just so excited!" and she hung up. The next seven messages all echoed her enthusiasm.

Had the idea not come from my trial judge, I would never have embarked on the attempt. Judge Rosenbaum became one of my strongest supporters, and he was the toughest trial judge in the Minnesota federal district. So many impossible twists and turns occurred in my journey and I had no answers for any of them. It all boiled down to *grace*, something given to me that I could never earn or deserve.

I turned to Barbara and we embraced. Another miracle had come our way, and it was a huge one. In the life of a convicted felon, a presidential pardon is life changing. At one time I breezed through life as a normal person, but once the tag of felon was hung around my neck, it all changed. Rapists, murderers, drug dealers, child molesters, and drunken pilots are all lumped together and no distinction is ever made for the remainder of one's life. Jobs close, people turn away, and doors slam shut. Nothing can ever counterbalance the label of *felon*.

I served my time and "paid my debt to society." But I would be forever crippled as a felon. Most of my day-to-day life was unaffected, but the felony conviction reared its ugly head at the most unexpected and inopportune times. It was like having a piece of toilet paper stuck to my shoe; all I had to do was look down and it was always there. The presidential pardon changed all that.

I was an avid hunter, but had turned to bow hunting because I was forbidden to ever own or use a firearm. Now that my felony conviction had been lifted, I was free to live life back in the normal lane.

I went to the woods with a rifle in my hands for the first time in October 2001. On the first morning, I took a large six-point deer. My son rushed over, laughing and excited, as he picked me completely off the ground, swung me around, and hugged me. It had been eleven years, and a long time in coming.

My record was not expunged, nor should it have been, in my view. I committed a felony criminal act when I flew drunk which can never be undone. So while it remains on my record, the presidential pardon rests right beneath it.

Reporters from all over the country mobbed me once more. Many wanted to know what the big deal was since I already served my time. They simply didn't know, nor *could* they know, because they hadn't been where I had been. There is nothing about walking out of prison that implies forgiveness for the act committed. Society, in fact, continues to punish. The pardon said to me, "Okay...finally...we forgive you and we welcome you back into our midst." The emotional and psychological impact it brought was as meaningful as the privileges it gave back. It meant I was whole once again.

The pardon is beautifully framed on the office wall in my home. Barbara chuckles each time someone not familiar with my story is drawn to the large words "Executive Grant of Clemency" and immediately walks over and begins to read it.

Epilogue

My former copilot became a 747 captain with a major cargo airline. He made an unsuccessful bid to return to Northwest in 2004, when he finally brought his fourteen year-old termination grievance to an arbitrator. He is a good and decent man, a class act in every way. He was also the least culpable among us. His life since the Northwest Flight 650 incident has been exemplary, and he's displayed the attitude of a champion. The arbitrator, however, chose to narrowly confine the issue to the termination and whether it was justified, ignoring any other consideration.

The second officer who was with me is currently employed. He made an attempt to return to Northwest Airlines in 1993 and was initially supported by the Air Line Pilots Association. He was deceptive in the process and lost that support.

He later wrote and published his own account of this story in 2009 and I read it. It was full of events that never occurred, conversations that never took place, and it was a disturbing example of self-delusion. The few situations that were marginally recognizable were so skewed with embellishment and exaggeration that they were beyond the realm of truth and fact.

He had been employed with Northwest for barely twelve months before being terminated; I was there thirty years before retiring. Fifty-four of my fellow pilots and thirteen flight attendants wrote letters of outrage to the publisher of his book. A letter from John Dasburg, who'd been President and CEO of Northwest during the incident, also went to the publisher and his letter alone was enough to debunk the published version. I offered to pay for polygraph tests for myself and the second officer and even offered to go to his hometown to do that. I received no response other than an acknowledgement that all the letters had been received.

There is no doubt that he and his family suffered horribly, as we all did. After reading his account, I sought counsel from long standing members in my recovery community. I even discussed it with Ted Koppel and Laura Palmer, two professional journalists with a different perspective. Eventually, and very slowly, I managed to move from anger to pity and sympathy for him. I wish him and his family well, but I continue to maintain as much distance between us as possible.

Judge James M. Rosenbaum became Chief Judge of the Federal District, serving in Minnesota. On September 23, 2002, Barbara and I traveled to Washington, D.C., and we met the judge and his wife, Marilyn (also a judge). Twelve years had passed, and it was the first time since the trial that I had seen him. We spent two hours visiting in the lobby of the Mayflower Hotel. Like the early days of my journey, when things seemed horribly surreal, this visit also had a sense of the surreal but for much different reasons. This time it was because I was with a man who had played an enormous role in my life, one that began with each of us in a courtroom in opposite and different roles. Judge Rosenbaum retired from the bench in August of 2010.

John Dasburg, Northwest Airlines President and CEO, left Northwest Airlines in 2000 and became CEO of Burger King. He later became CEO of DHL, an all-cargo airline. I will always wonder where his courage came from to bring me back and allow me to fly again. He and I remain friends and have occasional contact with each other through cards and letters. My experience with him has been nothing short of remarkable.

O.C. Miller still flies as a captain for Northwest Airlines. He and I will always remain friends. I will never be able to thank him enough for the faith and confidence he placed in me, and the personal risks he took on my behalf. He continues to enjoy a position of trust and leadership at Northwest, and is highly respected by both management and the pilot group.

Jerome T. Arnold, the U.S. Attorney in Minneapolis during my trial, encountered his own difficulty with alcohol two years later. A small article discreetly placed in the back pages of a Minnesota newspaper reported that he was fined $700 for driving while his blood alcohol content was over the legal limit. The article stated, "Arnold was on his way to a residence he has at Schultz Lake on February 10 [1992] when he inadvertently entered the Air National Guard Base in Duluth."

Betsy de la Vega, Assistant U.S. attorney, the prosecutor in my trial, took a transfer to California. I last saw her on a TV tabloid program where she continued to proclaim "a conspiracy of silence" among airline pilots, contrary to the open and available information about alcoholism and recovery programs in the airline industry. I declined an invitation to appear on the same program.

My attorney, Peter Wold, got married and has two young sons. He continues a successful law practice in Minneapolis, Minnesota. We have remained close friends. "I believe in you, and I'm staying to the end...wherever that is," will always ring in my heart each time I think of him.

Judge Juanita Marsh, founder of Anchor Hospital, retired from the Georgia state bench. She lost a son who was physically and mentally damaged by drugs. During the course of her tenure at Anchor, she helped thousands of people. She remains a beautiful example of what people can do with a dream.

Marion E. Carl retired from the U.S. Marine Corps in 1973 as a Major General and returned to his Oregon home in a rural area on the banks of the Umpqua River, just outside Roseburg.

It was twenty years after Vietnam, in 1986, when I finally made contact again with my former boss. I wrote a brief note to the general saying, "I was your aide for only four months in Vietnam so you probably don't remember me, but I wanted to write and wish you and your family well." In a nice letter back to me, he said, "During the time I was a general I had a total of nine aides. I only remember three of them and I remember you the most." I was completely surprised and deeply touched. My time with him had been memorable but I had no idea he would remember me.

He asked if I would write my memories of my time with him and many of them appear in his book, *Pushing the Envelope,* which he finally wrote with Barrett Tillman.

He asked if I would like to pack into the mountains on an elk-hunting trip in 1989 and I jumped at the chance. I knew his small group was mostly WWII friends and outsiders weren't normally asked. We sat around mountain campfires at night and listened to stories his friends told. Marion, as he insisted I call him, was never a participant. He was just never very impressed with himself. A year later I was in the headlines, disgraced, and headed for prison. General Carl never turned away from me and he supported me unconditionally the entire time. He and I made another trip to the mountains in 1995. He was 79, experiencing some health problems, and it was his last hunting trip. We had a memorable time and it warms my heart that I could share that last hunting adventure with him.

On June 28, 1998, he died as he lived, acting heroically as he came to the aid of his wife, Edna. A 19-year-old local punk with an extensive criminal past invaded their home that evening to rob them. Marion, age eighty-two, was asleep in the back bedroom. Edna attempted to appease the robber but he fired a shotgun and several pellets struck her, wounding her in the scalp and waking the general. Seeing his wife bleeding, Marion Carl acted as he always did, and with no thought of his own personal safety he attacked the young shooter. Edna told me later that Marion was within three feet of subduing the attacker, when the gun discharged again, mortally wounding one of America's greatest heroes.

I sat next to the stained carpet in their home as Edna told me how she cradled him in her arms while waiting for help to arrive. Quietly, I looked around and remembered the hours I spent in their home during the days before each of our hunting trips. I remembered Edna's laughter and Marion's comments as they exchanged with each other. My time with them had been very special for me. But now I looked down to my right and saw the stains of Marion's blood, and could only imagine what it must have been like for Edna as she held him for the last time and tried to comfort him.

While there I met the general's son, Bruce Carl. Bruce is a strikingly handsome man who clearly bears the resemblance of his famous father. Bruce and I walked outside in the yard and he said his father often told him about me. It was, Bruce said, almost as if I was a brother he never met. *I had no idea* and felt a rush of emotion as I fought to hold myself in check. That this quiet man, this Marine legend, even remembered me was outside my sphere of expectation. This revelation from Bruce completely disarmed me.

Edna asked Barbara and me to sit with the family at the funeral the next day as a throng of a thousand or more gathered in a college auditorium to pay their respects. Some of America's greatest Marine aces from WWII were there to honor their fallen comrade, a man who gave so much to his country. Once more I listened to "Taps" and watched the missing man formation fly overhead as F4 Phantom jets and World War II F6F aircraft paid a final tribute.

One of my greatest life experiences, serving briefly as Marion Carl's aide, was an assignment I fought to avoid. What I would have missed had I been successful. Edna Carl has since passed away and left one more void in our lives.

The young killer will spend the rest of his life without parole in an Oregon prison.

Our family afterwards:

Our daughter Dawn and I healed our relationship and remain close. Dawn is now 40 and is remarried to her second husband, Fred, whom we love and happily welcomed into our family. Dawn will always be my "little girl." She has given us two wonderful grandkids: Chance, age 17, and Lauren, age 21, whom we love very much.

Our youngest son, Jay, is now forty-six. We had virtually no contact with him for eight years. He must deal with his own problems and we accept that he has his own path to follow. He recently contacted us and is trying, once again, to get sober. We hold him in our prayers.

Our oldest son, Scott, is forty-seven, and is married to Susan, a tall, beautiful blonde girl. She is as pretty and sweet internally as she is externally. I congratulated him on maintaining the normal male Prouse tradition of outclassing ourselves with our mates! Susan is more our daughter than daughter-in-law. They have given us three wonderful grandchildren, two extraordinary boys, Cole, age ten, and Austin, age twelve, and beautiful little Ava, age five. We are extremely close to all of them and they add richness to our lives. Scott has his MBA and retired from the Marine Corps Reserve as a Lieutenant Colonel, having served five years on active duty and sixteen more in the reserves.

Barbara has only gotten more beautiful and gracious with time. She is an instant hit with those she meets and that has not changed since the first day of our marriage. My demure South Texas wife has grown into all her strengths and wears them well. She has been severely tested and has come through with blazing, bright colors. I still wonder why and how I was so lucky to share a life with her.

At age seventy-two, I continue to maintain my FAA First Class medical certificate and am still flying. For the past fifteen years I've been involved in Angel Flights, which are charitable flights. As with everything I've done, I fully disclosed my story to the Angel Flight organization and they welcomed me aboard. I am also involved in animal rescue flights.

There is never a time when I watch a young mother and baby get in my plane that I am not reminded of the day I risked the lives of fifty-eight passengers and my fellow crew members when I flew drunk. The deeply valued gift of trust comes with sobriety.

I was unable to return to my native community due to the shame I carried, but I received a phone call in 1994 from one of my native brothers in Wichita. I tensed as I recognized Chuck's voice and his words came through the phone. Finally, I told him I had been too ashamed to return. His voice softened as he replied, "I think you forget the things our people respect the most." I didn't respond. He paused at my silence then continued, "You have forgotten, haven't you?" I quietly said, "I guess so...." He replied with the perfect words of reminder, "Honesty and humility...and you have those."

Barbara and I went home to the Wichita powwow that summer. For three days I danced and walked among the people I grew up with, many of them now elderly and struggling with health issues. My native family immediately fell in love with Barbara and drew her into their midst. As I danced once more, I felt my youth return as my heart responded to the drum in the way it always had.

Again, the circle closed and my healing was complete in all quadrants. I have been active in Native American sobriety programs since that time.

Barbara and I are extraordinarily happy. We laugh continuously, and are never far away from a hug and a kiss. There are no *bad* days. Some are better than others–but none are *bad* today. We have learned to handle life's bumps with a smile, and we accept them because we're powerless over most of them. "God, grant me the serenity to accept the things I cannot change, the courage to change the things I can, and the wisdom to know the difference." We know we cannot change people, places, or things. And we try to summon the courage to change the things we can. What I can change mostly is my attitude, and I work on that daily.

Gratitude is the driving force in our lives and it overshadows all else.

I often interrupt Barbara in the middle of a sentence. "Gosh, you're pretty," I'll say, and she never fails to smile in an almost embarrassed way. And the nice thing about my comment is that it's always genuine and spontaneous; it's exactly what I'm thinking as I'm looking at her at that very moment. She has only gotten more beautiful with each passing year.

Someday she'll lose me or I'll lose her, but in the meantime we both know how grateful and blessed we are to have each other. If I make that ultimate flight West ahead of her, as I begin the turn for the final approach, I hope I will be able to look up into those beautiful brown eyes one last time. We have had a wonderful life together. She is and has always been the wind beneath my wings.

I sometimes end a talk with something I heard from Father Martin. He was a giant in recovery and beloved the entire world over.

I do not wish you joys...without a sorrow,
Nor endless days without the healing dark.
Nor brilliant sun without the restful shadow,
Nor tides that never turn against your bark.
I wish you strength...and faith, and love, and wisdom.
And goods – gold enough to help some needy one.
I wish you songs, but also blessed silence...
And God's sweet peace, when every day is done.

Frank Frey was a former Marine pilot and a close friend I loved. He was a gentle soul who succumbed to the disease of alcoholism in his early 40s. He bequeathed my closing to me. He used it, and he smiled when I asked if he'd mind if I also did. I have closed with it for many years now and I hope Frank approves, as he looks down and smiles once again.

Blue skies,
Lyle Prouse
Captain, Retired, Northwest Airlines

24935150R00172

Made in the USA
Lexington, KY
06 August 2013